# The Republican Manual

# Also from Westphalia Press

westphaliapress.org

# The Republican Manual

History, Principles, Early Leaders, Achievements
of the Republican Party

## by E. V. Smalley

with a new introduction by Paul Rich

WESTPHALIA PRESS
An imprint of Policy Studies Organization

The Republican Manual: History, Priciples, Early Leaders, Achievements
of the Republican Party
All Rights Reserved © 2014 by Policy Studies Organization

**Westphalia Press**
An imprint of Policy Studies Organization
1527 New Hampshire Ave., NW
Washington, D.C. 20036
info@ipsonet.org

**ISBN-13: 978-1-63391-086-7**
**ISBN-10: 1633910865**

Cover design by Taillefer Long at Illuminated Stories:
www.illuminatedstories.com

Daniel Gutierrez-Sandoval, Executive Director
PSO and Westphalia Press

Rahima Schwenkbeck, Director of Media and Marketing
PSO and Westphalia Press

Updated material and comments on this edition
can be found at the Westphalia Press website:
www.westphaliapress.org

# Introduction

# Selling the Northwest and the Republicans

On December 30, 1899, The New York Times reported, "St. Paul, Dec. 29 – E.V. Smalley, the editor of *The Northwestern Magazine* and Secretary of the National Sound Money League, who has been suffering with nervous dyspepsia and nervous prostration for some time, died here to-night."

Smalley began his career as a boy working in a print shop, and then served in the Civil War in the Seventh Ohio Infantry, being wounded in the battle of Port Republic. In 1865 he bought a newspaper in Youngstown, Ohio, which was in the congressional district of James Garfield. In 1870 he became the Washington correspondent for the *New York Tribune*. His articles led to efforts by President Grant to suppress the Ku Klux Klan in South Carolina. He frequently wrote for *The Century Magazine* on an amazing variety of topics, including the Supreme Court, the oil industry, General Sherman, the Pension Office, sheep farming, flour making, Western history and geography.

He was the personal friend of both Presidents Hayes and Garfield; even writing a life of Garfield. Briefly his private secretary, Smalley owed to Garfield his appointment as clerk of the committee on military affairs in Washington. His anti-slavery views fired his enthusiasm for the Republican Party, as he writes in this volume:

> Twenty-five years ago the Republican party was married to liberty. And this is our silver wedding, fellow-citizens. A worthily married pair love each other better on the day of their silver wedding than on the day of their first espousals; and we are truer to liberty today and dearer to God than we were when we spoke our first word of liberty.

In 1884 Smilley left Washington for St. Paul, Minnesota, where he founded the *Northwest Illustrated Monthly Magazine*. The magazine was closely associated with the Northern Pacific Railroad and of its president, the entrepreneur Henry Villard, who understandably wanted to help Smalley in promoting the region where the railroad did its business. The magazine had a one man band in its editor, who wrote articles, answered mail personally, and organized groups of prospective settlers to visit possible homesites. His later life was spent on the magazine and promoting the region and its future. In his very last years, Smalley was in the National Sound Money League which promoted the gold standard.

At Smalley's death his journal claimed 30,000 subscribers and 150,000 readers. Although he never succeeded in making it into a national journal with the influence of the *Atlantic Monthly*, for which he at one time wrote, he earned a permanent place in the history of the Northwest.

Paul Rich
Garfield House, Washington

JAMES A. GARFIELD.

# THE

# REPUBLICAN MANUAL.

History, Principles, Early Leaders, Achievements,

OF THE

# REPUBLICAN PARTY,

WITH BIOGRAPHICAL SKETCHES OF

## JAMES A. GARFIELD

AND

## CHESTER A. ARTHUR.

By E. V. SMALLEY.

NEW YORK:
AMERICAN BOOK EXCHANGE,
TRIBUNE BUILDING,
1880.

# TABLE OF CONTENTS

———◆———

# INTRODUCTION.

THE purpose of this work is to describe very briefly the origin, rise, and growth of the Republican Party, its great achievements in moulding public opinion, and its important work of administration and legislation. Since the party was formed, a new generation of voters has come upon the stage of political action, to whom its early history is little more than a tradition. A brief résumé of that history must be interesting and instructive to these young Republicans who have taken up its work and are to carry it on after all its founders have passed away, and the older members of the party can hardly fail to find some pleasure and profit in reviewing the story of its organization and victories. No party ever had such a record. It has freed four millions of slaves ; it has suppressed the most formidable rebellion the world ever saw ; it has preserved and strengthened the credit of the nation ; it has conferred equal rights of suffrage and citizenship upon all the inhabitants of this Republic, and it has administered the Government for twenty years with signal fidelity, honor, and intelligence. Within the compass of a work so limited as this, it is not possible to go into many interesting details concerning the career of this great historic party. Very little can be said about its action in State campaigns and its position upon State issues. Its history as a national organization alone is dealt with in the following pages, and that, too, in as condensed a form as is consistent with the presentation of all important facts.

# A BRIEF HISTORY

# REPUBLICAN PARTY.

---

## EARLY PARTIES IN THE UNITED STATES.

ALL political parties that have exerted marked influence upon their times, have had their beginnings far back of the period of their organization. Parties are somewhat like generations of men. The characteristics of any single generation cannot properly be studied without some knowledge of those that have gone before. It occasionally happens that a party comes up suddenly on some transient wave of popular excitement, growing out of events essentially temporary in their nature, or springs from some fictitious issue, magnified into importance for the time being by the lack of any real fundamental question affecting the Government and the interests of the people. The roots of such parties are never worth seeking, because the plant itself bears no seed and soon withers and disappears.

The Republican Party was the child of the conscience of the North, aroused, at length, to assertion by the growth of the institution of slavery. In its embryonic forms, it existed almost from the very beginning of the Government. It did not

gain strength and individuality, however, until more than half
a century after the adoption of the Federal Constitution. A
brief examination of the history of the parties preceding it is
essential to an understanding of the changes in public sentiment
which at last developed this most important, most powerful,
and most moral of all the political organizations that have thus
far arisen in the United States.

During the Revolution there were but two parties in the
country ; the Patriot Party, supporting the effort for separate
national life ; and the Tory Party, which opposed the severing
of the Colonies from the mother country. After the recognition of American Independence parties soon divided on the
question of forming a closer union between the States. One,
known as the Federalist Party, favored the adoption of a Constitution creating a strong, enduring National Government, and
the other, called the Anti-Federalist Party, desired to uphold
the rights of the States as separate and sovereign, and to continue the mere league between them formed by the Articles of
Confederation. The feebleness of the old system became more
and more apparent, and a convention, called in 1787, for the
purpose of amending and strengthening the Articles of Confederation, adopted a Constitution, after a four months' session,
and thus created a new government, with independent and sovereign powers within its own prescribed functions. The new
government had no model in history. The Swiss Republic was,
at that time, a league of cantons, closely resembling our own
form of government prior to the adoption of the Constitution.
No model was found in antiquity for the experiment. It was,
therefore, only natural that the scheme of resting a central authority upon thirteen independent State Governments should
awaken scepticism and resistance. The Anti-Federalist Party
opposed the ratification of the Constitution, and were successful
in several States in delaying, for a time, their assent to it. The
position of the Anti-Federalists was that a single executive head

was dangerous. They feared above all things, that the country would lapse back into a monarchical condition and lose its liberties. The value and necessity of a National Government was, however, so clear, that the Federalists were in a large majority in the country and held the administration for twelve years. In 1788 they elected George Washington, President, and John Adams, Vice-President. At that time the Constitution required the electors to vote for two candidates for President. The one having the highest number of votes became President, and the one next highest, became Vice-President. This system continued until 1804, when the present plan was adopted. During Washington's first administration, a fresh cause for division of parties was found in the French question. The Anti-Federalists, led by Jefferson, were warm sympathizers with France, and desired that the new American Republic should, in some form, give assistance to its recent ally. The Federalists favored a strict neutrality between Republican France and her enemies. Party feeling ran high at the second Presidential election in 1792, but Washington again received the unanimous vote of the Electoral College. Adams was again chosen Vice-President, receiving 77 votes, against 55, of which 50 were cast for George Clinton, the candidate of the Anti-Federalists.

About this time the Anti-Federalists began to drop their party name and to take the name of Democrats. Thomas Jefferson, their great leader, objected, however, to the use of the word Democrat and sought to secure the adoption of the name Republican. Backed by his influence, this name struggled for a time for recognition and was used to some extent in a few States, but was not generally adopted. Most of the old Anti-Federalists preferred the term Democrat as implying more fully hostility to the assumption of governmental powers threatening the individual rights of citizens. In 1796 the Federalists elected John Adams, President. He received 71 electoral votes and Jefferson, his opponent, receiving 68, became Vice-Presi-

dent.   Troubles with France arose and nearly resulted in war.
During these troubles Congress passed two acts, known as the
Alien and Sedition Laws ; one empowering the President to
order aliens who were conspiring against the peace of the
United States to quit the country, and the other providing for
the punishment of seditious libels upon the Government.   These
laws created much party feeling and were denounced by the
Democrats as tyrannical and unconstitutional.   They contributed very largely to the overthrow of the Federal Party at the
Presidential election of 1800, when Mr. Adams was a candidate
for re-election.   The Democrats voted for Jefferson and Burr,
and gave them 73 votes each in the Electoral College, while
Adams received 65, Pinckney 64, and John Jay 1.   The
election was thrown into the House of Representatives by a tie
between Jefferson and Burr.   Jefferson was chosen President
and Burr Vice-President.   When Jefferson entered the Executive office, his old views about diminishing the powers of the
General Government were considerably modified.   He gave the
country a vigorous and successful administration and was re-
elected in 1804, by 162 electoral votes.   The Federalists voted
for Pinckney of South Carolina, and Rufus King of New York,
and were able to control only 16 electoral votes.   Jefferson
declined to be a candidate for a third term, and the Democrats
selected as their nominee his friend, James Madison, whose
home near Charlottesville, Va., was almost in sight from Jefferson's house at Monticello.   During the last year of Jefferson's
administration, the Federalists gained considerable fresh vitality
through the popular opposition to what was known as the Embargo, an act of Congress prohibiting American vessels from
trading with foreign ports.   It was adopted out of revenge for
the insolent actions of Great Britain and France, which arbi-
trarily searched American ships on the high seas and often seized
them and confiscated their cargoes.   The embargo was fatal
for a time to the commercial interests of the United States,

and was repealed in 1809. At the election of 1808, the name Democrat was almost universally adopted by the party supporting Madison. Madison received 122 votes and George Clinton 113, while the Federal candidates, C. C. Pinckney, and Rufus King, received 47 each. The war of 1812 which practically began in 1811, by British emissaries inciting the Indian tribes of the Northwest to hostile acts, nearly obliterated party lines for a time. Both of the parties supported the war when it was fairly begun. The Federalists continued their organization, however, and at the election of 1812, gave 89 votes for De Witt Clinton, against 128 for Madison. The Democrats nominated for President, James Monroe, Mr. Madison's Secretary of State, Madison himself declining a third term. It is difficult at this distance to understand what were the issues of the contest, but it is plain that the old political parties had nearly exhausted their motives of controversy and that the issues were rather the traditions of old struggles than anything fresh and vital. Monroe received 183 votes, against 24 given to Rufus King by the States of Massachusetts, Connecticut, and Delaware. Now began what is known in our political history as the era of good feeling. No one was disposed to longer question the utility of the Federal Government, and on the other hand, no one was disposed to assert for it any dangerous or monarchical powers. Both the Democrats and the Federalists supported Monroe, and he was re-elected in 1820, by all of the electoral votes save one.

---

## CHAPTER II.

### THE BEGINNING OF THE ANTI-SLAVERY MOVEMENT.

Up to 1820, the existence of slavery in the United States had been regarded as a misfortune by the people of all sections of the country. Indeed, among the causes of grievances brought

against Great Britain, was her action in forcing the slave trade
upon the colonies against their will.   With scarcely an exception, the early statesmen of the Republic regarded the institution of slavery as an evil which would gradually be got rid of
by wise emancipation measures.   Looking to that end, the slave
trade was prohibited and ranked with piracy, as a crime, as
early as 1808.   Mr. Jefferson, the head of the Democratic
party, was one of the most enlightened opponents of slavery, and was far from foreseeing that the party which he had
founded would in after-years, become its chief defender.   The
first anti-slavery society in the country was formed by the
Quakers of Pennsylvania, but there were, at an early period,
organizations of emancipationists in the South who kept up
some agitation in behalf of measures for getting rid of the institution by the action of the State Governments.   One after another of the Northern States where slavery existed provided for
its gradual abolition, and the sentiment in the North was so
nearly unanimous in opposition to fastening slavery permanently upon the country that it insisted that for every new Southern
State which came in, a Northern free State should be admitted.
Thus, Vermont, Ohio, and Indiana compensated for Kentucky,
Tennessee, and Louisiana ; and later, Maine counterbalanced
Alabama.   Thus far, the number of free and slave States was
equal.   Then the question arose in 1820 about admitting Missouri with a slave Constitution.   It gave rise to a vehement
public discussion which was rather sectional than political.   The
people of the Northern States insisted that a clause, prohibiting
slavery, should be inserted in the Missouri Constitution as a
condition of the admission of the State.   The struggle went on
in Congress for over two years.   While it aroused the anti-
slavery sentiment of the North, which had been almost dormant,
it had the effect of inciting the South to a united and earnest
defence of an institution which had before been regretted, even
in that section, as undesirable and temporary in its nature.

A compromise settled the struggle for the time being, in which the South gained a victory. Missouri was admitted with slavery, but an act was passed prohibiting slavery in all the new territory lying north of latitude 36 degrees and 30 minutes, known as "Mason and Dixon's Line." This settlement became known as the "Missouri Compromise." The North gained nothing that did not belong to it before and the South secured the admission of a new slave State, north of the old line separating freedom from slavery. The "Missouri Compromise" laid the foundation of the future Republican Party, by creating in the mind of the North, a distrust of the South and by developing a political force in the country which received the significant designation of the Slave Power. This force, in the course of time, suppressed all opposition to slavery in the South and asserted the right to convert the whole unoccupied territory of the United States into slave States, and to carry its human chattels into the Northern States under the protection of the Federal Government, in defiance of the laws of those States. Resistance to the slave power and its demands formulated itself in the course of time into the Republican Party.

---

## CHAPTER III.

### THE WHIG AND DEMOCRATIC PARTIES.

Monroe's administration is chiefly famous in history for its recognition of the Spanish-American Republics and its declaration of what is known as the "Monroe Doctrine," an assertion that any attempt on the part of European Governments to extend their system to any portion of the American Continent would be considered to be dangerous to the peace and safety of the United States. The destruction of party lines under Monroe's administration went so far that in the election of 1824,

no reorganization on the basis of old ideas was practicable.
There were four candidates for the Presidency. Andrew Jackson received 99 votes, John Quincy Adams 84, William H. Craw-
ford 41, and Henry Clay 37. The election was thrown into the
House of Representatives, and Mr. Adams was chosen President. The administration of the new President, who was a son
of the great Federalist, John Adams, might have been expected
to restore the Federal Party, but that party had outlived its
usefulness. It had witnessed a complete success of its ideas
respecting the National Government and there was no occasion
for its revival. The supporters of Mr. Adams called themselves
National Republicans, but the name did not long survive. Mr.
Adams's policy did not differ much from that of Mr. Monroe.
The distinguishing event of his administration was the adoption
of the protective tariff system. It was favored by the North and
opposed by the South. Parties degenerated into factions and
the personal popularity of the political leaders had more to do
with their success than any principles they professed. In 1828,
Mr. Adams was a candidate for re-election, but was defeated by
Andrew Jackson, who had 178 votes, to Adams's 83. Jackson
was a narrow-minded man of limited education, strong prejudices, violent temper, and little schooling in statesmanship.
His popularity grew out of his success as a military commander.
He introduced personal government at Washington to a far
greater extent than any of his predecessors or successors.
Fealty to him, personally, was the chief test of merit in his
eyes. For a time the country was divided into a Jackson party
and an anti-Jackson party, all other names being lost sight of.
Jackson introduced into American politics the theory that " to
the victors belong the spoils ;" he was the first President who
removed from office all persons not favorable to him politically.
John Quincy Adams had made a few removals of officials in
high position, but there was a great public clamor against him
for this act. Jackson swept the entire public service of every-

body who had not favored his election, and filled the offices
with his personal partisans. The corruption of American politics in more recent times is largely due to this high-tempered,
bigoted, and egotistical man ; but his glaring faults almost
merit complete forgiveness, in view of his great service to the
country in suppressing the nullification movement in South
Carolina.

Up to this time, the South, and particularly the Democratic
Party in the South, had asserted the doctrine, that the Constitution is a federal compact between sovereign States, and that
in such compacts between sovereigns who are equal there is
no arbiter, each State being the rightful judge, as a party to the
compact, of the constitutionality of any measure of the General
Government. This view was asserted by the Legislatures of
Virginia and Kentucky, in what are generally called the resolutions of 1798. The doctrine that each State can judge for
itself whether the laws or the action of the Government is constitutional or not became in time a part of the platform of
principles of the Democratic Party, and was held to with particular zeal by the people of the South. In 1832, South Carolina, under the lead of John C. Calhoun, endeavored to resist
the enforcement of the new tariff law, by a process called nullification. Less from statesmanship and patriotism, probably,
than from motives of personal hostility to Mr. Calhoun,
President Jackson threw himself with all the force of his resolute nature upon the other side, and declared his intention to
treat nullification as treason, and to hang the men who resisted
the authority of the United States. He ordered a large armed
force to Charleston and thus put an end to the incipient movement for dissolving the Union. His vigorous conduct caused
the total abandonment of the theory that a State can set aside
the laws of the United States at its pleasure. The South
shifted its policy, and soon began to rally on a new position,
namely, that when a State does not like the conduct of the

General Government, it has a right to secede from the Union.

The nullification question was not taken up as a party issue, and, indeed, Jackson gave it very little time to ferment in the public mind.    He furnished the country with an issue, however, by assailing the Bank of the United States, an institution modelled somewhat after the Bank of England and having close relations to the Government.    It is said that Jackson's hostility to the bank arose from the refusal of one of its branches in the South to cash his checks when he was carrying on the Florida War.    In 1832, the President recommended the removal of the public funds from the bank.    Congress refused to authorize the removal.    Then Jackson, on his own responsibility, ordered the Secretary to withdraw the deposits and place them in certain State banks.    That officer refusing, he was removed and Mr. Taney appointed to his place.    The bank was broken down, a great financial panic followed, and serious commercial distress afflicted the country.    The opponents of Jackson's policy toward the bank organized themselves under the name of the Whig Party, taking this name because the Whig Party in England had resisted the arbitrary measures of the king.    Thus, by a curious change of the political situation, the leader of the Democrats, the party formed to resist strong government in this country, became the type and exemplar of the strong government idea, and the Whigs, the successors of the Federalists, became, as they imagined, the defenders of the people against the encroachments of Executive power.    In 1832, just before the bank question came up, Jackson was re-elected by 219 electoral votes, against a divided opposition, casting 49 votes for Henry Clay, 11 for John Floyd, and 7 for William Wirt. A short-lived popular excitement against secret societies, and especially against the Masons, sprang up, and Wirt was the candidate of a new party called the Anti-Masonic Party.    He got the electoral vote of Vermont.    Martin Van Buren was chosen

Vice-President. In 1836, General Jackson put forward Mr. Van Buren as his successor. The bank question, the tariff question, and opposition to the personal government of Jackson were the chief issues. Jackson had made a powerful impression on the rather unorganized public sentiment of the country by his boldness and independence, and his influence was sufficient to secure the election of Van Buren. He received 170 electoral votes. The Whig vote was divided between William Henry Harrison, 73 ; Hugh L. White, 26 ; Daniel Webster, 14 ; and Willie P. Mangum, 11. Up to 1832 national nominating conventions were unknown. A party caucus of members of Congress selected the candidates for President and Vice-President, and not unfrequently State Legislatures put candidates in the field. Van Buren's administration was exceedingly unpopular. The commercial crisis of 1837 and the hard times which followed reacted powerfully against the dominant party. The administration was charged with the dullness of trade, the stagnation of industry, the scarcity of good money, and the alarming number of business failures. More to the hard times than to any other cause was due the overwhelming success of the Whigs in 1840. The Whigs held a national convention at Harrisburg, in December, 1839, and nominated General Harrison for President, and John Tyler for Vice-President. The Democrats held their convention at Baltimore, in May, 1840, and unanimously nominated Van Buren for re-election. The campaign was the most exciting, demonstrative, and dramatic that had ever taken place in this country, and the result was that Harrison and Tyler received 234 electoral votes, and Van Buren 60. The Democratic vote for Vice-President was divided. Harrison's popular vote was 1,275,011, and that of Van Buren 1,128,702. Although Harrison's majority of the popular vote was a very small one, his electoral majority was enormous, a discrepancy which strikingly illustrates the peculiarity of our electoral system.

Harrison died a month after his inauguration—worried to death by office-seekers, it is said. His successor, John Tyler, proved treacherous to the Whig Party, espoused the views of the Democrats, changed his Cabinet, and finally went over to the Democratic side.

## CHAPTER IV.

### REVIVAL OF THE SLAVERY AGITATION—THE LIBERTY PARTY.

In 1844, the Democrats nominated James K. Polk for President, and the Whigs nominated Henry Clay. The question of the extension of slave territory entered largely into the canvass. A treaty had been negotiated for the annexation of Texas, then an independent Republic, but still claimed by Mexico as a part of her dominions. The treaty was rejected by the Senate and the Democratic Party throughout the country took it up and declared in their conventions that it was a great American measure. The Whigs were nearly unanimous in their opposition to the Texan scheme ; in the North, because of their unwillingness to give the slave power another State ; in the South, on various grounds of expediency. The opposition of the Whigs was not sufficiently clear and earnest, however, to draw to their support all the voters hostile to the annexation project. A party was organized which took broad grounds against the extension of slavery and assumed for itself the name of the Liberty Party. It was, in fact, an offshoot from the anti-slavery organizations throughout the North. A struggle arose in the American Anti-slavery Society as to the duty of its members. One faction, headed by William Lloyd Garrison, abstained wholly from voting, on the ground that the Constitution was a covenant with the slave power to protect slavery. The other faction insisted that the way to fight slavery was to use the weapon of the ballot. This faction became the Liberty

Party, and nominated James G. Birney for President. It was a very small party, but an exceedingly earnest one, and although it never had a majority in any State, and probably not in any county, it frequently held the balance of power, and exerted considerable influence on the two great parties. Just before the election of 1844, Mr. Clay wrote a letter which dissatisfied the Liberty Party and also the anti-slavery Whigs in the State of New York. About 16,000 votes were cast in New York for Birney and were mostly withdrawn from the Whig ticket. This defection caused the loss of the State to Clay, defeated him for the Presidency, and changed the whole subsequent history of the country. The result of the election was 174 votes for Polk and Dallas, and 105 for Clay and Frelinghuysen, the vote of New York turning the scale. Under Polk's administration, Texas was admitted and war was waged with Mexico. The war was opposed by most of the Northern Whigs who had begun to be considerably tinctured with anti-slavery sentiments and still more strongly opposed by the Liberty Party men and the Garrisonians, now called by the name of Abolitionists, who thought that the purpose of the conflict was to secure more territory to be made into slave States.

The decline of the Whig Party dates from this period. As a national organization it was obliged to cater to the South, where a large part of its strength lay, and no positive declaration against the extension of slavery could be got from its conventions. At the same time a feeling of hatred to the slave power had obtained a firm lodgment in the mind of a large portion of its Northern members. The Whig Party embraced in its membership a much larger portion of the intelligent and educated classes of the country than its rival, the Democratic Party. In the South, these classes contented themselves with opposition to extreme pro-slavery measures threatening the perpetuity of the Union, but in the North they began more and more to demand such action as should stop the growth of the slave power and secure to freedom all the unoccupied territory of the United States.

## CHAPTER V.

### THE WILMOT PROVISO—THE FREE SOIL PARTY—THE CAMPAIGN OF 1848.

IT became apparent before the end of the war, that the defeat of Mexico would be followed by the cession of a large part of her territory to the United States, and the question began to be agitated in Congress as early as 1847, of what should be the condition of the territory in reference to slavery.   At a consultation of members of the House from the free States, who felt that the extreme limit of justifiable concession to slavery had already been reached, David Wilmot, of Pennsylvania, presented the following proviso, to be offered to any bill for the organization of new Territories : "That as an express and fundamental condition to the acquisition of new territory from the Republic of Mexico, by the United States by virtue of any treaty that may be negotiated between them, and to the use by the Executive of any moneys herein appropriated, neither slavery nor involuntary servitude shall ever exist in any part of said territory, except for crime whereof the party shall first be duly convicted."   This was the famous Wilmot Proviso which played a large part in the political history of the succeeding years.   It served to bring together many members of both the Whig and Democratic organizations who were opposed to the extension of slavery.   Its advocates were called in the political nomenclature of the day, " Wilmot Proviso Men," although they adhered for a time to their old party connections.   The proviso was offered to the bill for negotiating a treaty with Mexico, but it was defeated in the House.

In 1848 the Democrats nominated for President, General Lewis Cass, of Michigan.   His principal competitors in the convention were   James Buchanan and Levi Woodbury.   The nominee for Vice-President was General William O. Butler, of

Kentucky. The New York Democrats divided into two factions, one, called " Barn-burners," opposed the extension of slavery, and the other, styled " Hunkers," sympathized fully with the South. The " Barn-burners " bolted from the Democratic convention, and sent delegates to a national convention held at Buffalo, which organized a new party, called the Free Soil Party. The Free Soil Party was the legitimate successor of the Liberty Party of 1848. The Buffalo Convention nominated Martin Van Buren for President, and Charles Francis Adams for Vice-President. Van Buren's nomination weakened the moral force of the new movement, for while President he had been a tool of the slave power, and only since his retirement to private life had he expressed himself against the extension of slavery to the Territories. The motive of his nomination was to secure the votes of " Barn-burners " of New York and to defeat Cass.

The Whig National Convention met in Philadelphia and nominated General Zachary Taylor, of Louisiana, for President. His chief competitors for the nomination were Henry Clay, General Scott, and Daniel Webster. Taylor's nomination was exceedingly popular in the country on account of his brilliant service in the Mexican War and his lack of any political record with which fault could be found. The Democrats, in their convention, refused to endorse the extreme Southern view, that slaves were property and could be carried into the Territories under the protection of the Government. The Whigs dodged the slavery question altogether. The Free Soilers claimed that the Constitution was hostile to slavery and intended to limit it to the States where it existed by virtue of local laws, and further, that the Federal Government should relieve itself from all responsibility for the existence of the institution. At the election, General Taylor carried 15 States, with 163 electoral votes ; and General Cass 15 States, with 137 electoral votes. Van Buren carried no State, but had a large vote throughout the North.   The entire popular vote stood, Taylor and Fillmore, 1,360,752 ; Cass and Butler, 1,219,962 ; Van Buren and Adams, 291,342.   The general effect of the canvass was to show that the Democrats were pretty thoroughly committed to the slave power and that the Whigs did not dare to antagonize it.   The agitation produced by Van Buren's candidacy served a good purpose in further arousing public sentiment in the North to the encroachments of slavery.

---

## CHAPTER VI.

### THE COMPROMISE OF 1850 AND THE FUGITIVE-SLAVE LAW.

SOON after the peace with Mexico, which secured to the United States all the territory comprised in the present States of California and Nevada, and the Territories of Utah, Arizona, and New Mexico, gold was discovered in California, and an immense rush of emigration occurred.   In a short time there were people enough there to form a State Government.   They adopted a Constitution prohibiting slavery, and applied for admission to the Union.   At that time there were 15 slave States and 15 free States, and the admission of California would place the free States in the majority of one.   It was therefore vehemently opposed by the representatives of the slave power.   Many slave States threatened secession if the new State should be admitted without some concessions to secure the equality of the South in the future.   They demanded a recognition of their claim that slavery could not be prohibited in the Territories or its existence be made an objection to the admission of a new State. They also demanded a guarantee against the abolition of slavery in the District of Columbia, and a stringent fugitive-slave law.   The contest in Congress lasted nearly two years, and was finally settled by what is known as the Compromise of 1850.

Zachary Taylor, who though a slaveholder did not sympathize with the extreme Southern view, had died before the controversy culminated, and Millard Fillmore, his successor, openly espoused the side of the pro-slavery leaders. The compromise was advocated by Henry Clay, and received, also, the support of the great Northern Whig leader, Daniel Webster, who abandoned his anti-slavery position and went over, with his great intellect and influence, to the slave power. His action divided the Whig Party in the North and practically gave it a death-blow. Wm. H. Seward became the leader of the anti-slavery Whigs. The compromise of 1850 admitted California with its free Constitution, and left for future settlement the status of the rest of the conquered territory in respect to slavery; rejected the Wilmot Proviso, and paid Texas $10,000,000 for a visionary claim to the Territory of New Mexico; prohibited slave auctions in the District of Columbia, and enacted the odious fugitive-slave law. This law shocked the sense of justice of the more intelligent portion of the Northern people and exerted a powerful influence in preparing men's minds for the advent of the Republican Party. It provided for the return of alleged fugitives without trial by jury, allowing their captors to take them before a United States Commissioner, who was empowered to remand them on the *ex-parte* depositions of the slave-catchers. The Commissioners were paid ten dollars in case they directed the return of the alleged fugitive, and five dollars if, for any cause, they decided against the claimant. In effect, therefore, they were offered a bribe to decide against the person claimed as a slave. Slave-catchers were authorized to summon bystanders to their aid, and all good citizens were commanded to assist in the arrest of alleged fugitive slaves. The law, in effect, ordered the people of the North to turn slave-catchers and threatened them with heavy penalties in case they harbored or assisted any fugitive. Numerous cases of extreme brutality arose from the execution of this law. Professional slave-hunters invaded the North and captured colored persons without much regard to whether they had run away from slavery or not. In some cases there was resistance on the part of the people, and trials occurred which served to increase the irritation in the public mind. The law was vehemently denounced by the anti-slavery Whigs, the anti-slavery Democrats, and the Free Soilers, and the Abolitionists found in it a new text for the crusade they preached with so much earnestness and self-denial against the "sum of all villainies." Some of the Northern States passed what were known as "Personal Liberty Bills," practically nullifying the fugitive-slave law and punishing as kidnappers persons who sought to carry off alleged slaves without trial by jury. These personal liberty bills furnished a notable illustration of the powerlessness of theories of government, when human rights are involved. Hitherto the slave States had alone maintained extreme State rights doctrines, but now the free States practically asserted such doctrines in their legislation hostile to the Federal authority. The personal liberty bills set at naught the authority of the United States so far as it was sought to be exercised in the enforcement of the fugitive-slave law. They asserted the right of the State to protect the people within her borders from arrest and imprisonment without trial and from being carried off as slaves. They fell back upon the clause in the Constitution which says, "In any suits at common law, whereof the value of the controversy shall exceed $20, the right of trial by jury shall be preserved." Fugitives were claimed to be property exceeding that value, and it was asserted that they could not be deprived of their liberty without a jury trial. Public agitation against the fugitive-slave law increased from year to year, and it finally became impracticable in most parts of the North, save in the great cities, to reclaim fugitives. Not only was this the case, but associations were formed in many parts of the North for the purpose of aiding slaves to escape to Canada. The lines over which the fugitives were forwarded by day and by night, by the anti-slavery people, were known as the "Underground Railroad." Many thousands of negroes escaped from the border States to Canada by the aid of this institution, and became industrious and valuable citizens of the British dominions.

---

## CHAPTER VII.

### CAMPAIGN OF 1852—DEFEAT OF THE WHIG PARTY.

THE Whig and Democratic Parties had been fully committed by the action of their representatives in Congress to the endorsement of the compromise measures of 1850, and it was evident before their national conventions met in 1852 that they would rival each other in professions of fidelity to those measures. Indeed, a public pledge had been signed by Henry Clay, Howell Cobb, and about fifty other members of Congress, of both parties, agreeing to abide by the compromise as a final adjustment of the controversy between the free and the slave States. The Democratic Convention surprised the country by dropping General Cass, James Buchanan, and Stephen A. Douglas, who were the leading candidates for the nomination, and taking up Franklin Pierce of New Hampshire, a man almost unknown outside of his own State. On the 50th ballot Pierce was nominated. Wm. R. King of Alabama, was nominated for Vice-President on the second ballot. The convention declared that the compromise of 1850 was a finality and that the Democratic Party would resist all attempts at renewing the agitation of the slavery question. The Whig National Convention nominated General Winfield Scott for President. The other candidates were Millard Fillmore and Daniel Webster. Scott was nominated on the 52d ballot, and Wm. O. Graham of North Carolina was put on the ticket for Vice-President. The platform endorsed the compromise of 1850, including the fugitive-slave law, and declared that the system it established was essential to the nationality of the Whig Party and the integrity of the Union. The Whigs went into the canvass with a good deal of apparent vitality, but before the close it was evident that the poison of slavery had sapped the vitality of the party.

The Free Soilers met at Pittsburg, in August, and nominated John P. Hale of New Hampshire, for President, and Geo. W. Julian of Indiana, for Vice-President. Their platform was opposition to the extension of slavery and their battle-cry was "Free soil, free speech, free States, and free men." In some States the supporters of Hale and Julian took the name of Free Democrats, in others they called themselves, Free Soil Democrats, and in still others, simply Free Soilers. They did not poll as large a vote as in 1848. Numbers of New York Democrats who then voted for Van Buren, returned to their old allegiance. They had, however, a pretty effective organization in all of the Northern States, sustained a number of influential newspapers, and placed in the field many able stump-speakers. Most of their vote was drawn from the Whigs. The result of the election was that the Democrats carried all the States in the Union except Massachusetts, Vermont, Kentucky, and Tennessee, choosing 254 electors. General Scott received only 42 electoral votes. The popular vote was, Pierce, 1,601,474 ; Scott, 1,386,578 ; Hale, 156,149. The disaster to the Whigs was so overwhelming that it killed their party. They kept up some form of an organization for four years longer, but it was merely a shadow. The party had no longer an excuse for living. Its former principles of a protective tariff and a wise system of internal improvements had very little hold upon the public mind. The country was rapidly dividing on the slavery question, and as the Democratic party was generally recognized to be the principal ally of the slave power, there was no room for another organization not definitely opposed to that power.

The dead party was sincerely mourned, particularly by a class of its adherents in the North, represented by Seward and Greeley, who had hoped to lead it over to anti-slavery ground. It was also regretted by a considerable element of educated and conservative people in the South, sincerely attached to the Union, and apprehensive of grave dangers to the peace of the country from the extreme ground taken on the slavery question by the Democrats. The disappearance of the Whigs as an organization from the field of politics opened the way for the formation of the Republican Party, by a new and formidable agency, which will be described in the next chapter, coming in to complete the work.

---

## CHAPTER VIII.

### RISE AND FALL OF THE KNOW-NOTHING OR AMERICAN PARTY.

BETWEEN the years 1853 and 1855 there suddenly arose a party of phenomenal growth and extraordinary ideas. It took for itself the name of the American Party, but its members were generally known by the popular slang term of " Know-Nothings," which they did not themselves object to. They were organized into secret lodges, with pass-words and grips, and were sworn to vote for no one for a public office who was not a native. They proposed that citizenship should not be conferred, so far as the right of voting was concerned, until after twenty-one years' residence. They were peculiarly hostile to the Catholics, and claimed that the priests of that Church controlled the votes of their parishioners. The growth of this new organization was marvellous. It spread like wild-fire over the country and before it was two years old managed to carry many important local and State elections. It must not be supposed, however, that it was absolutely without roots in the past. Native Americanism as a sentiment had existed since about the year 1830, and had in several localities in the East assumed at different periods the form of political organizations. It rested on a not unreasonable apprehension of the growing power of the foreign element in the large cities of the country. This element, in large part ignorant of our system of government, frequently banded together to carry municipal elections, and elected objectionable persons to office. When the idea of nativism spread to the whole country and became the basis of a national party it was illogical and unpatriotic, because the growth of the United States had been largely the result of foreign immigration and a great part of its wealth had been produced by the labors of its foreign-born citizens. Many of these citizens were men of marked intellectual and moral worth, who had studied thoroughly the American system of free government, and had come to this country to escape the despotic limitations of life in the Old World. In seeking to exclude such men from voting and holding office in the land of their adoption the Know-Nothing movement was evidently unjust.

The rapid spread of the secret Know-Nothing lodges cannot be accounted for by the principles of ordinary political action. A study of the laws of mind which govern the propagation of intellectual delusions and produce phenomenal movements in the world of religion as well as of politics would be necessary for a philosophical treatment of the matter. Undoubtedly, the decay of the Whig party had much to do with the rise of this new movement. Men were suddenly cut adrift from their old party politics. In this situation they easily became a prey to a movement which had the fascination of secrecy and laid claims to lofty motives of patriotism. The Know-Nothing party culminated in 1855. It nominated Millard Fillmore for President in 1856, but it was already on the wane at that time, and shortly after the slavery question had so completely absorbed the public mind that Know-Nothingism subsided as rapidly as it had risen, and in a single year disappeared from the field of politics. It played a part of some importance in the work of forming the Republican Party, by making a sort of bridge upon which many old Whigs crossed over to that organization.

---

## CHAPTER IX.

### THE ANTI-SLAVERY SOCIETIES AND THEIR WORK.

BEFORE proceeding with the chronological order of our narrative, it is time that we should pause for a moment to consider the work of the anti-slavery societies in the North. Their members were few in number and were usually despised by the masses of people as impractical theorists and negro-worshippers, who threatened the tranquillity of the country and the permanence of the Union, but they were men of earnest convictions and lofty moral purpose, who, by their tireless exertions, gradually wore into the Northern mind a conception of the atrocity of slavery. These societies were strongest in New England, on the Western Reserve of Ohio, and in the Quaker communities of Pennsylvania, Ohio, and Indiana. They supported a number of eloquent public lecturers, who traversed the country and addressed meetings in school-houses, churches, and in the open air. Often these orators were received with opprobrium and insult ; sometimes they were brutally treated by angry mobs ; but they kept on heroically with their noble task. The condition of public sentiment in the North on the slavery question, prior to 1850, can scarcely be understood by the present generation. Even the church organizations were, as a rule, bitterly hostile to all forms of anti-slavery agitation. The Abolitionists, as the anti-slavery men were generally called, were looked upon as no better than criminals. A bigoted, unreasoning, and often brutal devoteeism to the slavery system had taken possession of the public mind, and whoever questioned the constitutionality or

perpetuity of that system ran the risk of ostracism in his social
and business relations, and if he publicly advocated his ideas,
actually took his life in his own hands.    This sentiment caused
the anti-slavery men to draw closely together for mutual encouragement and assistance.    They believed in the sacred
humanity of their work.    Their lecturers were entertained like
brethren at the homes of the members of the society where-
ever they went, and every anti-slavery man regarded every
other anti-slavery man in the light of a near personal friend.  In
some parts of the country, they held annual conventions under
tents or in groves.  A number of newspapers advocated their
ideas, chief among which was the *Liberator*, published in Boston
by William Lloyd Garrison, who was generally recognized as
the head of the movement.    Horace Greeley, in his "American Conflict," divided the opponents of slavery in the period
preceding the formation of the Republican Party into four
classes :

1. The Garrisonians, who regarded the Federal Constitution
as a covenant with death and an agreement with hell.    They
pledged themselves to wage against slavery an unrelenting war,
to regard and proclaim the equal and inalienable rights of every
innocent human being as inferior or subordinate to no other,
and to repudiate all creeds, rituals, constitutions, governments,
and parties that rejected these fundamental truths.    They generally declined to vote, believing the Government and all political parties so corrupted by slavery that no one could take any
part in politics without moral defilement.

2. The members of the Liberty Party who, regarding the
Federal Constitution as essentially anti-slavery, swore with
good conscience to uphold it and to support only candidates
who were distinctly, determinedly, and permanently champions
of liberty for all.

3. Various small sects and parties which occupied a middle
ground between the above positions, agreeing with the latter

in interpreting and revering the Constitution as consistently anti-slavery, while refusing with the former to vote.

4. A large and steadily increasing class who, though decidedly anti-slavery, refused either to withhold their votes or to throw them away on candidates whose election was impossible, but persisted in voting at nearly every election so as to effect good and prevent evil to the extent of their power.

The influence of all the various forms of anti-slavery agitation in opening the way for the advent of the Republican Party, and laying the foundation for that great organization, can scarcely be overstated.

---

## CHAPTER X.

### THE KANSAS-NEBRASKA STRUGGLE.

The result of the election of 1852 was to place the Democrats in complete control of the National Government. They had the President and a large majority in both houses of Congress. Their party was now completely dominated by the pro-slavery element. Franklin Pierce had been nominated by Southern votes and was wholly subservient to the slave power. In spite of the professions of the Democrats in their platform of 1852, in which they declared the compromise measures of 1850 to be a finality, settling forever the contest between the free and the slave States, Congress had scarcely met in 1853 before the South began to agitate for the repeal of the prohibition of slavery north of the line of 36 degrees 30 minutes. The vast plains lying beyond the States of Ohio and Missouri were known to be fertile and adapted for settlement. To remove the Indian tribes occupying them and make out of the region two new slave States, thus flanking the free States on the west and securing for slavery all of the vast region beyond the Missouri River, was the ambitious scheme of the Southern leaders. It mattered not that the faith of the South had been pledged, first by the compromise of 1820 and then by that of 1850, adopted as a final settlement of the slave agitation. The pro-slavery leaders felt their power and determined to exercise it. After a tremendous struggle in both houses of Congress, they passed a bill repealing the prohibition of 1820, and opening all of the new Northwest to slavery. The extreme pro-slavery Democrats asserted that the Missouri Compromise was unconstitutional and that Congress had no power to prohibit slavery in the territory of the United States. They further asserted that the people of the new Territory had no power themselves, by their own territorial statutes, to interfere with the holding of slave property. A more moderate wing of the party, headed by Stephen A. Douglas, broached what was known as the popular sovereignty doctrine, which was that the people of the Territories should themselves decide whether they would have free or slave States, and that Congress had no authority to interfere with them. Abraham Lincoln once characterized this doctrine as, in effect, that one man had the right to enslave another, but a third man had no right to interfere. Mr. Douglas's position prevailed, and the act organizing the Territories of Kansas and Nebraska, passed in 1854, permitted the introduction of slaves into those Territories and left the people free to regulate their domestic institutions in their own way.

The passage of this act created intense public excitement in the North. It was regarded as a breach of faith on the part of the South and as the forerunner of measures designed to extend slavery over the whole country. In every Northern State large numbers of men of influence broke loose from the old political organizations, and were styled " Anti-Nebraska Men." Public meetings were held denouncing the measure, and a great popular movement, hostile to the encroachment of slavery, arose spontaneously on a wave of excitement which swept over the entire North. The Territory of Nebraska was too far away from the slave States to be occupied to any great extent by emigrants from the South, but a fierce struggle arose for the possession of the Territory of Kansas. Armed men from Missouri moved over the border at once to occupy the region and keep out Northern immigrants. The Indian titles were quickly extinguished by the Democratic administration and the public lands thrown open for settlement. The first party of emigrants from the free States were visited by an armed mob and ordered to leave the Territory. The spirit of the North was fully aroused, however, and thousands of brave, intelligent men went to Kansas, determined to make it a free State. A contest ensued which lasted for several years, and was generally called at the time "The Border Ruffian War." Reckless and lawless men from the Missouri border harassed the Northern settlers. Many free State men were brutally murdered. The town of Lawrence was sacked and burned in part by an armed force of pro-slavery men. A regiment of wild young men from the South was recruited in Alabama by Colonel Buford, and invaded the Territory for the avowed purpose of subjugating the Northern settlers. The North supported her emigrants with fresh re-enforcements and with consignments of rifles and ammunition. Numerous encounters occurred with more or less loss of life. At the village of Ossawatomie, a pitched battle was fought, wherein 28 free State men led by John Brown defeated, on the open prairie, 56 border ruffians led by Captain Pate of Virginia.

In the struggle for Kansas, the South fought against the laws of nature. Very little of the Territory was adapted for the raising of cotton, and slavery had been found profitable only in the cotton regions. Few emigrants from the South went with their negroes to the new Territory, while resolute Northern farmers and mechanics poured in year after year in large numbers. The slave power then undertook to secure possession of Kansas by fraud. At the first election for a Territorial Legislature, thousands of Missourians crossed the Kansas border and

voted.  The free State men disregarded this election, held
another, and organized a legislature of their own, so that for a
time there were two legislatures in session.  In the same
manner, two State Constitutions were formed, one at Lecompton, by a convention composed of members chosen in great
part by fraudulent Missouri votes, and one at Lawrence, by a
convention representing the anti-slavery settlers of the Territory.  The administration at Washington endeavored to force
the pro-slavery Constitution upon the people.  Great efforts
were made to this end through the agency of the Federal office-
holders in the Territory, supported by detachments of Federal
troops, and these efforts were abandoned only when it became
evident that the free State men were in an overwhelming
majority and were determined to have their rights.  The Kansas War finally degenerated into a series of plundering raids
by parties of Missourians, but these in time became too hazardous to be continued.  Some Democrats in Congress opposed the
course of the administration toward Kansas and were called
Anti-Lecompton Democrats, but the bulk of the party stood
steadily on the side of the South as long as the Democrats held
power in Congress.  Kansas, with its free State Constitution,
was refused admission to the Union.

Every incident of the long struggle in Kansas was promptly
reported in the Northern papers, and the anti-slavery element in
the North followed the conflict with intense interest, and
looked upon the men who took their lives in their hands and
went to the new Territory to secure it for freedom as heroes of
a just and patriotic cause.  It was the Kansas and Nebraska
Bill and the struggle between freedom and slavery beyond the
Missouri which finally crystallized the anti-slavery sentiment of
the North into the organization known as the Republican
Party.

## CHAPTER XI.

### THE OSTEND MANIFESTO, THE DRED SCOTT DECISION, AND THE ATTACK ON CHARLES SUMNER.

THREE events occurring in the period we are now describing contributed powerfully towards increasing the alarm in the North at the purposes and spirit of the slave power. In August 1854, Secretary of State William L. Marcy secretly directed James Buchanan, John Y. Mason, and Pierre Soule, our ministers at London, Paris, and Madrid, respectively, to meet in some European city and confer about the best method of getting possession of Cuba. The conference took place at Ostend, and resulted in a dispatch to our Government, known as the "Ostend Manifesto," which recommended the immediate purchase of Cuba, and threatened Spain with a forcible seizure of the island in case she should refuse to sell it. The purpose of the Cuban annexation scheme thus developed was to prevent the island from ever becoming a free republic like San Domingo, and to make out of it one or more slave States to reenforce the slave power in Congress. Nothing came of the manifesto, save the resulting anger of European nations and the increased determination created in the North to oppose the schemes of the pro-slavery leaders.

The Supreme Court of the United States at this time was thoroughly in sympathy with the projects of the pro-slavery Democracy. The leaders of that party determined by a bold stroke to cut the Gordian knot of controversy as to the power of the Government over slavery in the Territories, and for this purpose they procured from the court what was known as the Dred Scott decision. Dred Scott was a negro belonging to an army officer who had taken him into a free State. This act entitled the slave to his liberty, and when he was afterward taken back to Missouri he sued for his freedom. The case was carried up to the Supreme Court. A majority of the judges decided that persons of African blood were never thought of or spoken of except as property when the Constitution was formed, and were not referred to by the Declaration of Independence, which says that all men are created free and equal and entitled to life, liberty, and the pursuit of happiness. Such persons, the court declared, had no status as citizens, and could not sue in any court, and were so far inferior that they had no rights that a white man was bound to respect. Proceeding then to the question of slavery in the Territories, the court, through its Chief-Justice, Roger B. Taney, held that the clause of the Constitution which says that "Congress shall have power to dispose of and make all needful regulations respecting the territory or other property belonging to the United States," applied only to territory that belonged to the United States when the Constitution was framed, and that in all other territory the slaveholder had the right to take his slaves, and Congress had no right to prevent him. This partisan decision was practically agreed to in 1855, but was held back until after the campaign of 1856, and made public early in 1857. It was designed to prohibit Congress from making any laws respecting slavery in the Territories, and to exclude all of the inhabitants of the United States of African blood, or mixed blood, from all of the privileges of citizenship, so far as such privileges were guaranteed and protected by the Federal Government. The decision shocked the humanity of the North, but was received in the South with great satisfaction. The slaveholders thought that they had at last secured from an authority that could not be disputed an absolute endorsement of their most extreme theories and had thrown over the institution of slavery the protecting shield of the highest tribunal in the land. They little dreamed of what the future had in store for them.

In May, 1856, a brutal and wanton attack was made upon Charles Sumner, a Senator from Massachusetts, by Preston

Brooks, a Representative from South Carolina. Mr. Sumner had made a speech upon the Kansas question, in which he had sharply criticised the State of South Carolina and had reflected somewhat severely upon Butler, one of her Senators. After the Senate had adjourned he was sitting at his desk engaged in writing, when Brooks approached him from behind, felled him to the floor with a blow from a heavy cane, and continued to beat him about the head till he was unconscious. A South Carolina member named Keitt and a Virginia member named Edmonson stood by at the time to prevent interference with the dastardly outrage. Mr. Sumner was severely injured and never fully recovered his former health. A disease of the spine ensued, and he was obliged to resort to a painful form of treatment which kept him for two years out of his seat in the Senate. The outrage produced great indignation throughout the North, which was intensified by the ovations paid to the ruffian Brooks when he returned home to South Carolina.

## CHAPTER XII.

### ORGANIZATION OF THE REPUBLICAN PARTY—CAMPAIGN OF 1856.

THE necessity for the organization of a national party to resist the encroachments of slavery was felt throughout the North immediately after the passage of the Kansas-Nebraska Bill. Events had already shaped the platform for such a party. It was in all men's minds, and might have been formulated in a single sentence, " The freedom of the Territories from the curse of slavery." Interference with slavery in the States where it existed by virtue of State law had not been thought of, save by the Abolitionists, who did not count as a political force. The men who were prepared to join a new party organization deter-

mined that slavery should be wedged in within the region where
it already existed, and that no protection should be given by
Federal law to property in slaves in the States whose laws declared that no such property should exist. The elements prepared for crystallization into a new party were the late Free
Soilers, the anti-slavery Whigs, and a small number of Democrats calling themselves anti-Nebraska men. The question
of when the Republican Party first originated, and who gave it
its name, has been much disputed, but within the past three
years it has come to be pretty generally acknowledged that the
Michigan State Convention, held at Jackson, early in June,
1854, was the first State representative body to take the name
of Republican. The title was suggested in a letter from Horace
Greeley to a delegate to that convention. This letter was shown
to the late Senator Howard and several other influential men.
The suggestion was deemed a good one, and the name was
formally adopted in the resolutions of the convention. A few
weeks later it was adopted by State conventions in Maine, Ohio,
Indiana, Illinois, Wisconsin, and Iowa. In most of the New England States, in Pennsylvania, and in the entire South, the Whig
Party still kept alive and ran tickets that year. The success of
the Republicans in all the States where they ran straight tickets
of their own gave a great impetus to the further extension of
the party. It won its first national triumph in the House of
Representatives elected in 1854, which convened in December,
1855, when the Republican candidate for Speaker, N. P. Banks
of Massachusetts, was elected.

In a single year, the Republican Party had carried most of
the Northern States and had secured a controlling influence in
the lower house of Congress. Its leaders were mostly men of
anti-slavery convictions from the old Whig Party, like Fessenden, Sumner, Greeley, Seward, Chase, Wade, and Chandler, but
there were among them several former Democrats. No account
was made of old political affiliations, however, and the only
test of membership was opposition to the encroachments of the

slave power. In 1855, the Republicans strengthened their State organizations and were successful in most of the Northern States. The Whig Party gave some last feeble signs of life in Maine, New Hampshire, Massachusetts, and Ohio. At the South, the Whigs almost in a mass merged themselves into the Know-Nothing or American organization. Conservative men in that section, opposed to reopening the slavery controversy, did not venture to ally themselves with the Republicans of the North, but took refuge in the American Party, where they were able for a brief time to combat the ultra pro-slavery element.

Thus far the Republicans had no national organization. On the 22d of February, 1856, the first Republican National Convention was held in Pittsburg, Pennsylvania. Its purpose was to better organize the party and to prepare the way for the Presidential campaign. A second convention, to nominate a President and Vice-President, met in Philadelphia on the 17th of June, and was presided over by Henry S. Lane, of Indiana. John C. Fremont, the intrepid Western explorer, was nominated for President on the first ballot, receiving 359 votes, to 196 for John McLean. William L. Dayton, of New Jersey, received 259 votes for Vice-President on an informal ballot, to 110 for Abraham Lincoln, and 180 scattering. Mr. Dayton was then unanimously nominated. The platform welcomed to the party all who were opposed to the repeal of the Missouri Compromise and the extension of slavery in the Territories, and who favored the admission of Kansas as a free State. It demanded the prohibition of slavery in all of the Territories of the United States, and denied the authority of Congress or a Territorial Legislature to give legal existence to slavery in any Territory, freedom being the public law of the national domain under the Constitution. It asserted the right and duty of Congress to prohibit in all Territories those twin relics of barbarism, slavery and polygamy.

The Democratic Convention met in Cincinnati on the 2d of June, and nominated James Buchanan for President on the

17th ballot. The voting at first was close between Buchanan and Pierce, Douglas having a small following. Toward the end, all the opposition to Buchanan centred on Douglas. The nominee for Vice-President was John C. Breckinridge of Kentucky. The platform denounced all attempts to prevent slavery in the Territories or the District of Columbia by legislation, and all objection to the admission of a new State on the ground that it established slavery. It revived the Kentucky and Virginia resolutions of 1797 and 1798, which contained an assertion of extreme State rights doctrines. It also recognized the right to maintain slavery in any part of the public domain, and promised the faithful execution of the fugitive-slave law.

The Know-Nothings, now calling themselves Americans, met in Philadelphia, on the 22d of February, and nominated for President Millard Fillmore of New York, and for Vice-President, Andrew Jackson Donelson of Tennessee. Their platform demanded that none but natives should hold office and that foreigners should not vote until they had lived twenty-one years in the country. On the 17th of September an insignificant remnant of the once powerful Whig Party convened in Baltimore and ratified the nomination of Mr. Fillmore. Their meeting attracted very little public attention.

The Presidential contest of 1856 was exceedingly animated in all of the Northern States. Colonel Fremont, although without any record as a politician, proved an exceedingly popular candidate. The Republicans carried every Northern State except Pennsylvania, New Jersey, Indiana, Illinois, and California, and gave to their ticket 114 electoral votes. The Americans carried but one State, Maryland. Buchanan's electoral vote was 174. Of the popular vote, Buchanan received 1,838,169 ; Fremont, 1,341,264 ; Fillmore 874,534. Buchanan had therefore a decided plurality but he lacked 377,629 votes of a majority over both of his competitors.

## CHAPTER XIII.

JOHN BROWN'S RAID—HELPER'S "IMPENDING CRISIS."

AN event that had a powerful effect in exciting the South, and in aggravating the growing sectional feeling in the North, took place in 1859. John Brown, who had distinguished himself as a brave free State leader in the Kansas war, invaded Harper's Ferry, Virginia, on the 17th of October, with an armed force consisting of 17 white men and 5 negroes. The invaders tore up the railroad track, cut the telegraph wires, and took possession of the United States Armory ; doing this by the authority of God Almighty, they said. Brown issued a proclamation calling upon the slaves of the South to rise and demand their liberty. The frightened inhabitants of the place appealed to the State authorities to come to their aid, and the State called upon the General Government. A force of United States marines was promptly despatched to Harper's Ferry, and a large body of Virginia militia was soon on the ground. Brown and his followers defended themselves in the armory building. A sharp conflict ensued. Hemmed in on all sides, Brown sent out a flag of truce, but the bearer, Stephens, was instantly shot down by the Virginians. One of Brown's men was captured by the Virginia militia, dragged out upon the railroad bridge, and shot in cold blood. Four of Brown's party attempted to escape by crossing the river, but three were mortally wounded. Brown made his last stand in an engine house, where he repulsed his assailants, who lost two killed and six wounded. The fight went on all day ; at night Brown's forces were reduced to three unwounded whites besides himself. Eight of his men, including two of his sons, were already dead, another lay dying, and two were captives, mortally wounded. Next morning the marines charged the engine house, battered down the door, and captured Brown with his surviving followers. The pur-

pose of the raid upon Harper's Ferry was to stimulate an insur-
rectionary movement throughout the South. Brown had drawn
up a sketch for a provisional government, and had nominated
several of his followers to the principal executive offices. He
was held a prisoner for about six weeks, tried at Charlestown,
Virginia, and hanged on the 2d day of December, exhibiting
to the last a heroic fortitude and an exalted frame of mind which
won for him the admiration of even his bitter enemies, the Virginians, and excited deep sympathy throughout the North. The
South was profoundly stirred by this invasion, insignificant as it
was in its dimensions and its results. The Southern people, in
their excited frame of mind undoubtedly believed that the
John Brown raid had the indorsement of the Republican Party
of the North, and was the beginning of an effort to destroy
slavery by inciting the slaves to a general insurrection. The
horrible history of the San Domingo massacre had always been
a terror to the Southern people, and a rumor of a negro rising
had, on several occasions in the past, sufficed to throw them
into a convulsive state of anger and apprehension. It was not
strange, therefore, that an effort to organize an insurrection, led
by courageous white men from the North, should provoke their
fiercest animosity.

John Brown had few apologists though a great many sympathizers in the North. His movement was his own secret and
was not abetted by any body of anti-slavery men. Just how
great an influence it exercised on the subsequent history of the
country it would, of course, be impossible to measure, but the
feelings it produced and the memories it left in the South were
a principal agency in inclining the Southern people to separate
from the North and set up a Government of their own.

A book published about this time on the slavery question
added to the irritation in the South. It was called " The Impending Crisis," and its author was Hinton R. Helper, a North
Carolinian, who had migrated to California. The book was

addressed to the slaveholding whites of the South, and was a powerful argument, re-enforced by statistics drawn from United States census reports, to prove that slavery cursed the industries of the Southern States.• The poverty of those States in respect to accumulated wealth and agricultural products in comparison with the States of the North, was forcibly set forth and the non-slaveholding Southern whites were urged to throw off the control of the small minority of slaveholders and take the affairs of their States into their own hands. The circulation of this book was everywhere prohibited in the South. It was regarded as an incendiary document, although it contained nothing but calm reasoning and indisputable statistics. Several Republican members of the House signed a letter endorsing the volume, and their conduct was made the subject of an acrimonious discussion. At one time a resolution came near passing, affirming that no man who recommended the book was fit to be Speaker of the House. "The Impending Crisis" had an immense sale and though its effect in the South was only to aggravate the pro-slavery feeling, it opened the eyes of many people in the North to the blighting effect of slavery upon industry, manufactures, and trade.

## CHAPTER XIV.

### THE CAMPAIGN OF 1860.

THE Republicans were not discouraged by their defeat in 1856. They saw that if they had carried the States of Pennsylania and Indiana they would have succeeded, and felt that they had formed what was destined to be the great party of the future, and that their principles would prevail in time. The promulgation of the Dred Scott decision immediately after the inauguration of Mr. Buchanan gave new vigor to the Republican cause, showing as it did that the pro-slavery party intended to fully subjugate the whole country and make of it a vast slave empire. The conduct of Buchanan in continuing the efforts of Pierce to force slavery upon the Territory of Kansas kept alive the discussion of the question of the freedom of the Territories until the next Presidential election. Buchanan was as fully subservient to the South as Pierce had been. His administration was controlled by ultra pro-slavery men, and directed its energies to carrying out the schemes of the slave power.

In 1856, Abraham Lincoln and Stephen A. Douglas contested the State of Illinois for the United States Senatorship, and made a memorable canvass which attracted great attention throughout the country. Douglas advocated what was known as his squatter sovereignty policy, which was that Congress should abstain from all legislation as to slavery in the Territories and allow the people to settle the question for themselves. Mr. Lincoln advocated the right and duty of Congress to prohibit slavery in the Territories. Although Lincoln had a majority of the popular vote, Douglas had a majority in the Legislature and was elected. The South was not satisfied with the Douglas squatter sovereignty plan, the theory of the pro-slavery leaders being that slavery could not be prohibited in the Territories by any power whatever. This theory was repugnant to a great majority of the Democrats of the North, and the conflict between it and the Douglas theory led to a disruption of the Democratic party. The Democratic national convention met at Charleston, on the 23d of April, 1860, and immediately got into a heated controversy upon the subject of slavery. Finally, by a close vote, it was resolved that as differences had existed in the party as to the nature and extent of the powers of the Territorial Legislatures and as to the powers and duties of Congress under the Constitution, over the institution of slavery within the Territories, the Democratic party would abide by the decision of the Supreme Court on the question of constitutional law. This exceedingly guarded and neutral declaration angered the

Southern delegates, and most of them withdrew from the convention. An adjournment was carried until the 18th of June, when the convention reassembled in Baltimore. The seceding delegates met and adopted an extreme pro-slavery platform, and adjourned to assemble in Richmond June 11th. The regular convention reassembled in Baltimore and nominated Stephen A. Douglas, of Illinois, for President, and Benjamin Fitzpatrick, of Alabama, for Vice-President. Fitzpatrick subsequently declined, and Herschel V. Johnson, of Georgia, was substituted by the National Committee. The Baltimore Convention affirmed Douglas' squatter sovereignty theory. The Bolting Convention met in Richmond and adjourned to meet again in Baltimore, June 23d, when it adopted the Charleston platform and nominated John C. Breckinridge, of Kentucky, for President, and Joseph Lane, of Oregon, for Vice-President.

A new party, composed mainly of former members of the now dead American party in the South and a few stubborn old Whigs in the North, was formed at Baltimore May 9th. It took the name of the Constitutional Union party, and nominated for President John Bell, of Tennessee, and for Vice-President Edward Everett, of Massachusetts. This party declared that it recognized no political principles other than the Constitution of the country, the union of the States, and the enforcement of the laws. This last phrase was intended to refer to the Fugitive Slave law. The Republican National Convention met in Chicago May 16th, 1860. It was generally supposed, prior to the meeting of the convention, that William H. Seward would be nominated for President. He was recognized as the chief leader of the new party, and its greatest teacher on the political bearings of slavery. His principal competitor was Abraham Lincoln, of Illinois. The other candidates were Simon Cameron, of Pennsylvania, Salmon P. Chase, of Ohio, Edward Bates, of Missouri, William L. Dayton, of New Jersey, John McLean, of Ohio, and Jacob Collamer, of Vermont. Mr. Seward led on the first and second ballot, but the argument that he would not be a popular candidate in the States of Pennsylvania, Indiana, and Illinois—the States lost by the Republicans in 1856—led to the nomination of Lincoln on the third ballot.   Hannibal Hamlin, of Maine, was nominated for Vice-President.   The platform was substantially that adopted in 1856.   Its chief planks were those referring to slavery in the Territories.   It declared freedom to be the normal condition of the Territories, and denounced the new dogma that the Constitution, with its own force, carried slavery there.

In the campaign of 1860 the Republicans were united and confident, while the Democrats were divided into two factions, which fought each other about as vigorously as they did their common enemy.   These factions were known by the name of their leaders, one being called Douglas Democrats, and the other Breckinridge Democrats.   There were few Douglas men in the South and few Breckinridge men in the North.   The strength of the new Constitutional Union party was almost wholly confined to the South.   Every free State but New Jersey was carried by the Republicans, and in New Jersey the refusal of a part of the Douglas men to support the fusion ticket allowed four of the Lincoln electors to slip in.   The electoral vote was divided as follows : Lincoln, 180, all from the North ; Breckinridge, 72, all from the South ; Bell, 39, from Virginia, Kentucky, and Tennessee ; and Douglas, 12, from Missouri and New Jersey.   The popular vote was, Lincoln, 1,857,610 ; Douglas, 1,291,574 ; Breckinridge, 850,082 ; Bell, 646,124.

The very large vote given to Mr. Douglas was due, in some part, to his personal popularity.   He was the idol of the Democratic party of the North, and had the South chosen to give him its support, instead of seceding from the convention and nominating Breckinridge, he would probably have been elected President.   With his comparatively moderate views on the subject of slavery, which were becoming more and more modified in the right direction as he saw the tendency of the pro-slavery leaders, it is not unlikely that he would have averted or at least postponed the war.

---

## CHAPTER XV.

### SECESSION—REBELLION—WAR.

As soon as the election of Lincoln and Hamlin was known to be beyond dispute, movements for seceding from the Union began in the South. The Southern-leaders did not wait to learn what the policy of the new administration would be, but made haste to break the relations of their States with the Union and to form a separate government, under the title of the Confederate States of America. As early as December South Carolina seceded ; other States followed during the winter, and in February a complete Rebel government was organized at Montgomery and a Rebel army put into the field. A considerable party in the Southern States, composed mostly of old Whigs, opposed secession, but were overpowed by the more active, unscrupulous, and determined supporters of the movement. During the session of Congress just prior to Mr. Lincoln's inauguration great efforts were made in the way of conciliatory propositions to induce the Southern States not to renounce their allegiance to the Union. The Republicans were willing to go to the farthest extent possible not involving the vital principle of their party that the Territories of the United States were free soil by virtue of the Constitution. The plan known as the Crittenden Compromise received a large vote in both Houses, although opposed by most Republicans. Its principal provision was that all of the territory north of latitude 36 degrees and 30 minutes should forever be free, and that all of the territory south of that line should be given up to slavery.

Senator Anthony, a Republican, was willing to admit New Mexico as a slave State, because slavery already existed there, but this was as far as he or any other Republican proposed to go concerning the disputed question of the condition of the Territories. A series of resolutions, accompanied by a constitutional amendment, passed both Houses, however, guaranteeing slavery in the States where it existed against any interference on the part of the Federal Government, and recommending the Northern States which had passed laws obstructing the recovery of fugitives to repeal them. A Peace Conference, invited by the Legislature of Virginia, sat in Washington in February. Thirteen Northern States and seven Southern States were represented. Its propositions had no effect in staying the rising tide of rebellion. The Southern leaders had fully made up their minds to dissolve the Union, and although many of them remained in Congress up to the time of Lincoln's inauguration, they did so avowedly for the purpose of resisting legislation which might be hostile to their section.

It is not the purpose of this work to trace the history of the war for the preservation of the Union further than is necessary to show the action of the political parties concerning its prosecution. The Republican party was the war party from the beginning to the end of the struggle, holding the Union to be a perpetual bond, and not a league which could be dissolved at the pleasure of any of its members. It also held that the Republic was indestructible, and that the duty of the United States Government was to enforce obedience to its authority.

The Democratic party in the North was in an extremely awkward predicament when the storm of war burst upon the country. For a whole generation it had maintained the theory of the Virginia and Kentucky resolutions, that the States were sovereign and were themselves the judges of the constitutionality of the Federal laws and acts. Out of this theory grew logically another, that the Government had no right to coerce sovereign States. This was the theory upon which Mr. Buchanan's administration proceeded during the three months in which the Rebellion organized itself throughout the South. It continued to be held by a considerable portion of the Northern Democracy, but the patriotic feeling which followed the attack upon Fort Sumter caused it to be exceedingly unpopular for a while, and it was rarely avowed in public during the first year of the war. For a time there was but one political party in the North, and that was the party of the Union. As the war went on, however, and it became evident that it was going to be a long struggle and no holiday parade, as many had imagined, the Democrats took courage and reorganized their party as an anti-administration party. They did not avowedly oppose the prosecution of the war at that time ; some of them, indeed, insisted that if they were in power they would push it more vigorously, but the spirit of their movement was one of dissatisfaction with the contest. In 1862, after the disaster to our armies on the Peninsula and at the second battle of Bull Run, a feeling of discontent arose throughout the North which took the form of hostility to the Republican party in the fall elections of that year. The Democrats carried the great central belt of States, beginning with New York and ending at the Mississippi River. Fortunately, in only one State was there a Governor to be elected. That was in the State of New York, where the Democrats chose Horatio Seymour, by the aid of enormous election frauds committed in the City of New York. The Republicans were barely able to secure a majority in the new House, and were for a time greatly discouraged by their reverses and apprehensive that the Democratic triumphs might lead to the ultimate success of the Rebellion. In 1863, however, the capture of Vicksburg by General Grant and the decisive victory at Gettysburg completely turned the current of public sentiment. The Republicans recovered that year every State they had lost in 1862.

Wherever the contest was the hottest there their victory was the greatest. The great political battle of the year occurred in Ohio, where the Democrats nominated Clement L. Vallandigham for Governor. He was an avowed opponent of the war and an open sympathizer with the South. The majority against him was the largest ever given at any election in the State, running up to nearly 100,000.

In 1863, the Democratic party in most of the Northern States threw off all pretension of sympathy with the Union cause. On this account they were given by the Republicans the name of "copperheads." In some parts of the West they wore pins made of the butternut, to typify their sympathy with the South, the Southern soldiers being frequently clad in homespun dyed with the juice of that nut.

A long and bloody riot occurred in the City of New York in 1863, in which thousands of Democrats resisted the draft and held possession of many parts of the city for several days, murdering a number of people. The Democratic Governor of the State, Horatio Seymour, addressed the mob in front of City Hall, at the height of the riot, and styled the lawless persons composing it "my friends." The riot was finally suppressed by United States troops, after considerable slaughter. In the State of Indiana a formidable conspiracy under the title of the "Sons of Liberty," was organized by the Democratic sympathizers with the South, but was suppressed by the vigilance and courage of Oliver P. Morton, the Republican Governor of the State.

In several of the States the Republicans in 1863 dropped their party name and took that of the Union party, in order to save the feelings of the war Democrats who desired to co-operate with them. The voting force of these war Democrats was comparatively small, but among them were a number of men of undoubted patriotism and high position in the country. Most of them continued to co-operate with the Republican party during and after the war.

The Republican party did not enter the war with the purpose of abolishing slavery. A few far-sighted men saw that the struggle must end either in the separation of the South or the freedom of the slaves, but the masses of the party did not look beyond the suppression of the Rebellion and the preservation of the Union. President Lincoln said that if he could save the Union with slavery he would save it, and that if he could save it without slavery he would save it. As the war went on, the folly of recognizing and protecting an institution which gave the rebels a large force of laboring men to stay at home and raise food for their armies became plainly apparent, and there was a general demand for the abolition of slavery as a war measure. It was not, however, till April, 1862, that slavery was abolished in the District of Columbia, nor till June, 1864, that the Fugitive Slave laws were repealed. In the early military operations against the Rebellion great care was taken not to excite insurrections among the slaves, and the negroes who came into our lines were treated as contraband property, so as not to be restored to their masters. On September 22d, 1862, President Lincoln issued his first proclamation of emancipation, which was, in effect, a threat to the States then in rebellion that they would lose their slaves unless they returned to the Union. He declared that on January 1st following all persons held as slaves in any State which should be then in rebellion should be then and forever after free. On January 1st, 1863, no rebel State having returned to the Union, he issued his second proclamation, designating the States and parts of States in rebellion, and ordering and declaring that all persons held as slaves in such regions " are and shall be free," and pledging the Government to maintain their freedom. " On this measure," said Lincoln, " I invoke the considerate judgment of mankind and the gracious favor of God." This celebrated proclamation professed to be a war-measure, adopted by authority of the President as the commander-in-chief of the army and navy.

The Thirteenth Amendment of the Constitution prohibiting slavery in the United States passed the Senate in April, 1864, and the House in January, 1865, but was not ratified by a sufficient number of States to make it valid until nearly a year after the end of the war. It was essentially a Republican measure, all of the Republicans in Congress voting for it, and nearly all of the Democrats voting against it. It will stand for all time as the noblest of the many monuments which mark the brilliant history of the Republican party. Public sentiment was slow to take shape in favor of the total abolition of the curse of slavery, but its progress was certain, and when the amendment was ratified it was approved by the entire Republican party. For some time afterward the Democratic party continued to denounce the Thirteenth Amendment, declaring it void and of no effect, but long ago even the most bigoted and stubborn Democrats came to acquiesce not only to its validity but in its justice and wisdom.

---

## CHAPTER XVII.

### THE PRESIDENTIAL CAMPAIGN OF 1864.

ANXIOUS to secure the co-operation of all men who favored the prosecution of the war, the Republicans, in 1864, called a Union National Convention to meet in Baltimore. The convention renominated Abraham Lincoln for President, and nominated Andrew Johnson, of Tennessee, for Vice-President. The nomination of Lincoln was by acclamation, but there were a number of candidates for the Vice-Presidency, prominent among whom were Hannibal Hamlin and Daniel S. Dickinson. Prior to the

Baltimore Convention a small number of Republicans, dissatisfied with the administration, and especially with its leniency
toward rebels, met at Cleveland and nominated John C. Fre-
mónt for President, and John Cochrane for Vice-President.
Their convention demanded the suppression of the rebellion
without compromise, and the confiscation of the lands of the
rebels, and their distribution among soldiers and actual settlers.
General Fremont accepted the nomination but repudiated the
confiscation plank of the platform.   Subsequently both the candidates withdrew from the field, and the whole movement col-
lapsed.   The Democrats held their convention in Chicago, and
manifested open hostility to the continuance of the war.   Bitter speeches were made, denouncing the administration.   A
platform was adopted declaring the war a failure, and attacking those who carried it on for disregarding the Constitution,
treading upon public liberty, perverting right, and impairing
justice, humanity, and material prosperity.   The convention
nominated for President General George B. McClellan, whose
half-hearted, dilatory course while in command of the army of
the Potomac was largely responsible for whatever failure had
characterized the war up to that time.   George H. Pendleton,
of Ohio, was nominated for Vice-President.   The platform
crippled the Democratic party in the canvass, for scarcely had it
been published when news came that Sherman had taken
Atlanta, and that Farragut had carried the defences of Mobile.
In the face of such victories as these the declaration that the
war was a failure sounded absurd and treasonable.

In the canvass of 1864 the Democrats attacked the administration for exceeding its constitutional powers in suspending the
habeas corpus and imprisoning rebel sympathizers and agents
in the North without trial.   They did not openly avow their
old theory, that the States could not be coerced; but they had
a great deal to say about the " bloody and endless war, brought
on by the anti-slavery agitators in the North." They denounced

the emancipation proclamation and appealed to the prejudice
against the negroes, still very strong in the North, by asserting
that the war was an abolition war, carried on not to restore the
Union but to free the slaves. The Republicans had practically
but one argument to make, and that was, that it was the duty
of every patriot to sustain the Government in its efforts to crush
the Rebellion and save the Union. The result of the election
was the success of the Republicans by very large majorities.
Mr. Lincoln had the electoral vote of every State not in the
rebellion, except Kentucky, Delaware, and New Jersey. He
received 212 electoral votes against 21 cast for McClellan. His
popular vote was 2,213,665 against 1,802,237. The success
of the Republicans in this critical campaign assured the ultimate triumph of the Union arms in the field, confirmed the
emancipation of the slaves, and opened the way to the termina-
tion of the war. Had the Democrats prevailed, there is little
reason to doubt that the war would have ended by a recognition
of the independence of the rebel States.

## CHAPTER XVIII.

### SECURING THE FRUITS OF THE WAR—THE STRUGGLE WITH ANDREW JOHNSON.

AFTER the Republican party had carried the war through to
a successful issue, destroying upon the battle-field the doctrine
of secession, and forcing the surrender of the rebel armies, it
was called upon to meet a new and very grave issue, involving
the security of the results of its past efforts.

Lincoln was assassinated in April, 1865, very soon after his
second inauguration. The Vice-President, Andrew Johnson,
became President. At first he was so radical and violent in
his treatment of the conquered rebels that it was feared that

he intended to depart wholly from the policy of kindly firmness followed by Mr. Lincoln. Before many months, however, he changed his attitude completely, and undertook to defeat the will of his party in Congress in respect to the reorganization of the rebel States. He had been bitterly opposed to the dominant element of the South all his life—coming of ignorant, poor white stock, and representing in his early career the antagonism of the non-slaveholding element in Tennessee against the slaveholders ; but all at once, when trusted with the reins of government, he manifested a stubborn purpose to carry out the wishes of the leading Southern men and to give them control of their local affairs.

The problem of restoring the Southern States to their relations to the Union was a difficult one, and the Republicans were not at first wholly agreed as to its proper solution. After nearly two years of consideration of the question, the party, however, came with substantial unanimity to the ground that the rebel States had forfeited their rights as States of the Union by the act of rebellion, and had become unorganized communities, held under the Constitution by conquest, and to be dealt with as Congress might see fit. Their re-entry into the Union must, it was maintained, be under such conditions as Congress should prescribe. In the mean time they were kept under military government, and were divided, for the purpose, into military districts. The Democrats held that so soon as hostilities ceased each rebel State had a right to reorganize its own State Government, and to enter into all of the privileges of a member of the national Union, without any interference or dictation on the part of Congress. This was the theory advocated by Andrew Johnson. Its purpose was to reinstate the white men of the South in full control of their local governments, leaving them to deal with the emancipated negro populations as they saw fit, under the solitary restraint of the Thirteenth Amendment.

After having emancipated the slaves, the Democrats held that Congress had nothing more to do with them. The temporary governments organized by the whites in several of the Southern States proceeded to pass codes of black laws, which reduced the negroes to a condition of serfdom, differing practically but very little from the old condition of slavery. President Johnson did not avowedly go over to the Democratic party : he kept Mr. Seward and several other Republicans in his Cabinet, but his policy toward the South was essentially a Democratic policy, and was sustained by very few people in Congress or the country except the Democrats. A small body of office-holders stood by him in order to retain their places, and became popularly known as "the bread and butter brigade." In 1867, the Republicans passed a series of acts, known as the Reconstruction laws, providing for the establishment of new State governments in the South. These laws allowed every man to vote, black or white, except such as had previously taken an oath to support the Constitution of the United States and had participated in the Rebellion. This limitation disfranchised a very large portion of the active and influential white men. President Johnson vetoed the Reconstruction acts, and they were passed over his veto, the Republicans having at that time and throughout his administration a two-thirds majority in both Houses.

The conduct of Johnson created a good deal of irritation and bad feeling. He was regarded as a traitor to the Republican party and the stubbornness with which he clung to his idea of the rights of the Southern States under the Constitution was generally believed among the Republicans to arise from a settled purpose on his part to betray his party and to destroy the substantial results of its victory over the Rebellion. The intense dislike and strong suspicion of Johnson which animated the greater portion of the Republican party resulted in the passage of articles of impeachment against him, on the 22d of February, 1868. The specifications were based on the President's illegal removal of Edwin M. Stanton from the office of the Secretary of War, his expressions in party speeches of contempt of Congress, and his hindrance of the execution of some of its acts. The trial began in the Senate on March 23d, and lasted nearly two months, attracting the closest attention of the whole country. Johnson was acquitted for lack of a two-thirds majority against him, the vote on the several articles of impeachment standing, guilty 35, not guilty 19. A few Republicans, led by Mr. Fessenden, of Maine, not believing him guilty of an offence warranting his removal from office, voted with the Democrats for his acquittal. The general effect of his obstinate resistance to Congress was to strengthen the Republican party, and the men that deserted its ranks to follow him were so few in number that they were scarcely missed. At one time Johnson appeared to contemplate the formation of a new party, of which he was to be the leader ; but he ended, after his term of office closed, in joining the Democratic party, which sent him to the Senate from Tennessee.

The Fourteenth Amendment to the Constitution was adopted in June, 1866, by Republican votes exclusively, in both Houses of Congress. This amendment made the freed negroes citizens of the United States and of the States in which they lived, and prohibited any State from abridging or limiting the privileges or immunities of citizens. It left each State to regulate the right of voting, but if a State excluded any of its citizens on account of race, color, or previous condition of servitude, it lost its representative and electoral strength proportionately. The amendment also provided that no person should hold office in the United States or any State who, not having taken the oath to support the Constitution of the United States, and had joined in the Rebellion ; but Congress might remove this disability by a vote of two-thirds of each branch. It provided, further, that neither the United States nor any State should assume or pay any debt accrued in the aid of the Rebellion, or from any of the

losses from the emancipation of the slaves. The Democratic
party vehemently opposed this amendment, and it was not fully
ratified by the requisite number of States until July, 1868.
Long after its ratification the Democrats were in the habit of
condemning it as revolutionary, unconstitutional, null and void.
Subsequent experience did not justify all of its provisions. The
section creating a class of persons under disabilities in the
South was after a time deemed unwise by a large majority of
the Republicans, and was greatly modified by successive amnesty measures.

In 1866, the Civil Rights act was passed, providing severe
penalties against any person who under color of any law or
ordinance should attempt to deprive the freedmen of equal
rights or subject them to any penalty or prohibition different
from those to which the whites were subjected. This act as well
as Amendment XIV was vetoed by President Johnson, opposed by the Democrats, and passed by the Republicans over
that veto and in spite of that opposition.

---

## CHAPTER XIX.

### THE CAMPAIGN OF 1868.

THE Presidential campaign of 1868 was fought upon the issues
growing out of the Reconstruction acts of Congress, the Amendments to the Constitution, and the suffrage and citizenship they
conferred upon the colored race. The Republican National
Convention met in Chicago, May 20th, and nominated General
Ulysses S. Grant for President by acclamation. A sharp contest took place over the Vice-Presidency. The first ballot resulted as follows : Schuyler Colfax, of Indiana, 115 ; Benjamin
F. Wade, of Ohio, 147 ; Reuben E. Fenton, of New York, 126 ;
Henry Wilson, of Massachusetts, 119 ; Andrew G. Curtin, of

Pennsylvania, 51 ; Hannibal Hamlin, of Maine, 28 ; James M.
Speed, of Kentucky, 22 ; James Harlan, of Iowa, 16 ; J. A. J.
Creswell, of Maryland, 14 ; W. D. Kelley, of Pennsylvania, 4 ;
S. C. Pomeroy, of Kansas, 6. On the fifth ballot Schuyler
Colfax was nominated, receiving 541 votes. The chief features
of the platform were the indorsements of the constitutional
amendments securing the political and civil equality of the
blacks and of the Reconstruction acts of Congress.

The Democratic National Convention met in New York, July
4th, and nominated Horatio Seymour, of New York, for President, and Francis P. Blair, of Missouri, for Vice-President.
An attempt was made to liberalize the party and induce it to
cease its opposition to the results of the war, by the nomination of Salmon P. Chase, of Ohio, who stood a little aloof
from the Republican party and held rather a neutral attitude.
It was unsuccessful. Moderate ideas prevailed, however, in the
platform, which was cautiously worded so as not to offend a
considerable number of Democrats who were in favor of what
was called " accepting the situation." Among the candidates
for the Presidency before the convention was General W. S.
Hancock, who received a large vote from men who desired to
make use of his military reputation as an offset to that of General Grant. The majority of the convention were not willing,
however, to nominate any man whose record of hostility to all
of the Republican measures during the last ten years was in any
way doubtful. The Democratic campaign was so bad a failure
that before it closed the leading Democratic newspaper organ demanded a change in the ticket as the only way of securing the
possibility of success. General Grant was elected by a popular
vote of 3,012,833 against 2,703,249. He carried all the States
except Delaware, Georgia, Kentucky, Louisiana, Maryland, New
Jersey, New York, and Oregon. Three States—Virginia, Mississippi, and Texas—had not gone through with the process of reconstruction and therefore had no vote. Of the electoral votes

Grant received 214, and Seymour 80.   After this overwhelming
defeat a growing sentiment in favor of accepting the results of
the war and ceasing the hopeless contest against the inevitable
took possession of the Democratic Party.   The election was
exceedingly important in its influence upon the history of the
country.   Had the Republicans been defeated the whole policy
of equal suffrage and citizenship would probably have been
overturned.   That policy was completed and firmly secured a year
later by the Fifteenth Amendment to the Constitution, which
provided that neither the United States nor any State should
abridge the right of any citizen to vote on account of race,
color, or previous condition of servitude.   The ratification of
this amendment by the requisite number of States was proclaimed March 20th, 1870.

---

## CHAPTER XX.

### CONDITION OF THE SOUTH—CARPET-BAG-GOVERNMENT—THE KU-KLUX KLAN CONSPIRACY.

ENCOURAGED by President Johnson's opposition to the Reconstruction acts to believe that they would in the end be set
aside, the white people of the States which had joined the Rebellion very generally refrained from taking part in the elections under these acts, and thus the newly enfranchised negroes
became suddenly possessed of almost unlimited political power.
With them acted a few respectable white natives who had
conscientiously opposed the war, a few enterprising Northern
emigrants who went South to invest their means and better
their fortunes, and a few adventurers attracted by the prospect
of office.   This was a poor foundation on which to rear a stable
structure of local government.   The mass of the white population
looked upon the negroes as they would upon so many cattle or
horses which they had been robbed of by the National Govern-

ment, and regarded them in their quality of voters and citizens with undisguised hatred and contempt. The State Governments established under the new order of things were the subject of constant insult in the Southern papers, and were despised and detested by the great mass of the native tax-paying people. The poor whites were fully as hostile as the better classes. To some extent the new governments merited the condemnation they received. Most of them were ignorant and rapacious, borrowing and wasting large sums of money, raising heavy taxes, and creating numberless scandals. It made no difference, however, what was the character of the men connected with these governments—they were all denounced as thieves. Northern white men who had settled in the South, whether they held office or not, were stigmatized as " carpet-baggers," and every native white man who joined the Republican Party was denounced as a " scallawag," and cut off from all social relations with his neighbors. The carpet-bag governments, as they were called, could not have existed for a moment without the support of the national authority. Troops were stationed in every capital and principal city through the South, for the purpose of awing the disaffected people and compelling obedience to the local authorities. Even these means were not wholly effective, however. A secret organization sprang up as if by magic in all parts of the South, whose members were exclusively white men, hostile to the new order of things, and sworn to accomplish the destruction of negro rule. This organization was called the Ku-Klux Klan. Its ostensible purpose at first was to keep the blacks in order and prevent them from committing small depredations upon the property of the whites, but its real motives were essentially political. The members met in secret conclaves, and rode about the country at night wearing long gowns of black or scarlet cloth, with hideous masks or hoods enveloping their heads. They murdered many of the negro leaders, and in pursuance of their scheme for overawing the colored population took the poor blacks out of their cabins at night and brutally flogged them. In some neighborhoods scarcely a colored man escaped a visitation from these terrible midnight riders. The negroes were invariably required to promise not to vote the Republican ticket, and threatened with death if they broke their promises. In some places the Ku-Klux Klan assaulted Republican officials in their houses or offices or upon the public roads ; in others they attacked the meetings of negroes and dispersed them. Their action took almost every form of lawlessness, and was adopted with the single purpose of breaking down the authority of the Republican State and local governments, and preparing the way for a Democratic victory at the elections. The Ku-Klux Klan order and its variations extended throughout the entire South. In some localities it was called by other names, such as the " White League," or the " Knights of the White Camellia," and sometimes its members appeared without disguise and made their murderous attacks upon their political opponents in broad daylight. In such cases it was given out by the Southern newspapers that a riot had occurred, in which the blacks were the aggressors. Wherever the facts were obtained by the investigations of committees of Congress, it was found that this explanation was a false one, and that whites were always the attacking party.

The Ku-Klux Klan were particularly active in the Northern counties of South Carolina, and these counties were selected by President Grant for the enforcement of an act of Congress, passed by the Republicans, with the view of suppressing these treasonable and murderous organizations. The habeas corpus was suspended by Executive order in the five counties referred to, a considerable body of troops was stationed there, and large numbers of arrests were made by the soldiers. Nearly three hundred Ku-Klux were imprisoned at one time at Yorkville, South Carolina, under military guard. Their disguises and other articles were captured, and several of them made full confession of the atrocities in which they had been engaged. A few were selected for trial and were convicted and sentenced to imprisonment in the Albany Penitentiary. The rest were released on their pledges of good behavior. The result of these severe measures was to break up the Ku-Klux organizations throughout the South. Hostility to negro suffrage and Republican government subsequently took other forms of violence, but the whipping and killing of defenceless people by masked midnight riders was abandoned.

The Republicans of the North earnestly sustained the measures of the Government for the punishment of conspiracy and of crime, and for the defense of the rights of their brethren in the South. The inefficiency and corruption which characterized most of the Southern State governments produced, however, considerable effect upon the Northern mind, and in course of time a large portion of the Northern Republicans grew weary of the effort to sustain those governments by armed force. Thus there came to be a division in the party, one element believing it to be the duty of the administration to continue its policy of interference in Southern affairs, and the other contending that the difficult problem of good government and equal rights in that section could be best worked out by the Southern people themselves, without any outside pressure. The stories of Southern outrages grew monotonous and wearisome. Many people doubted their authenticity, because from their own experience in the law-abiding communities of the North they could not conceive of a state of things so wholly foreign to anything they had observed at home. It did not seem reasonable that men should be guilty of such barbarous acts as were done in the South for the purpose of gaining political power. All reference to those acts and arguments drawn from them were characterized, in the political parlance of the time, as " waving the bloody shirt," and lost their effect upon the public mind. Nevertheless only a small part of the truth concerning the state of affairs in the South between 1867 and 1876 was ever made known. It is not extravagant to assert that more men lost their lives during that period for the sole crime of being Republicans than fell on any one battle-field of the war

In the course of eight years of President Grant's administration the white Democrats of the South succeeded in getting possession of all of their States except South Carolina, Florida, and Louisiana—overcoming the Republican majorities by a system of intimidation, violence, and fraud.    The three remaining States passed into their hands immediately after the accession of President Hayes.    President Grant's policy toward the South was not uniform and consistent.    At times he was exceedingly firm in his defense of the so-called carpet-bag governments, but at other times he was yielding or indifferent, and allowed the processes for the destruction of those governments to go on without interference.    Toward the close of his official career he came to the conclusion that it was unwise to longer attempt to support by Federal bayonets authority which was obnoxious to the influential and intelligent tax-paying classes of the South. In this conclusion a large portion of the Republicans sympathized, but their opinion did not in the least modify their feelings of condemnation of the methods by which the Southern Democrats had overturned the Republican State governments in that section.

## CHAPTER XXI.

### DEFENDING THE NATIONAL HONOR AND THE PUBLIC CREDIT.

IT is now time to refer to a portion of the career of the Republican Party which reflected great honor upon it, and entitled it anew to the respect and gratitude of the country.    At the end of the war the United States owed an enormous bonded debt.    In addition it had outstanding a large volume of paper

currency, issued with the understanding that it should be redeemed in coin as soon as the Government was able to do so.
In 1867, after the floating obligations remaining from the war
had been gathered in and funded, the question of how to deal
with the debt and the currency was taken up in earnest by the
Republicans in Congress. Their plans met with vehement opposition from a large portion of the Democratic Party. A new
and preposterous theory was advanced, to the effect that the
notes of the Government, called greenbacks, were actual money
instead of promises to pay money, and that the bonded debt of
the United States could be lawfully and honorably discharged
with these notes. This theory started in the West and was
called at first "Pendletonism," from the fact that Pendleton,
the Democratic candidate for Vice-President in 1864, was
among its early and prominent advocates. It was claimed by
the supporters of this theory that as greenbacks were real money
the country ought to have a large supply of them. They favored an immediate issue of hundreds and even thousands of
millions of dollars. All of the bonds that were not specifically
made payable in coin they proposed to pay off at once in greenbacks, and thus stop the interest upon them. The paper money
idea soon developed into a great popular mania in the West.
Many Republicans were carried away by it, but the majority of
the party firmly resisted it. Not much headway was made by
this dangerous and dishonest heresy east of the Alleghany
Mountains, but beyond that line, clear through to the far West,
the excitement raged for several years. It must be said, in
credit of the Democrats of the East, that they gave no assistance
to the greenback idea. As a party, however, the Democrats
may truthfully be said to have advocated it, since the great bulk
of the Democratic representation in Congress came from the
West and the South, where the mania was widely prevalent.
However much praise the few Democrats who opposed the
scheme are entitled to, it is certain that it could not have been

defeated had not the Republican Party as a national organization set its face firmly against it.

Many of the advocates of inflation having cut loose from the principles of common honesty soon became repudationists, and formed a party by themselves, called the Greenback party. They proposed to pay off the whole of the debt in greenbacks, and never redeem the greenbacks, but let them wear out and perish. They even went so far as to pass resolutions in their conventions declaring that all taxation should cease and that the Government should support itself by issuing paper money. A constant struggle against inflation schemes was kept up by the Republicans in Congress for more than a decade, and was only ended by the successful resumption of specie payments on the first of January, 1879. In all of this time the Republican Party was vigilant and firm in defending the national honor, and preventing its credit from suffering by the repeated assaults upon it. which came from the Democratic and Greenback Parties. The party which saved the Union and abolished slavery was called upon to save the credit and honor of the country, and prevent its currency from becoming worthless, and it nobly responded to the call.

---

## CHAPTER XXII.

### THE LIBERAL DEFECTION AND THE CAMPAIGN OF 1872.

CONSIDERABLE dissatisfaction was felt in the Republican Party at the course of President Grant's administration. A small element of conscientious men, many of whom had aided in forming the party, believed that his policy toward the South was unwise, and that it was time to inaugurate an era of peace, reconciliation. and good feeling. They also wanted to see a policy of civil service reform established, by which merit should

be the test for public office, and Government officials should
stick to their legitimate business, and, not devote their time to
managing caucuses and conventions in the interest of party
leaders who had secured them their appointments.

Grant's project for annexing San Domingo created a good
deal of opposition, and many of his appointments to office were
of a character not to commend themselves to the public judgment. An open breach occurred between him and several Republican leaders in Congress, chief among whom were Senators
Sumner, Schurz, and Trumbull. Long and acrimonious debates
over the San Domingo matter and a sale of arms to the French
Government served to widen the breach. The opponents of
General Grant believed that his control over all of the Federal
office-holders was so great and their control over the machinery
of the conventions was so perfect that his renomination would
be brought about in spite of any amount of antagonistic feeling
that might exist in the party, so they determined to make a
demonstration which would show to the country that they
would not in any event support Grant for a second term. They
took the name of " Liberal Republicans," and held a National
Convention in Cincinnati, in May, 1872. Once assembled they
were surprised at their own apparent strength and at the number of old-time Republicans who came to co-operate with them.
The plan of the leaders of the movement was to nominate
Charles Francis Adams for President. Some of them believed
that so excellent and fit a nomination would so commend itself
to the whole Republican Party that General Grant would be
dropped. Adams failed of a majority on the first ballot, and
the convention was stampeded by a movement in behalf of

ment as one of soreheads and bolters, and in their own convention, held in Philadelphia in June, nominated President
Grant for re-election by acclamation.   A brisk contest over the
Vice-Presidency occurred between Schuyler Colfax, the incum-
bent of the office, and Henry Wilson, a Senator from Massachusetts, in which Wilson was successful, receiving 364½ votes to
321½ for Colfax.   The platform of the Liberal Republicans demanded that sectional issues should be buried, that good-will
should be cultivated between sections, that the constitutional
amendments in all the settlements of the war should be regarded as finalities, that civil service reform should be under-
taken, and that specie payments should be immediately restored.
The platform of the regular Republicans rehearsed the glorious
history of the Republican Party and reaffirmed its well-known
distinctive principles of equal political and civil rights and a
firm maintenance of the national credit and honor.

The Democrats found themselves in a painful dilemma.   If
they nominated a ticket of their own there was not the slightest chance of electing it.   If they indorsed the Liberal Republican ticket they would have to abandon all of the ideas for
which they had been contending since 1860.   Their convention
met at Baltimore in July and chose the latter horn of the
dilemma.   In spite of the bald inconsistency of the proceeding,
the party which had defended slavery and opposed the suppression of the Rebellion nominated as its candidate for President a most conspicuous antagonist of slavery, a life-long opponent of the South, and a zealous advocate of all measures
which had been adopted for crushing the Rebellion and giving
freedom and citizenship to the blacks.   This apparent conversion of a great party and this acknowledgment of the error of
its ways would have been sublime if it had been sincere, but the
object of most of the Democratic leaders was only to obtain
office and political patronage.   Horace Greeley made no pledges
to them, and he avowed not the slightest alteration in his opin-

ions on the issues of the time. They hoped, however, that if
they succeeded in electing him a sense of gratitude would induce him to give them place and power. The campaign was a
very animated one at first, but after the Republicans carried
North Carolina in August and Pennsylvania in October it became evident that the Greeley coalition could not win, and
thenceforward the Democratic and Liberal canvass lost all
vitality. A large number of the Republicans left their party to
follow their old anti-slavery leader, Horace Greeley, but their
votes were more than counterbalanced by those of Democrats
who refused to support him. This class had a candidate of
their own in Charles O'Conor, who was nominated by a convention held at Louisville. He received but a small vote, however.
Most anti-Greeley Democrats contented themselves with staying at home on election day. Some of them voted for Grant,
to show in a marked manner their hostility to the course of
their party. Grant carried all the States except Georgia,
Kentucky, Maryland, Missouri, Tennessee, and Texas. His
popular vote was 3,597,070. The vote for Greeley was 2,834,-
079. O'Conor received 29,408 votes, and Black 5608. Horace
Greeley died before the electoral colleges met. The electoral
vote as cast by the colleges was as follows : Grant, 286 ; Hendricks, 42 ; Brown, 18 ; C. J. Jenkins, 2 ; David Davis, 1 ; un-
counted because cast for Horace Greeley, 17.

The Liberal defection seriously weakened the Republican
Party in the State campaigns of the three following years, but in
1876 the breach was fully healed, and with the exception of a
few leaders who joined the Democrats the whole body of Lib-
erals returned to their old party allegiance in the Presidential
campaign of that year.

## CHAPTER XXIII.

### PRESIDENT GRANT'S SECOND ADMINISTRATION—CAMPAIGN OF 1876.

REPUBLICAN divisions continued to a considerable extent during the second administration of President Grant. The dissatisfied members of the party did not, however, form any political organization, but contented themselves with holding themselves aloof from the State campaigns. Several painful scandals affecting the appointees and personal friends of President Grant added to the unpopularity of the administration. In 1874, the feeling of distrust and dislike culminated and resulted in an astonishing series of Democratic victories at the State and Congressional elections. A large number of Northern States that had been steadfastly Republican were carried by the Democrats. Even Massachusetts, which had given heavy Republican majorities ever since the party was formed, elected a Democratic Governor. In short, there was a reaction against the Republicans throughout the country of such magnitude and importance that many would-be prophets predicted the speedy death of the party, asserting that its mission was fulfilled, its work done, and its career closed. The Democrats elected a majority of the members of the National House of Representatives, and thus in the following year came into possession of one branch of Congress for the first time since 1860.

It was not long before the Republicans who had deserted their party and thus helped its enemy to a substantial victory began to realize that they had made a grave mistake. They saw that to trust the party of slavery and rebellion with the power in the National Government was to run the risk of seriously compromising the results of the war. The State elections of 1875 showed the result of this conviction, for most of the old Republican States which had been lost in 1874 were regained.

An exceedingly thorough and brilliant canvass was made in Ohio upon the financial question. The Democrats of that State fully indorsed what was known as the soft-money idea. They opposed the act for the resumption of specie payments, passed by Congress in January of that year, demanded the issue of more irredeemable greenbacks, and asserted that the interest on the public debt should be paid in paper money, and some of their orators and newspapers went so far as to demand the payment of the principal of the debt in the same kind of currency. The Democratic nominee for Governor was William Allen, popularly known as "old Bill Allen," who already held the place by virtue of the election of 1873. This venerable politician personified for a time the soft-money delusion, which got the name of "the Ohio idea," and was commonly ridiculed by its opponents as "the rag baby." The Republican candidate was Rutherford B. Hayes, who had been Governor for two terms, from 1868 to 1872. Taking ground in favor of honest money redeemable in coin and an honest payment of the national debt, the Republicans carried the State by a small majority and turned the tide of inflation. The campaign attracted national attention to Mr. Hayes, and made him the candidate of his State for the Presidential nomination in 1876.

The Republicans held their National Convention at Cincinnati on June 14th, 1876. James G. Blaine, of Maine, was the leading candidate, and his nomination was regarded as almost a certainty when the balloting began. The other prominent candidates were Oliver P. Morton, of Indiana ; Roscoe Conkling, of New York ; Benjamin F. Bristow, of Kentucky, and John F. Hartranft, of Pennsylvania. Bristow's power came, as a rule, from the element most dissatisfied with President Grant's administration. Bristow had been Secretary of the Treasury, and had differed with the President about the prosecution of certain persons in the West concerned in the frauds on the revenue. A personal quarrel arose, and Bristow resigned his place in the Cabinet. The supporters of Morton, Conkling, and Hartranft were, in the main, warm friends of the administration. Those of Mr. Blaine were drawn from both elements by his great personal popularity and his reputation as a Congressional leader. A combination between the forces of Morton, Conkling, Hartranft, and Hayes, and a portion of those of Bristow defeated Blaine and nominated Hayes on the seven a ballot, the vote standing, Hayes, 384 ; Blaine, 351 ; Bristow, 81. William A. Wheeler, an old and influential representative in Congress from the State of New York, was nominated for Vice-President with little opposition. Mr. Hayes' nomination proved to be a popular and fortunate one. He had an excellent military and civil record and no personal enemies, and he united all of the jarring elements of the Republican organization.

The Democratic Convention met in St. Louis on the 27th of June, and on the second ballot nominated Samuel J. Tilden, of New York for President. His principal competitors were, Hendricks, of Indiana ; Allen, of Ohio, and General Hancock, of the army. Tilden had just served a term as Governor of New York, and had won considerable reputation as a reformer by his hostility to the canal ring, and to the corrupt Tammany organization in the City of New York. The Democrats ran their canvass almost exclusively on what they called the reform line. They claimed that the Republican Party had grown corrupt with long lease of power. They vigorously attacked the administration of President Grant, made the most of all the scandals, true or false, which had grown out of it, and presented their candidate as a man who would sweep the public service clean of all abuses as with a new broom.

The Republican canvass consisted mainly of an attack on the bad record of the Democratic Party and a cry of alarm at the solidity of the section of the country late in rebellion. A good deal was made out of the enormous Southern claims presented in Congress for war damages, and an effective attack was kept up against Mr. Tilden on account of his failure to pay a large amount of money due from him to the Government as income tax, and also on account of his sharp financial operations in connection with certain Western railroads. Three insignificant minor organizations placed candidates in the field for the campaign of 1876. The Greenback Party, an organization of fantastic theorists and small demagogues, took up the so-called Ohio idea, which the Democrats had refused to indorse in their St. Louis platform, and endeavored to build upon it a great political organization. They nominated for President the venerable New York philanthropist, Peter Cooper, and for Vice-President Samuel F. Cary, of Ohio, a popular orator who had belonged to nearly every political organization which had existed in his life-time. The Prohibitionists held a convention in Cleveland and nominated for President Green Clay Smith, of Kentucky, and for Vice-President, Gideon T. Stewart, of Ohio, on a platform demanding a constitutional amendment prohibiting the liquor traffic. A mass meeting was held in Pittsburg, which attempted to start a new organization called the American National Party. James B. Walker, of Illinois, was nominated for President, and Donald Kirkpatrick, of New York, for Vice-President. The platform favored the recognition of God and the Sabbath in the Constitution, demanded prohibitory liquor laws, and denounced all secret societies. The movement proved abortive, and nothing was heard of it during the canvass.

The campaign of 1876 was exceedingly animated, and was closely contested in all parts of the Union except the Southern States, where the Democrats had already gained control. The popular vote was follows : Tilden, 4,284,757 ; Hayes, 4,033,- 950 ; Cooper, 81,740 ; Smith, 9,522. The electoral vote, as finally decided by a commission created to settle the dispute about the returns, was, Hayes, 185 ; Tilden, 184.

## CHAPTER XXIV.

### THE CONTROVERSY ABOUT THE ELECTORAL COUNT.

BOTH parties claimed to have carried the Presidential election of 1876, and before the question was decided the country was brought uncomfortably near to the verge of civil war. The result turned upon the votes of South Carolina, Florida, and Louisiana, which were certified by the State authorities to have been cast for Hayes and Wheeler. In each of those States Democratic electors claimed to have been elected, and sent contesting returns to Washington. Great excitement prevailed throughout the country. Politicians of both parties hurried to the disputed States to witness the counts of the popular vote and supervise the action of the rival electoral colleges. In South Carolina, which the Republicans had previously carried by majorities averaging 30,000, the Democrats organized rifle clubs during the campaign to systematically intimidate colored voters. These rifle clubs moved about the country fully armed, and uniformed in red shirts, broke up Republican meetings, and spread terror among the black population. The whole State seemed like an armed camp. The effect produced by this military organization on the minds of the timid colored people was greatly increased by the Ellenton and Hamburg massacres, in which a large number of negroes were killed. An account of these occurrences would be foreign to the purpose of this work. It is enough to say that the white Democrats were the aggressors and the colored Republicans the victims, and that the Republicans were convinced that both of the affairs grew out of the purpose of the Democrats to so terrify the blacks that a large proportion of them would be afraid to vote. As first returned there appeared to be a small majority for Tilden in South Carolina. The board of canvassers threw out the votes of two counties, acting in this matter by the plain authority of the laws of the State, and gave certificates to the Hayes electors. In Florida there was a little violence and a good deal of fraud, with the same result as in the case of South Carolina. In Louisiana the Republicans, judging from elections of previous years, had a large and certain majority. The Democrats selected five of the heaviest of the Republican parishes for a species of campaigning known as bulldozing. It was practically the South Carolina rifle club system, which, it may be mentioned, originated in Mississippi, in the State canvass of 1875, and was currently known in the South as the " Mississippi plan." In Louisana, however, it was somewhat modified and combined with features borrowed from the old Ku-Klux Klan. The scheme of the Democrats was well conceived, for if they could by their acts of violence overcome the Republican majorities in those five counties they could carry the State. The only alternative for the Republicans who controlled the State Government would, they thought, be to throw out the returns of the five counties entirely, and in that event the Democrats would also win the election. The returning board, composed of Republicans, was authorized by law to count and tabulate the votes and reject those from the precincts where the election had been vitiated by fraud or violence, and by this authority the board threw out the five bulldozed parishes, which left the Democrats a majority ; but it also threw out a number of precincts in other parishes, so that the Republicans had a majority on the final count. The action of the board was purely legal, but it was violently assailed as wicked and corrupt by the Democrats. In a moral point of view the defeat of the Democratic scheme for carrying the State by terrorizing the Republican voters in five of the strongest Republican parishes was certainly justifiable.

When the Democrats saw that they had lost South Carolina, Florida, and Louisiana, and that Hayes would have a majority of one in the electoral count, they attempted to set up a bogus electoral college in Oregon. Five thousand dollars were sent out from New York to pay expenses, and more money was promised if the plot succeeded. Governor Grover, a Democrat, making himself the judge of the qualifications of the Oregon electors, decided that one of them was not competent, and commissioned the defeated Democratic candidate, named Cronin, in his place. Cronin held an electoral college by himself, ⟨ ⟩ appointed two other Democrats to fill vacancies, and sent on a pretended return to Washington.

The Democrats had a majority in the House of Representatives and the Republicans in the Senate, and there was a deadlock for a time over the question of the powers of the two Houses concerning the electoral count. The Democrats held that if one House should reject a return it could not be counted, while the Republicans took the ground that a concurrence of both Houses was necessary for the disfranchisement of a State, or the rejection of any part of its vote. It was also maintained by many Republicans, though not by all, that the President of the Senate was empowered by the Constitution to count the returns, and that the two Houses were only present in joint convention as official witnesses. This opinion had the support of the authority of many of the framers of the Constitution, and it was beyond dispute that the returns of all the early Presidential elections were counted in this way. Fortunately, a compromise was reached and a bill was passed, providing that all returns objected to by either House should be referred to a commission composed of five Senators, five Representatives, and five Justices of the Supreme Court, and that the decisions of the commission should stand unless overturned by the concurrent vote of both Houses. With few exceptions the leading men of both parties united in this compromise. It was considered a patriotic thing to allay public excitement and avoid the growing danger of civil war by submitting the whole controversy to a judicial settlement. In the organization of the tribunal the representatives from the two Houses of Congress were evenly divided between the two parties. Two of the Supreme Court Justices selected had Republican antecedents and two Democratic, and the choice of the fifth justice was left to these four. The Democrats supposed that their choice would fall upon Justice Davis of Illinois, but Davis was elected to the Senate by the Legislature of the State, and having thus stepped down from the bench into party politics, was not available. Justice Bradley, of New Jersey, was therefore selected. The questions before the tribunal were argued for weeks by some of the ablest lawyers in the country. On divisions the vote invariably stood eight to seven, the eight Republicans voting together, and the seven Democrats showing equal solidity. The Republicans took the ground that Congress had no right to go back of the regular formal returns of any State, to take up questions concerning frauds in elections or counts. The Democrats abandoned for a time, in their extreme party necessity, their old State rights doctrine, and contended that Congress could set aside the regular returns and investigate the facts on which they were based. The adoption of this theory would have resulted in making Presidential elections useless, because no disputed election could ever be settled in the interval between the meetings of the electoral colleges in December and the time for the inauguration of the new President on the 4th of March. Either party could prolong an investigation till after March 4th, and thus enable the Senate to place its presiding officer in the Presidential chair.

The decisions of the commission made Rutherford B. Hayes President of the United States, giving him a majority of one electoral vote over Samuel J. Tilden. There was much menacing talk among the Democrats for a time about inaugurating Tilden and supporting him with the militia of the States having Democratic Governors. The House of Representatives passed resolutions declaring Tilden to be the lawfully elected President. An attempt was made by the Democrats of that body to filibuster so as to consume the time till noon on the 4th of March, and thus prevent the completion of the count. This scheme would have been carried out had it not been for the opposition of many of the Southern Democrats, who showed much more moderation and patriotism at this juncture than did their brethren at the North. The count was completed just in time, and Hayes was duly inaugurated without opposition. For years afterward, however, indeed up to the present time, it has been the fashion of the Democrats to denounce the Electoral Commission for which their own party leaders were as much responsible as those of the Republican Party, and to stigmatize Mr. Hayes as a fraudulent President. Mr. Hayes's title, legally and morally, is just as clear as that of any President who ever occupied the White House. He had a majority of the electoral votes legally returned and legally counted, and if a fair election had been permitted in the South by the rifle clubs and bulldozing organizations he would have had a large majority of the popular vote.

## CHAPTER XXV.

### PRESIDENT HAYES' ADMINISTRATION—THE SOUTHERN QUESTION—CIVIL SERVICE REFORM.

PRESIDENT GRANT went out of office with a great many opponents in his own party, and a great many devoted friends. His administration failed to keep the Republican Party united, but perhaps it was too strong and its majorities too large for harmony to prevail. It seems to be a law of parties that when one greatly overtops the other for a series of years it begins to crumble. If it has the binding force of principle, however, the disintegration only throws off some of the surface material, and ceases when it is brought down to about the size of the opposing party. The mistakes President Grant made in regard to persons and policy will hardly be remembered in history, and need not be dwelt on here. Future generations will think of only two things in connection with his eight years in the White House, and both will be regarded as bright and enduring honors worthily added to his great military fame—that he held the country firmly up to the results of the war, and that he stood like a rock to stem the current of the paper-money inflation mania. To the title of victor over the Rebellion which he won at Appomattox may truthfully be added that of defender of the public credit and protector of the principle of equal rights for all citizens.

When Mr. Hayes entered upon the duties of the Presidential office, rival State governments existed in South Carolina and Louisiana. The Florida imbroglio had been settled by the action of the State Supreme Court. In South Carolina the Republicans claimed to have elected Governor Chamberlain by the same vote which chose the Presidential electors. The Democrats claimed that Wade Hampton was lawfully elected. Each party had inaugurated its Governor, and each had a Legislature in session—the Republicans in the State House, protected by a force of United States troops, the Democrats in a building hired for the purpose. After a delay of over a month, which was unfortunate because irritating to the public mind both North and South, the President ordered the troops to withdraw from the State House, and the Chamberlain government instantly ceased to exist. The Hampton government took possession of the State House without opposition, admitted a portion of the members of the Republican Legislature, and, professing an intention to forget the past and to treat all citizens fairly, assumed complete control of the State.

In Louisiana the condition of things was more complicated than in South Carolina. The Republicans, under Governor Packard, had a complete State government installed in the State

House in New Orleans, but it could not make its authority respected in the State, and was actually a close prisoner in the Capitol building. The Democrats, under Governor Nicholls, ran a government in Odd Fellows Hall, and having a large force of well-disciplined white militia at their command were able to enforce their authority. With their troops and with the police of New Orleans they so overawed the Republican officials, legislators, and guards that they did not venture to cross an imaginary line drawn through the middle of the streets surrounding the State House. In a building adjoining the State House a regiment of United States troops was quartered, and a passage was opened between the two structures so that the soldiers could go to the assistance of Governor Packard in case of an attack. Throughout the State the Democrats had displaced the Republican local officials chosen at the fall election, and thus controlled the judiciary and the county offices in all the parishes except those in the sugar-planting region, where the blacks were in an overwhelming majority. A few unprincipled colored men went back and forth between the two Legislatures, making a quorum in whatever body they appeared. President Hayes sent a commission to New Orleans to effect a compromise if possible. Its members were Judge Lawrence, of Illinois, General Hawley, of Connecticut, Wayne McVeagh, of Pennsylvania, Judge Harlan, of Kentucky, and ex-Governor Brown, of Tennessee. It was finally arranged that the Nicholls government should be allowed to go on, that a Legislature should be made up of the two conflicting organizations, that the troops should be withdrawn from protecting Packard, and that no prosecutions for political reasons should be commenced against Republicans. Governor Packard did not assent to these terms. Seeing that he could not sustain himself, he abandoned the State House, and the Nicholls government moved in. The Democrats soon broke faith by beginning criminal suits against members of the Returning Board for

the purpose, as was generally reported, of forcing the administration to give them control of the New Orleans Custom House
patronage. The State Supreme Court finally put a stop to these
proceedings. The Senate at Washington admitted Kellogg,
the Senator chosen by the Packard Legislature, thus virtually
recognizing the legality of the Packard government, but in the
case of South Carolina it seated Butler, whom the Democratic
Legislature had chosen, while still in a fragmentary and illegal
condition. This was done as a compromise, but two years later
the Democrats sought to unseat Kellogg, and were only prevented by three or four Southern Senators breaking away from
the party caucus, and sustaining Kellogg on the ground that
his case was *res adjudicata.*

President Hayes' action in the South Carolina and Louisiana
affairs gave rise to severe criticism and active opposition in the
Republican Party. A portion of the Republicans calling themselves "stalwarts" insisted that the titles of Chamberlain and
Packard were just as good as that of Mr. Hayes, and should
have been defended with the whole power of the Government,
if necessary. Another element believed that the experiment of
sustaining Southern governments with Federal bayonets had
failed to produce order, prosperity, and security of the civil
rights of the negroes, and that the only course left was to
let the Southern States alone to manage their own affairs.

Whatever might be the legal and moral title of Packard and
Chamberlain, this latter class argued, it was impolitic to sustain
with armed force authority which could not make itself respected. This class hoped that the policy of non-interference
would soon lead to the division of the Southern whites, to the
blotting out of the color line in Southern politics, and to the
growth of a new Republican organization, composed of both
whites and blacks. They were encouraged in this belief by
the statements of many prominent Southern men, who said,
" Give us home rule, and the feeling of intolerance toward the

Republican Party will cease." Thus far the hope of a division in the " solid South" has not been verified. Opposition to the Democratic Party in that section is still regarded as in some sort treason to the interests of the South, as though the South were not a component part of the United States, but a political entity separate and apart. In most of the Southern States no opposition is made to the negroes voting as they please, but the counting and return of the votes are in the hands of the Democratic officials, and public opinion, so far as it is shaped by the respectable white classes, justifies any fraud that is necessary to wipe out Republican majorities. In Louisiana, in 1878, unprovoked and brutal massacres of negroes took place in three parishes, with the evident purpose of preventing the Republicans from carrying the election.

Besides the Southern question, there came up another issue upon which Republicans disagreed. An agitation began during President Grant's administration for a reform in the civil service. Grant yielded to it so far as to create a comission which prescribed rules for the examination of candidates for office. The movement went beyond this and demanded that appointments should not be made as a reward for party service ; that the public offices should not be dispensed by Senators and Congressmen to their followers and favorites, and that public officials should not employ their time in managing caucuses and conventions, and in working for the success of candidates. The Cincinnati platform promised this sort of reform, and President Hayes believed in it. He attempted to carry it out by disregarding, when he saw fit, the recommendations of Senators and Representatives concerning appointments and removals in their States or districts, and by issuing an order commanding office-holders to refrain from taking part in caucuses, conventions, and other forms of party work. On the one side it was held that this policy weakened the party organization and deprived the officials of their rights as citizens to take an active part in politics ; on the other it was maintained that the policy was a good one, tending to elevate politics and to release the party from the rule of cliques of office-holders, who organized " machines" to override the will of a large majority of the voters.

These dissensions so weakened the party that in 1877 it lost several of the States it had carried in 1876. Time and good sense have healed them in a large measure, however. The order to office-holders is not enforced ; and the administration, while preserving a proper degree of independence for the appointing power, gives due weight to the recommendations of the people's representatives in Congress. The Republican Party recovered its compactness in 1878, in the defense of the Specie Payment Act against the assaults of the Democrats. It was powerfully aided, too, by an exposure made by the *New York Tribune* of a secret correspondence in cipher, carried on during the winter of 1876-7 between Mr. Tilden's nephew Pelton and other confidential friends in New York and certain agents sent out to capture the electoral votes of the States of South Carolina, Florida, Louisiana, and Oregon. The employment of corrupt means to bribe electors or returning authorities in those States was plainly shown by these dispatches. The disposition of some Republicans to think Mr. Tilden might possibly have been fairly elected and unjustly kept out of the Presidency vanished when the means adopted by his close friends to secure him the office were thus exposed.

---

## CHAPTER XXVI.

### THE RESUMPTION OF SPECIE PAYMENTS—THE ELECTION LAWS— DEMOCRATIC ATTEMPT TO COERCE THE EXECUTIVE.

THE act of 1875 providing for a return to specie payments on the first of January, 1879, was a Republican measure, and for four years was defended by the Republicans against the attacks of the Democrats. A few Western Republicans joined in these attacks, and a few Eastern Democrats helped repulse them ; but the great mass of one party favored the redemption of the greenback notes in coin, and the great mass of the other wanted the law repealed. Many Democrats embraced the notion of " fiat money," asserting that the government by its fiat can make absolute money out of paper or any other valueless material. Gold and silver money was a relic of barbarism, they declared, to use valuable metals for currency when paper, which cost next to nothing, would answer the purpose much better, being wasteful and foolish. These deluded people wanted all the greenbacks and the national bank notes retired and replaced by a new kind of Government notes, bearing no promise to pay on their faces, but simply declaring themselves to be money of different denominations. These notes were to be issued in quantities sufficient " to meet the wants of trade," and were never to be redeemed.

As the time fixed for resumption drew near, the clamor against the law increased. Every business failure was ascribed by the Democratic press in the West and South to the effect of the act, and the speedy ruin of the business of the country was predicted. John Sherman, who as Secretary of the Treasury made careful preparation for resumption, and opposed any postponement of the date, was a special target for criticism and abuse. Specie payments were resumed on the day appointed by law, without the slightest shock or disturbance to business interests. Industrial and commercial prosperity began to return to the country shortly afterward, and now the wisdom of the Resumption Act is acknowledged by every one. Even the fanatical paper-money doctrinaires, who formed a party by themselves, because the Democrats did not go far enough in the direction of repudiation and inflation to satisfy them, have ceased to demand in their platforms the repeal of the law. Like the former inflationists in the Democratic Party, they have come down to a demand for the retirement of bank-notes and the substitution of greenbacks for them.

In the Congress which closed March 4th, 1879, the Democrats controlled the House and the Republicans the Senate. The Democrats sought to accomplish the repeal of the Federal election laws in spite of the opposition of both the Senate and the President. These laws were passed in 1870, after an investigation of the gigantic frauds perpetrated in the City of New York at the election of 1868. They were always objectionable to the Democrats, theoretically because they conflicted with their traditional views about State rights, and practically because they prevented the repetition of the frauds of 1868 for the benefit of the Democratic Party. The Republicans defended the laws because of their demonstrated utility in securing fair elections, and because they were based on the sound constitutional principle of the right of Congress to regulate elections that are national in their character. The Democrats tacked a section repealing the election laws upon a general appropriation bill. They also placed on the Army Appropriate Bill a section prohibiting the use of troops at elections to keep the peace or suppress riots. Rather than abandon these " riders" they let the bills fail, and forced an extra session of Congress.

In the new Congress the Democrats controlled both Houses, and had only the President to grapple with. Mr. Hayes resolved to defend the election laws with his veto power. As for the matter of troops at the polls, he exposed the issue as a fictitious one, showing that there were already ample provisions of law forbidding the use of troops for political purposes. He refused to abandon for the Executive the right to enforce obedience to law, with the military arm if necessary, at places where elections were held, as well as elsewhere. So the issue was joined. The Democrats threatened to break down the Government by leaving it without means to exist if the President did not yield. Mr. Hayes stood firm, and answered them by a series of vetoes directed against their measures, which maintained, by arguments of remarkable force and clearness, the supremacy of the nation in all matters of national concern, and the independence of the Executive from Congressional dictation. Baffled at every point in the long struggle, the Democrats finally yielded and passed all the appropriations except the one providing for the payment of the United States marshals. They declared, however, that they would renew the contest at the next session, but the fall elections went against them, and they did not resume hostilities in the session which began December, 1879. Only a remnant of the controversy was preserved in a proviso, which they put upon an appropriation bill at the close of the session, prohibiting the payment of deputy marshals for services at elections.

---

## CHAPTER XXVII.

### THE CAMPAIGN OF 1880—NOMINATION OF JAMES A. GARFIELD.

THE idea of electing General Grant in 1880 for a third term was in the minds of many prominent Republicans from the day he left the White House. Most of these men had favored his nomination in 1876, but considerable feeling arose in the country against a third term, and to assure the people that the party did not meditate conferring upon Grant greater honors then Washington had received, several Republican State Conventions passed resolutions in 1875 declaring that they were opposed to the election of any President for more than two terms. General Grant went abroad in 1877 and spent two years in foreign travel, making the circuit of the globe and visiting nearly all the great nations of the earth. He was received, wherever he went, with honors such as are only accorded to reigning monarchs. Regarded as the representative of the great

American Republic and the most distinguished of living military chieftains, his journey was a succession of brilliant official and popular demonstrations. These remarkable honors were almost as flattering to his countrymen as to him, and served to keep his name and fame fresh in their minds. Before he returned to the United States, in the fall of 1879, it was plain that a strong movement would be made to secure his nomination. With characteristic reticence he neither assented nor objected to this movement, but remained perfectly passive. Most of the politicians who had held positions under his administration naturally desired his return to power, and there was besides a considerable body of Republicans who had not been office-holders and did not expect to be, who believed he would be the most popular candidate the party could nominate, and urged his candidacy on the ground of expediency. His most prominent supporters were the three influential Senators from New York, Pennsylvania, and Illinois—Conkling, Cameron, and Logan. The Southern Republicans were almost unanimous in his favor. A considerable majority of the Northern Republicans opposed his nomination, however, because they believed it would be a violation of the tradition of two terms only, and a step toward personal government. Besides, they thought it would furnish the Democrats with a popular issue—opposition to a third term—on which the Republicans would be placed in the position of defending an innovation upon a safe, conservative, long-established custom. The discussion of the question of nominating Grant began in earnest in December, 1879, and lasted without intermission until the National Convention met at Chicago on the 10th of June following. Most of the anti-third-term men supported Senator James G. Blaine, of Maine, the most popular of the Republican leaders. A considerable number favored the Secretary of the Treasury, John Sherman, of Ohio, making his excellent record as a Republican and his brilliant success in the resumption of specie payments the ground of their choice. Senator Geo. F. Edmunds, of Vermont, had the backing of his own State and of Massachusetts ; Elihu B. Washburne, ex-minister to Paris, had a small Western following, and Senator William Windom, of Minnesota, was supported by that State. Neither candidate had votes enough to nominate him. The first ballot in the convention stood : Grant, 304 ; Blaine, 284 ; Sherman, 93 ; Edmunds, 34 ; Washburne, 30 ; Windom, 10. On the second ballot one vote was given to Garfield, and on most of the subsequent ballots, during the first day's voting he had 2. The above figures were pretty closely preserved for thirty-three ballots. The Grant men could have controlled the nomination if they had been willing to drop their candidate and take up a new man, but they stuck to the ex-President with absolute fidelity. Both the Blaine men and the Sherman men were equally devoted to their leaders. The dead-lock was finally brought to an end by the Wisconsin delegation voting for Garfield on the 34th ballot, against his protest. As the leader of the Ohio delegation, Garfield was a supporter of Sherman, and he objected to being put in an apparent attitude of willingness to abandon the Ohio candidate. On the next ballot, however, Indiana followed Ohio, and on the 36th ballot nearly the whole body of anti-third term men swung into line for Garfield, giving him the nomination by the following vote : Garfield, 399 ; Grant, 306 ; Blaine, 42 ; Sherman, 3 ; Washburne, 5. The result was a fortunate one. General Garfield was acceptable to all the elements in the convention, and the whole party dropped at once all former causes of difference and rushed to his support. Chester A. Arthur, of New York, an earnest Grant man, was nominated for the Vice-Presidency, with a view of making the ticket represent both wings of the party lately engaged in a contest over the question of Grant's candidacy. The vote was—Arthur, 468 ; Washburne, 193 ; Jewell, 44 ; Maynard, 30 ; Bruce, 8. General Arthur's experience as chairman of the New York Republican

State Committee made him peculiarly available, and his prominence as a Grant man made him specially acceptable to the element which had before controlled Republican politics in New York. The ticket was instantly indorsed by the entire Republican press and by men of all shades of Republican opinion.

By a happy inspiration the convention selected, instead of the obscure man of only local fame who usually comes out of such close contests with the nomination, one of the best known, most trusted, and ablest of the national leaders of the Republican Party. At the same time it secured a man with extraordinary elements of personal popularity in his career—a man who rose from the ranks of toil, who gained the means for his education at the carpenter's bench and on the tow-path of a canal, who served with distinguished bravery in the war, and who has won his way, by pure merit and honest effort, to the highest walks of statesmanship and scholarly culture.

The Democratic National Convention met at Cincinnati on the 22d of June. The party had been suffering from the standing candidacy of Samuel J. Tilden, who had a claim upon the nomination based on the assertion by the Democratic leaders and newspapers that he was elected in 1876 and defrauded of the office. He personified the "fraud issue," and it was manifestly impossible for the party to make that issue prominent without making him its candidate. Mr. Tilden wrote a letter just before the convention assembled, declining in terms the nomination. The letter presented, however, in a masterly manner, the arguments in favor of his candidacy, and was generally regarded as intended to strengthen his chances for the nomination. On the first ballot the delegates scattered their votes as follows : Hancock, 171 ; Bayard, 153½ ; Field, 65 ; Morrison, 62 ; Hendricks, 49½ ; Thurman, 68½ ; Payne, 81 ; Tilden, 38 ; Ewing, 10 ; Seymour, 8 ; scattering, 28.

After this ballot the convention adjourned until the next day, and during the night the opponents of Tilden managed to combine upon General Hancock, who was nominated next morning. The second ballot stood : Hancock, 319 ; Randall, 129½ ; Bayard, 113 ; Field, 65½ ; Thurman, 30 ; Hendricks, 31 ; English, 19 ; Tilden, 6 ; scattering, 3.    Changes were made before the vote was announced which nominated Hancock, he having 705 votes to Hendricks, 30 ; Bayard 2, and Tilden 1.

Hancock had been the standing candidate, since 1868, of those Democrats who wanted to repeat the McClellan experiment with a better soldier than McClellan.    A National Greenback Convention met in Chicago, June 11th, and nominated J. B. Weaver, of Iowa, for President, and E. J. Chambers, of Texas, for Vice-President.

## CHAPTER XXVIII.

### A FEW WORDS IN CONCLUSION.

In the foregoing chapters the main current of Republican action has been clearly traced, beginning with the hostility of the party to the extension of slavery, and continuing through its successive defence of the integrity of the American Union, its emancipation of the slaves, its reorganization of the rebellious States, its establishment of equal suffrage and equal citizenship for all, its defence of the public credit, and its resumption of specie payments.    Outside of this main channel of patriotic activity it has accomplished many things which should not be overlooked, even in so brief a sketch as is given in these pages. It has steadily reduced the debt resulting from the war, and has paid off and cancelled the enormous amount of $837,-000,000 in the period between 1865 and 1880.    At the same time it has been so successful in funding the principal of the remaining debt in low-interest bonds that it has effected a saving, in the matter of interest alone, of $71,000,000 a year, thus further lessening the burden of the debt. It steadily reduced taxation and public expenditures as long as it remained in power in Congress. It has greatly improved and simplified the protective tariff system, originated by the Whig Party, and has by its legislation of the past twenty years so encouraged and shielded American manufactures that they have increased more than fourfold and are now able to command our own markets and to compete in many lines with the manufactures of older countries in the markets of the world. While opposing all monopolies, the Republican Party has had for its central idea in its tariff legislation the fact that the perpetuity of free institutions in this country requires an intelligent laboring class, and that such a class cannot exist upon the pauper wages paid to the laborers of the Old World. The party has also carried out the policy of internal improvements, originated by the Whig Party, and by a system of judicious legislation has opened the great rivers of the country to navigation, improved its harbors, and connected the Atlantic with the Pacific coast by great railway lines. It has established a national banking system which saves the people millions of dollars annually by protecting them against the losses incident to the old State banking systems which preceded it. It has greatly improved the postal system, giving to the country fast mails and letter-carrier deliveries. It has established the principle of international arbitration as a means of averting war. A catalogue of the wise measures it has adopted would be far too long to be given here. Nearly all of these measures were resisted at the time of their adoption by the opposition party, but with scarcely an exception they have come to be approved by that party as wise and patriotic. No one can see into the future of American politics, but it is evident that the party which has been able to meet all of the issues of the most important epoch in the nation's history with such signal intelligence and such remarkable success is not near the end of its career. The day is probably far distant when a complete and final history of the Republican Party can be written. The author presents these pages only as a brief outline sketch of the first quarter of a century of its existence.

# REPUBLICAN PRINCIPLES.

## FIRST REPUBLICAN NATIONAL PLATFORM.

### ADOPTED AT PHILADELPHIA, JUNE 17TH, 1856.

THIS convention of delegates, assembled in pursuance of a call addressed to the people of the United States, without regard to past political differences or divisions, who are opposed to the repeal of the Missouri Compromise, to the policy of the present administration, to the extension of slavery into free territory ; in favor of admitting Kansas as a free State, of restoring the action of the Federal Government to the principles of Washington and Jefferson, and who purpose to unite in presenting candidates for the offices of President and Vice-President, do resolve as follows :

*Resolved*, That the maintenance of the principles promulgated in the Declaration of Independence and embodied in the Federal Constitution is essential to the preservation of our republican institutions, and that the Federal Constitution, the rights of the States, and the Union of the States, shall be preserved.

*Resolved*, That with our republican fathers we hold it to be a self-evident truth that all men are endowed with the inalienable rights to life, liberty, and the pursuit of happiness, and that the primary object and ulterior designs of our Federal Government were to secure these rights to all persons within its exclusive jurisdiction ; that as our Republican fathers, when they had abolished slavery in all of our national territory, ordained that no person should be deprived of life, liberty, or property without due process of law, it becomes our duty to maintain this provision of the Constitution against all attempts to violate, for the purpose of establishing slavery in any territory of the United States, by positive legislation, prohibiting its existence or extension therein. That we deny the authority of Congress, or of a Territorial Legislature, of any individual or association of individuals, to give legal existence to slavery in any Territory of the United States, while the present Constitution shall be maintained.

*Resolved,* That the Constitution confers upon Congress sovereign power over the Territories of the United States for their government, and that in the exercise of this power it is both the right and the duty of Congress to prohibit in the Territories those twin relics of barbarism—polygamy and slavery.

*Resolved,* That while the Constitution of the United States was ordained and established by the people in order to form a more perfect union, establish justice, insure domestic tranquillity, provide for the common defense, and secure the blessings of liberty, and contains ample provisions for the protection of the life, liberty, and property of every citizen, the dearest constitutional rights of the people of Kansas have been fraudulently and violently taken from them ; their territory has been invaded by an armed force ; spurious and pretended legislative, judicial, and executive officers have been set over them, by whose usurped authority, sustained by the military power of the Government, tyrannical and unconstitutional laws have been enacted and enforced ; the rights of the people to keep and bear arms have been infringed ; test oaths of an extraordinary and entangling nature have been imposed as a condition of exercising the right of suffrage and holding office ; the right of an accused person to a speedy and public trial by an impartial jury has been denied ; the right of the people to be secure in their persons, houses, papers, and effects against unreasonable searches and seizures has been violated ; they have been deprived of life, liberty, and property without due process of law ; that the freedom of speech and of the press has been abridged ; the right to choose their representatives has been made of no effect ; murders, robberies, and arsons have been instigated and encouraged, and the offenders have been allowed to go unpunished ;—that all of these things have been done with the knowledge, sanction, and procurement of the present administration, and that for this high crime against the Constitution, the Union, and humanity, we arraign the administration, the President, his advisers, agents, supporters, apologists, and accessories, either before or after the facts, before the country and before the world, and that it is our fixed purpose to bring the actual perpetrators of these atrocious outrages and their accomplices to a sure and condign punishment hereafter.

*Resolved*, That Kansas should be immediately admitted as a State of the Union, with her present free Constitution, as at once the most effectual way of securing to her citizens the enjoyment of the rights and privileges to which they are entitled, and of ending the civil strife now raging in her territory.

*Resolved*, That the highwayman's plea, that " might makes right," embodied in the Ostend circular, was in every respect unworthy of American diplomacy, and would bring shame and dishonor upon any government or people that gave it their sanction.

*Resolved*, That a railroad to the Pacific Ocean, by the most central and practicable route, is imperatively demanded by the interests of the whole country, and that the Federal Government ought to render immediate and efficient aid in its construction ; and, as an auxiliary thereto, the immediate construction of an emigrant route on the line of the railroad.

*Resolved*, That appropriations by Congress for the improvement of rivers and harbors, of a national character, required for the accommodation and security of our existing commerce, are authorized by the Constitution, and justified by the obligation of Government to protect the lives and property of its citizens.

------

## SECOND REPUBLICAN NATIONAL PLATFORM.

### ADOPTED AT CHICAGO, MAY 17TH, 1860.

*Resolved,* That we, the delegated representatives of the Republican electors of the United States, in convention assembled, in discharge of the duty we owe to our constituents and our country, unite in the following declarations :

1. That the history of the nation during the last four years has fully established the propriety and necessity of the organization and perpetuation of the Republican Party, and that the causes which called it into existence are permanent in their nature, and now, more than ever before, demand its peaceful and constitutional triumph.

2. That the maintenance of the principles promulgated in the Declaration of Independence and embodied in the Federal Constitution, "that all men are created equal ; that they are endowed by their Creator with certain inalienable rights ; that among these are life, liberty and the pursuit of happiness ; that to secure these rights governments are instituted among men, deriving their just powers from the consent of the governed," is essential to the preservation of our republican institutions ; and that the Federal Constitution, the rights of the States, and the union of the States must and shall be preserved.

3. That to the union of the States this nation owes its unprecedented increase in population, its surprising development of material resources, its rapid augmentation of wealth, its happiness at home, and its honor abroad ; and we hold in abhorrence all schemes for disunion, come from whatever source they may ;

and we congratulate the country that no Republican member of Congress has uttered or countenanced the threats of disunion so often made by Democratic members without rebuke and with applause from their political associates ; and we denounce those threats of disunion in case of a popular overthrow of their ascendency as denying the vital principles of a free government, and as an avowal of contemplated treason which it is the imperative duty of an indignant people sternly to rebuke and forever silence.

4. That the maintenance inviolate of the rights of the States, and especially the rights of each State to order and control its own domestic institutions according to its own judgment exclusively, is essential to that balance of powers on which the perfection and endurance of our political fabric depends ; and we denounce the lawless invasion by armed force of the soil of any State or Territory, no matter under what pretext, as among the gravest of crimes.

5. That the present Democratic administration has far exceeded our worst apprehensions, in its measureless subserviency to the exactions of a sectional interest, as especially evinced in its desperate exertions to force the infamous Lecompton Constitution upon the protesting people of Kansas ; in construing the personal relation between master and servant to involve an unqualified property in persons ; in its attempted enforcement. everywhere, on land and sea, through the intervention of Congress and of the Federal courts, and of the extreme pretensions of a purely local interest ; and in its general and unvarying abuse of the power intrusted to it by a confiding people.

6. That the people justly view with alarm the reckless extravagance which pervades every department of the Federal Government ; that a return to rigid economy and accountability is indispensable to arrest the systematic plunder of the public treasure by favored partisans ; while the recent startling developments of fraud and corruption at the Federal metropolis

show that an entire change of administration is imperatively demanded.

7. That the new dogma that the Constitution of its own force carries slavery into any or all of the Territories of the United States is a dangerous political heresy, at variance with the explicit provisions of that instrument itself, with contemporaneous exposition, and with legislative and judicial precedent ; is revolutionary in its tendency, and subversive of the peace and harmony of the country.

8. That the normal condition of all of the territory of the United States is that of freedom ; that as our republican fathers, when they had abolished slavery in all of our national territory, ordained that " no person should be deprived of life, liberty, or property without due process of law," it becomes our duty, by legislation, whenever such legislation is necessary, to maintain this provision of the Constitution against all attempts to violate it ; and we deny the authority of Congress, of a Territorial Legislature, or of any individuals, to give legal existence to slavery in any Territory in the United States.

9. That we brand the recent reopening of the African slave trade, under the cover of our national flag, aided by perversions of judicial power, as a crime against humanity and a burning shame to our country and age ; and we call upon Congress to take prompt and efficient measures for the total and final suppression of that execrable traffic.

10. That in the recent vetoes, by their Federal Governors, of the acts of the Legislatures of Kansas and· Nebraska prohibiting slavery in those Territories, we find a practical illustration of the boasted Democratic principle of non-intervention and popular sovereignty embodied in the Kansas-Nebraska bill, and a demonstration of the deception and fraud involved therein.

11. That Kansas should, of right, be immediately admitted as a State under the constitution recently formed and adopted by her people, and accepted by the House of Representatives.

12. That, while providing revenue for the support of the General Government by duties upon imports, sound policy requires such an adjustment of these imposts as to encourage the development of the industrial interests of the whole country ; and we commend that policy of national exchanges which secures to the workingmen liberal wages, to agriculture remunerating prices, to mechanics and manufacturers an adequate reward for their skill, labor and enterprise, and to the nation commercial prosperity and independence.

13. That we protest against any sale or alienation to others of the public lands held by actual settlers, and against any view of the free homestead policy which regards the settlers as paupers or suppliants for public bounty ; and we demand the passage by Congress of the complete and satisfactory homestead measure which has already passed the House.

14. That the Republican Party is opposed to any change in our naturalization laws, of any State legislation by which the rights of citizenship hitherto accorded to immigrants from foreign lands shall be abridged or impaired, and in favor of giving a full and efficient protection to the rights of all classes of citizens, whether native or naturalized both at home and abroad.

15. That appropriations by Congress for river and harbor improvements of a national character required for the accommodation and security of an existing commerce, are authorized by the Constitution, and justified by the obligation of Government to protect the lives and property of its citizens.

16. That a railroad to the Pacific Ocean is imperatively demanded by the interests of the whole country ; that the Federal Government ought to render immediate and efficient aid in its construction ; and that as preliminary thereto a daily overland mail should be promptly established.

17. Finally, having thus set forth our distinctive principles and views, we invite the co-operation of all citizens, however differing on other questions, who substantially agree with us in their affirmance and support.

## THIRD REPUBLICAN NATIONAL PLATFORM.

### Adopted at Baltimore, June 7th, 1864.

*Resolved*, That it is the highest duty of every American citizen to maintain against all their enemies the integrity of the Union, and the paramount authority of the Constitution and laws of the United States ; and that, laying aside all differences of political opinion, we pledge ourselves as Union men, animated by a common sentiment, and aiming at a common object, to do everything in our power to aid the Government in quelling by force of arms the rebellion now raging against its authority, and in bringing to the punishment due to their crimes the rebels and traitors arrayed against it.

*Resolved*, That we approve the determination of the Government of the United States not to compromise with rebels, nor to offer any terms of peace except such as may be based upon an " unconditional surrender" of their hostility and a return to their just allegiance to the Constitution and laws of the United States, and that we call upon the Government to maintain this position and to prosecute the war with the utmost possible vigor to the complete suppression of the rebellion, the patriotism, the heroic valor, and the undying devotion of the American people to their country and its free institutions.

*Resolved*, That, as slavery was the cause, and now constitutes the strength, of this rebellion, and as it must be always and everywhere hostile to the principles of republican government, justice and the national safety demand its utter and complete extirpation from the soil of the Republic, and that we uphold and maintain the acts and proclamations by which the Government, in its own defense, has aimed a death-blow at this gigantic evil. We are in favor, furthermore, of such an amendment to the Constitution, to be made by the people in conformity with its provisions, as shall terminate and forever

prohibit the existence of slavery within the limits of the jurisdiction of the United States.

*Resolved,* That the thanks of the American people are due to
the soldiers and sailors of the army and navy, who have
perilled their lives in defense of their country, and in vindication of the honor of the flag ; that the nation owes to them
some permanent recognition of their patriotism and valor, and
ample and permanent provision for those of their survivors who
have received disabling and honorable wounds in the service of
the country ; and that the memories of those who have fallen
in its defense shall be held in grateful and everlasting remembrance.

*Resolved,* That we approve and applaud the practical wisdom,
the unselfish patriotism and unswerving fidelity to the Constitution and the principles of American liberty, with which Abraham Lincoln has discharged, under circumstances of unparalleled difficulty, the great duties and responsibilities of the Presidential office ; that we approve and indorse, as demanded by
the emergency and essential to the preservation of the nation,
and as within the Constitution, the measures and acts which
he has adopted to defend the nation against its open and secret
foes ; that we approve especially the proclamation of emancipation, and the employment as Union soldiers of men heretofore held in slavery ; and that we have full confidence in his
determination to carry these and all other constitutional measures essential to the salvation of the country into full and complete effect.

*Resolved,* That we deem it essential to the general welfare
that harmony should prevail in the national councils, and we
regard as worthy of public confidence and official trust those
only who cordially indorse the principles proclaimed in these
resolutions, and which should characterize the administration
of the Government.

*Resolved,* That the Government owes to all men employed in
its armies, without regard to distinction of color, the full pro-

tection of the laws of war, and that any violation of these laws of the usages of civilized nations in the time of war by the rebels now in arms, should be made the subject of full and prompt redress.

*Resolved,* That the foreign immigration, which in the past has added so much to the wealth and development of resources and increase of power to this nation, the asylum of the oppressed of all nations, should be fostered and encouraged by a liberal and just policy.

*Resolved,* That we are in favor of the speedy construction of a railroad to the Pacific.

*Resolved,* That the national faith, pledged for the redemption of the public debt, must be kept inviolate ; and that for this purpose we recommend economy and rigid responsibility in the public expenditures, and a vigorous and a just system of taxation ; and it is the duty of every loyal State to sustain the credit and promote the use of the national currency.

*Resolved,* That we approve the position taken by the Government that the people of the United States never regarded with indifference the attempt of any European power to overthrow by force, or to supplant by fraud, the institutions of any republican government on the Western Continent, and that they view with extreme jealousy, as menacing to the peace and independence of this our country, the efforts of any such power to obtain new footholds for monarchical governments, sustained by a foreign military force, in near proximity to the United States.

## FOURTH REPUBLICAN NATIONAL PLATFORM.

### ADOPTED AT CHICAGO, MAY 21ST, 1868.

THE National Republican Party of the United States, assembled in National Convention in the city of Chicago, on the 21st day of May, 1868, make the following declaration of principles :

1. We congratulate the country on the assured success of the reconstruction policy of Congress, as evidenced by the adoption, in the majority of the States lately in rebellion, of constitutions securing equal civil and political rights to all ; and it is the duty of the Government to sustain those constitutions and to prevent the people of such States from being remitted to a state of anarchy.

2. The guarantee by Congress of equal suffrage to all loyal men at the South was demanded by every consideration of public safety, of gratitude, and of justice, and must be maintained ; while the question of suffrage in all of the loyal States properly belongs to the people of those States.

3. We denounce all forms of repudiation as a national crime ; and the national honor requires the payment of the public indebtedness in the uttermost good faith to all creditors at home and abroad, not only according to the letter but the spirit of the laws under which it was contracted.

4. It is due to the labor of the nation that taxation should be equalized and reduced as rapidly as the national faith will permit.

5. The national debt, contracted as it has been for the preservation of the Union for all time to come, should be extended over a fair period for redemption ; and it is the duty of Congress to reduce the rate of interest thereon whenever it can be honestly done.

6. That the best policy to diminish our burden of debt is to so improve our credit that capitalists will seek to loan us money at lower rates of interest than we now pay and must continue to pay so long as repudiation, partial or total, open or covert, is threatened or suspected.

7. The Government of the United States should be administered with the strictest economy ; and the corruptions which have been so shamefully nursed and fostered by Andrew Johnson call loudly for radical reform.

8. We profoundly deplore the untimely and tragic death of Abraham Lincoln, and regret the accession to the Presidency of Andrew Johnson, who has acted treacherously to the people who elected him and the cause he was pledged to support; who has usurped high legislative and judicial functions; who has refused to execute the laws; who has used his high office to induce other officers to ignore and violate the laws; who has employed his executive powers to render insecure the property, the peace, liberty and life of the citizen; who has abused the pardoning power; who has denounced the national legislature as unconstitutional; who has persistently and corruptly resisted, by every means in his power, every proper attempt at the reconstruction of the States lately in rebellion; who has perverted the public patronage into an engine of wholesale corruption; and who has been justly impeached for high crimes and misdemeanors, and properly denounced guilty thereof by the vote of thirty-five Senators.

9. The doctrine of Great Britain and other European powers, that because a man is once a subject he is always so, must be resisted at every hazard by the United States, as a relic of feudal times not authorized by the laws of nations, and at war with our national honor and independence. Naturalized citizens are entitled to protection in all of their rights of citizenship, as though they were native born; and no citizen of the United States, native or naturalized, must be liable to arrest and imprisonment by any foreign power for acts done or words spoken in this country; and, if so arrested and imprisoned, it is the duty of the Government to interfere in his behalf.

10. Of all who were faithful in the trials of the late war, there were none entitled to more especial honor than the brave soldiers and seamen who endured the hardships of campaign and cruise, and imperilled their lives in the service of the country; the bounties and pensions provided by the laws for these brave defenders of the nation are obligations never to be

forgotten ; the widows and orphans of the gallant dead are the wards of the people—a sacred legacy bequeathed to the nation's protecting care.

11. Foreign immigration, which in the past has added so much to the wealth, development, and resources, and increase of power to this Republic, the asylum of the oppressed of all nations, should be fostered and encouraged by a liberal and just policy.

12. This convention declares itself in sympathy with all oppressed peoples struggling for their rights.

13. That we highly commend the spirit of magnanimity and forbearance with which men who have served in the Rebellion, but who now frankly and honestly co-operate with us in restoring the peace of the country and reconstructing the Southern State governments upon the basis of impartial justice and equal rights, are received back into the communion of the loyal people ; and we favor the removal of the disqualifications and restrictions imposed upon the late rebels in the same measure as the spirit of disloyalty will die out, and as may be consistent with the safety of the loyal people.

14. That we recognize the great principles laid down in the immortal Declaration of Independence as the true foundation of democratic government, and we hail with gladness every effort toward making these principles a living reality on every inch of American soil.

## FIFTH REPUBLICAN NATIONAL PLATFORM.

### ADOPTED AT PHILADELPHIA, JUNE 6TH, 1872.

THE Republican Party of the United States, assembled in National Convention in the City of Philadelphia, on the 5th and 6th days of June, 1872, again declares its faith, appeals to its history, and announces its position upon the questions before the country :

1. During eleven years of supremacy it has accepted with grand courage the solemn duties of the time. It suppressed a gigantic rebellion, emancipated four millions of slaves, decreed the equal citizenship of all, and established universal suffrage. Exhibiting unparalleled magnanimity, it criminally punished no man for political offenses, and warmly welcomed all who proved loyalty by obeying the laws and dealing justly with their neighbors. It has steadily decreased with firm hand the resultant disorders of a great war, and initiated a wise and humane policy toward the Indians. The Pacific Railroad and similar vast enterprises have been generously aided and success-fully conducted, the public lands freely given to actual settlers, immigration protected and encouraged, and a full acknowledg-ment of the naturalized citizen's rights secured from European powers. A uniform national currency has been provided, repu-diation frowned down, the national credit sustained under the most extraordinary burdens, and new bonds negotiated at low rates. The revenues have been carefully collected and honestly applied. Despite annual large reductions of the rates of taxa-tion, the public debt has been reduced during General Grant's Presidency at the rate of a hundred millions a year, great finan-cial crises have been avoided, and peace and plenty prevail throughout the land. Menacing foreign difficulties have been peacefully and honorably composed, and the honor and power of the nation kept in high respect throughout the world. This glorious record of the past is the party's best pledge for the future. We believe the people will not intrust the govern-mentto any party or combination of men composed chiefly of those who have resisted every step of this beneficent pro-gress.

2. The recent amendments to the National Constitution should be cordially sustained because they are right, not merely toler-ated because they are law, and should be carried out according to their spirit by appropriate legislation, the enforcement of

which can safely be intrusted only to the party that secured those amendments.

3. Complete liberty and exact equality in the enjoyment of all civil, political, and public rights should be established and effectually maintained throughout the Union by efficient and appropriate State and Federal legislation. Neither the law nor its administration should admit any discrimination in respect of citizens by reason of race, creed, color, or previous condition of servitude.

4. The National Government should seek to maintain honorable peace with all nations, protecting its citizens everywhere, and sympathizing with all peoples who strive for greater liberty.

5. Any system of the civil service under which the positions of the Government are considered rewards for mere party zeal is fatally demoralizing, and we therefore favor a reform of the system by laws which shall abolish the evils of patronage and make honesty, efficiency, and fidelity, the essential qualifications for public positions, without practically creating a life tenure of office.

6. We are opposed to further grants of public lands to corporations and monopolies, and demand that the national domain be set apart for free homes for the people.

7. The annual revenue, after paying current expenditures, pensions, and the interest on the public debt, should furnish a moderate balance for the reduction of the principal, and that revenue, except so much as may be derived from a tax upon tobacco and liquors, should be raised by duties upon importations, the details of which should be so adjusted as to aid in securing remunerative wages to labor, and promote the industries, prosperity, and growth of the whole country.

8. We hold in undying honor the soldiers and sailors whose valor saved the Union. Their pensions are a sacred debt of the nation, and the widows and orphans of those who died for their country are entitled to the care of a generous and grateful

people. We favor such additional legislation as will extend the bounty of the Government to all of our soldiers and sailors who were honorably discharged, and who in the line of duty became disabled, without regard to the length of service or the cause of such discharge.

9. The doctrine of Great Britain and other European powers concerning allegiance—" once a subject always a subject"—having at last, through efforts of the Republican Party, been abandoned, and the American idea of the individual's right to transfer allegiance having been accepted by European nations, it is the duty of our Government to guard with jealous care the right of adopted citizens against the assumption of unauthorized claims by their former governments, and we urge continued, careful encouragement and protection of voluntary immigration.

10. The franking privilege ought to be abolished, and the way prepared for a speedy reduction in the rates of postage.

11. Among the questions which press for attention is that which concerns the relations of capital and labor, and the Republican party recognizes the duty of so shaping legislation as to secure full protection and the amplest field for capital, and for labor, the creator of capital, the largest opportunities, and a just share of the mutual profits of these two great servants of civilization.

12. We hold that Congress and the President have only fulfilled an imperative duty in their measures for the suppression of violent and treasonable organizations in certain lately rebellious regions, and for the protection of the ballot-box ; and, therefore, they are entitled to the thanks of the nation.

13. We denounce repudiation of the public debt, in any form or disguise, as a national crime. We witness with pride the reduction of the principal of the debt, and of the rates of interest upon the balance, and confidently expect that our excellent national currency will be perfected by a speedy resumption of specie payment.

14. The Republican Party is mindful of its obligations to the loyal women of America for their noble devotion to the cause of freedom. Their admission to the wider fields of usefulness is viewed with satisfaction ; and the honest demand of any class of citizens for additional rights should be treated with respectful consideration.

15. We heartily approve the action of Congress in extending amnesty to those lately in rebellion, and rejoice in the growth of peace and fraternal feeling throughout the land.

16. The Republican party proposes to respect the rights reserved by the people to themselves as the powers delegated by them to the State and to the Federal Government. It disapproves of the resort to unconstitutional laws for the purpose of removing evils, by interference with rights not surrendered by the people to either the State or National Government.

17. It is the duty of the General Government to adopt such measures as may tend to encourage and restore American commerce and ship-building.

18. We believe that the modest patriotism, the earnest purpose, the sound judgment, the practical wisdom, the incorruptible integrity, and the illustrious services of Ulysses S. Grant have commended him to the heart of the American people, and with him at our head we start to-day upon a new march to victory.

19. Henry Wilson, nominated for the Vice-Presidency, known to the whole land from the early days of the great struggle for liberty as an indefatigable laborer in all campaigns, an incorruptible legislator and representative man of American institutions, is worthy to associate with our great leader and share the honors which we pledge our best efforts to bestow upon them.

## SIXTH REPUBLICAN NATIONAL PLATFORM.

### ADOPTED AT CINCINNATI, JUNE 15TH, 1876.

WHEN, in the economy of Providence, this land was to be purged of human slavery, and when the strength of government of the people, by the people, and for the people was to be demonstrated, the Republican Party came into power. Its deeds have passed into history, and we look back to them with pride. Incited by their memories to high aims for the good of our country and mankind, and looking to the future with unfaltering courage, hope, and purpose, we, the representatives of the party in National Convention assembled, make the following declaration of principles :

1. The United States of America is a nation, not a league. By the combined workings of the National and State Governments, under their respective constitutions, the rights of every citizen are secured, at home and abroad, and the common welfare promoted.

2. The Republican Party has preserved these governments to the hundredth anniversary of the nation's birth, and they are now embodiments of the great truths spoken at its cradle— " that all men are created equal ; that they are endowed by their Creator with certain inalienable rights, among which are life, liberty, and the pursuit of happiness ; that for the attainment of these ends governments have been instituted among men, deriving their just powers from the consent of the governed." - Until these truths are cheerfully obeyed, or if need be vigorously enforced, the work of the Republican Party is unfinished.

3. The permanent pacification of the southern section of the Union and the complete protection of all of its citizens in the free enjoyment of all of their rights is a duty to which the Republican Party stands sacredly pledged. The power to provide

for the enforcement of the principles embodied in the recent constitutional amendments is vested by those amendments in the Congress of the United States, and we declare it to be the solemn obligation of the legislative and executive departments of the Government to put into immediate and vigorous exercise all their constitutional powers for removing any just causes of discontent on the part of any class, and for securing to every American citizen complete liberty and exact equality in the exercise of all civil, political, and public rights. To this end we imperatively demand a Congress and a Chief Executive whose courage and fidelity to those duties shall not falter until these results are placed beyond dispute or recall.

4. In the first act of Congress signed by President Grant, the National Government assumed to remove any doubts of its purpose to discharge all just obligations to the public creditors, and " solemnly pledged its faith to make provision at the earliest practicable period for the redemption of the United States notes in coin." Commercial prosperity, public morals, and national credit demand that this promise be fulälled by a continuous and steady progress to specie payment.

5. Under the Constitution the President and heads of departments are to make nominations for office ; the Senate is to advise and consent to appointments, and the House of Representatives is to accuse and prosecute faithless officers. The best interest of the public service demands that these distinctions be respected ; that Senators and Representatives who may be judges and accusers should not dictate appointments to office. The invariable rule in appointments should have reference to the honesty, fidelity, and capacity of the appointees, giving to the party in power those places where harmony and vigor of administration require its policy to be represented, but permitting all others to be filled by persons selected with sole reference to the efficiency of the public service, and the right of all

citizens to share in the honor of rendering faithful service to the country.

6. We rejoice in the quickened conscience of the people concerning political affairs, and will hold all public officers to a rigid responsibility, and engage that the prosecution and punishment of all who betray official trusts shall be swift, thorough, and unsparing.

7. The public school system of the several States is the bulwark of the American Republic, and with a view to its security and permanence we recommend an amendment to the Constitution of the United States forbidding the application of any public funds or property for the benefit of any schools or institutions under sectarian control.

8. The revenue necessary for current expenditures and the obligations of the public debt must be largely derived from duties upon importations, which, so far as possible, should be adjusted to promote the interests of American labor and advance the prosperity of the whole country.

9. We reaffirm our opposition to further grants of the public lands to corporations and monopolies, and demand that the national domain be devoted to free homes for the people.

10. It is the imperative duty of the Government so to modify existing treaties with European Governments that the same protection shall be afforded to the adopted American citizen that is given to the native born ; and that all necessary laws should be passed to protect emigrants in the absence of power in the States for that purpose.

11. It is the immediate duty of Congress to fully investigate the effect of the immigration and importation of Mongolians upon the moral and material interests of the country.

12. The Republican Party recognizes with approval the substantial advances recently made toward the establishment of equal rights for women by the many important amendments effected by Republican legislatures in the laws which concern

the personal and property relations of wives, mothers, and widows, and by the appointment and election of women to the superintendence of education, charities, and other public trusts. The honest demands of this class of citizens for additional rights, privileges, and immunities should be treated with respectful consideration.

13. The Constitution confers upon Congress sovereign power over the Territories of the United States for their government, and in the exercise of this power it is the right and duty of Congress to prohibit and extirpate, in the Territories, that relic of barbarism—polygamy ; and we demand such legislation as shall secure this end and the supremacy of American institutions in all of the Territories.

14. The pledges which the nation has given to her soldiers and sailors must be fulfilled, and a grateful people will always hold those who imperilled their lives for the country's preservation in the kindest remembrance.

15. We sincerely deprecate all sectional feeling and tendencies. We therefore note with deep solicitude that the Democratic Party counts, as its chief hope of success, upon the electoral vote of a united South, secured through the efforts of those who were recently arrayed against the nation, and we invoke the earnest attention of the country to the grave truth that a success thus achieved would reopen sectional strife and imperil national honor and human rights.

16. We charge the Democratic Party with being the same in character and spirit as when it sympathized with treason ; with making its control of the House of Representatives the triumph and opportunity of the nation's recent foes ; with reasserting and applauding in the National Capitol the sentiments of unrepentant rebellion ; with sending Union soldiers to the rear, and promoting Confederate soldiers to the front ; with deliberately proposing to repudiate the plighted faith of the Government ; with being equally false and imbecile upon the overshadowing

financial questions ; with thwarting the ends of justice by its partisan mismanagement and obstruction of investigation ; with proving itself, through the period of its ascendency in the lower House of Congress, utterly incompetent to administer the Government ; and we warn the country against trusting a party thus alike unworthy, recreant, and incapable.

17. The national administration merits commendation for its honorable work in the management of domestic and foreign affairs, and President Grant deserves the continued hearty gratitude of the American people for his patriotism and his eminent services, in war and in peace.

Upon the reading of the resolutions, Edward L. Pierce, of Massachusetts, moved to strike out the eleventh resolution ; which, after debate, was disagreed to—yeas 215, nays 532.

Edmund J. Davis moved to strike out the fourth resolution and substitute for it the following :

*Resolved,* That it is the duty of Congress to provide for carrying out the act known as the Resumption Act of Congress, to the end that the resumption of specie payments may not be longer delayed.   Which, after a brief debate, was disagreed to on a *viva voce* vote.

The candidates were : Rutherford B. Hayes, of Ohio, for President ; William A. Wheeler, of New York, for Vice-President.

---

## SEVENTH REPUBLICAN NATIONAL PLATFORM.

### ADOPTED AT CHICAGO, JUNE 5TH, 1880.

THE Republican Party, in National Convention assembled, at the end of twenty years since the Federal Government was first committed to its charge, submits to the people of the United States this brief report of its administration : It suppressed a rebellion which had armed nearly a million of men to subvert the national authority. It reconstructed the Union of the States, with freedom instead of slavery as it corner-stone. It transformed 4,000,000 human beings from the likeness of things to the rank of citizens. It relieved Congress from the infamous work of hunting fugitive slaves, and charged it to see that slavery does not exist. It has raised the value of our paper currency from thirty-eight per cent to the par value of gold. It has restored upon a solid basis, payment in coin for all the national obligations, and has given us a currency absolutely good and equal in every part of our extended country. It has lifted the credit of the nation from the point where six per cent bonds sold at eighty-six to that where four per cent bonds are eagerly sought at a premium. Under its administration railways have increased from thirty-one thousand miles in 1860 to more than eighty thousand miles in 1879. Our foreign trade has increased from seven hundred millions to eleven hundred and fifty millions in the same time ; and our exports, which were twenty millions less than our imports in 1860, were $264,000,000 more than our imports in 1879. Without resorting to loans it has, since the war closed, defrayed the ordinary expenses of government besides the accruing interest on the public debt, and disbursed annually more than $30,000,000 for soldiers' pensions. It has paid $888,000,000 of the public debt, and, by refunding the balance at a lower rate, has reduced the annual interest charge from nearly $151,000,000 to less than $89,000,000. All the industries of the country have revived, labor is in demand, wages have increased, and throughout the entire country there is evidence of a coming prosperity greater than we have ever enjoyed. Upon this record the Republican Party asks for the continued confidence and support of the people, and this convention submits for their approval the following statement of the principles and purposes which will continue to guide and inspire its efforts :

1. We affirm that the work of the last twenty-one years has

been such as to commend itself to the favor of the nation, and
that the fruits of costly victories which we have achieved
through immense difficulties should be preserved ; that the
peace so gained should be cherished ; that the dissevered Union,
now happily restored, should be perpetuated, and that the liberties secured to this generation should be transmitted undiminished to future generations ; that the order established and
the credit acquired should never be impaired ; that the pension
promises should be paid ; that the debt so much reduced should
be extinguished by the full payment of every dollar thereof ;
that the reviving industries should be further promoted, and
that the commerce, already so great, should be steadily encouraged.

2. The Constitution of the United States is a supreme law, and
not a mere contract. Out of confederated States it made a sovereign nation. Some powers are denied the nation, while others
are denied the States. But the boundary between powers delegated and those reserved is to be determined by the National
and not the State tribunals.

3. The work of popular education is one left to the care of
the several States, but it is the duty of the National Government
to aid that work to the extent of its constitutional ability. The
intelligence of the nation is but the aggregate intelligence of
the several States, and the destiny of the nation must be guided,
not by the genius of any one State, but by the average genius
of all.

4. The Constitution wisely forbids Congress to make any law
respecting an establishment of religion, but it is idle to hope
that the nation can be protected against the influence of sectarianism while each State is exposed to its domination. We
therefore recommend that the Constitution be so amended as to
lay the same prohibition on the Legislature of each State, and
to forbid the appropriation of public funds to the support of
sectarian schools.

5. We reaffirm the belief avowed in 1876 that the duties levied for the purpose of revenue should so discriminate as to favor American labor ; that no further grant of the public domain should be made to any railroad or other corporation ; that slavery having perished in the States, its twin barbarity, polygamy, must die in the Territories ; that everywhere the protection accorded to a citizen of American birth must be secured to citizens by American adoption ; that we esteem it the duty of Congress to develop and improve our water-courses and harbors, but insist that further subsidies to private persons or corporations must cease ; that the obligations of the Republic to the men who preserved its integrity in the day of battle are undiminished by the lapse of fifteen years since their final victory, and their perpetual honor is and shall forever be the grateful privilege and sacred duty of the American people.

6. Since the authority for regular immigration and intercourse between the United States and foreign nations rests with the Congress of the United States and its treaty-making powers, the Republican Party, regarding the unrestricted immigration of the Chinese as an evil of great magnitude, invoke the exercise of that power to restrain and limit that immigration by the enactment of such just, humane and reasonable provisions as will produce that result.    .

7. That the purity and patriotism which characterized the earlier career of R. B. Hayes, in peace and war, and which guided the thought of our immediate predecessors to him for a Presidential candidate, have continued to inspire him in his career as Chief Executive, and that history will accord to his administration the honors which are due to an efficient, just, and courteous discharge of the public business, and will honor his interpositions between the people and proposed partisan laws.

8. We charge upon the Democratic Party the habitual sacrifice of patriotism and justice to a supreme and insatiable lust of

office and patronage ; that to obtain possession of the National
Government and State Governments, and the control of place,
they have obstructed all efforts to promote the purity and to
conserve the freedom of suffrage ; have labored to unseat lawfully elected members of Congress to secure at all hazards the
majority of the States in the House of Representatives ; have
endeavored to occupy by force and fraud the places of trust given
to others by the people of Maine, and rescued by the courage
and action of Maine's patriotic sons ; have, by methods vicious
in principle and tyrannical in practice, attached partisan legislation to appropriations, upon whose passage the very movements
of the Government depend ; have crushed the rights of the individual, have advocated the principles and sought the favor of
rebellion against the nation, and have endeavored to obliterate
the sacred memories of the war and to overcome its inestimably
good results of nationality, personal freedom, and individual
equality.   The equal steady and complete enforcement of the
laws and the protection of all our citizens in the enjoyment of
all privileges and immunities guaranteed by the Constitution, is
the first duty of the nation.   The dangers of a solid South can
only be averted  by a faithful performance of every promise
which the nation has made to its citizens.   The execution of
the laws and the punishment of all those who violate them are
the only safe method by which an enduring peace can be secured, and genuine prosperity established throughout the South.
Whatever promises the nation makes the nation must perform,
and the nation cannot with safety relegate this duty to the
States.   The solid South must be divided by the peaceful agencies of the ballot, and all opinions must there find free expression ; and to this end the honest voter must be protected against
terrorism, violence, or fraud.   And we affirm it to be the duty
and purpose of the Republican Party to use all legitimate
means to restore all States of this Union to the most perfect
harmony which may be possible.   And we submit to the prac-

tical, sensible people of the United States to say whether it would not be dangerous to the dearest interests of our country at this time to surrender the administration of the National Government to a party which seeks to overthrow the existing policy, under which we are so prosperous, and thus bring distrust and confusion where there is now order, confidence, and hope.

The Republican Party, adhering to the principle affirmed by its last National Convention, of respect for the constitutional rules governing appointments to office, adopts the declaration of President Hayes, that the reform of the civil service should be thorough, radical, and complete. To this end it demands the co-operation of the legislative with the executive department of the Government, and that Congress shall so legislate that fitness, ascertained by proper practical tests, shall admit to the public service.

# EARLY REPUBLICAN LEADERS.

BY

CHARLES T. CONGDON.

# EARLY REPUBLICAN LEADERS.

THERE is abundant evidence that slavery in America was never germane to the sentiment and conscience of the American people. The plea sometimes adduced during the anti-slavery discussion, that the slaves were forced upon the colonies by the commercial cupidity of the mother country, was not without a modicum of truth. It is historically true that both Virginia and South Carolina, in the eighteenth century, sought to restrict the importation of slaves. Massachusetts and Pennsylvania pressed the adoption of similar measures, but in each instance the veto of the colonial governor was interposed. It must be understood that, notwithstanding slave labor was in many of the colonies found profitable, there was always sturdy protest against it. The constant testimony of the Quakers against it is of record. John Wesley had denounced it as the sum of all villainies ; Whitefield had spoken to the planters of " the miseries of the poor negroes ;" Dr. Hopkins, the eminent theologian, had fitly characterized the traffic in its very centre, and to the faces of the Newport merchants engaged in it. The Continental Congress in 1774 had pledged the United Colonies to discontinue altogether the slave trade. Several of the slave colonies themselves joined in the declaration against the trade. These facts are worth remembering, because they show that even at that time there was a strong and conscientious feeling against slavery and in favor of justice and humanity. The defence of slavery upon moral, theological, and political grounds came afterward.

It is nearly a hundred years since the establishment of the Pennsylvania Society for Promoting the Abolition of Slavery, and Benjamin Franklin was made its president. There were other and similar societies in different States. The first anti-slavery national convention was held in 1795.

Perhaps the earliest abolitionist intimately connected with the anti-slavery agitation which culminated in such great results was Benjamin Lundy, a member of the Society of Friends, who, born in New Jersey in 1789, in 1815 had established an anti-slavery association called "The Union Humane Society," at St. Clairsville, Va. Lundy wrote, travelled, lectured, and everywhere maintained his crusade against the institution. In 1821 he started the *Genius of Universal Emancipation*, the office of which he removed to Baltimore in 1824. Having made the acquaintance of William Lloyd Garrison, he engaged the assistance of that gentleman in the editorial management of the newspaper. Lundy was the first to establish anti-slavery periodicals and deliver anti-slavery lectures. It is stated that from 1820 to 1830 Lundy travelled twenty-five thousand miles, five thousand on foot, visited nineteen States, made two voyages to Hayti, and delivered more than two hundred addresses.

The first number of Mr. Garrison's *Liberator* was published in Boston, in January, 1831. The history of the agitation which was then begun has already been partially written and is familiar to many still living. From this time forth to the bloody issue, and the final triumph of right and of justice, slavery began to be felt in the politics of the country. Undoubtedly a vast majority of both the Whig and Democratic Parties were upon its side. Upon the other there were two classes. There was that which would keep no terms with slavery, but at all times and seasons yielded not one jot or tittle, but demanded its immediate abolition. There were others who took more moderate ground ; who doubted the policy of instant abolition ; who ad-

hered to the parties with which they found themselves allied ;
but who nevertheless insisted upon the right of free discussion
and the right of petition. The great champion of this right in
the House of Representatives was John Quincy Adams. He had
gone from the White House to the House of Representatives with
no special feelings of kindness for the Southern States or for their
political leaders. But he was always careful to declare that personally he was not in favor of the abolition of slavery in the District, while he deemed the right of petition " sacred and to be
vindicated at all hazards.'' His position must not be misunder-
stood. Asserting energetically the right of the petitioners to be
heard, he had no sympathy with their opinions. He did not
regard the question of slavery in the District as of much consequence. He took no humanitarian ground. He fought the
battle, and fought it nobly, but it was as a constitutional lawyer,
and not as an abolitionist. He argued the matter as he argued
the famous Amistad case, upon strictly legal principles. Fortunately they happened to be upon the right side, and Mr.
Adams's services at this time were unquestionably of great value
to the cause of freedom.

.Among the few who took an entirely different ground, and
who avowed their sympathy with the prayer of the petitioners,
was William Slade, of Vermont, who was in the House from
1831 to 1843, and afterward Governor of Vermont. He said,
with manly precision and courage, " The petitioners wish the
abolition of slavery in the District of Columbia ; so do I. They
wish to abolish the slave-trade in the District ; so do I.'' But
protest at such a time was vain, and the petitions were laid
upon the table by a great majority. Agitation must at any cost
be arrested. Tranquillity must by any expedient be secured.
In the Senate at the same time a similar controversy was going
on. Singularly enough, the champion of the right of petition
here was Mr. James Buchanan, who spoke and voted for the
reception of the petitions, though he also advocated the instant

rejection of their prayer ; and he actually succeeded, to the great indignation of Mr. Calhoun, in carrying his point. Mr. Morris, of Ohio, vindicated the right, and declared that "no denial of it by Congress could prevent them from expressing it." Similar ground was taken by Mr. Prentiss, of Vermont. Mr. Webster, not then so regardless of the popular opinion as he afterward became, advocated the reference of the petitions to the proper committees.

Among those who in those dark days of Northern subserviency nobly stood up for free speech and a free press, was Governor Joseph Ritner, of Pennsylvania, who in one of his messages said : "Above all, let us never yield up the right of free discussion of any evil which may arise in the land, or any part of it." Thaddeus Stevens, then chairman of the Judiciary Committee of the Pennsylvania House, took ground equally brave and independent. The Southern Legislatures had asked of the Northern States the enactment of laws for the suppression of free discussion. "No State," said Mr. Stevens, "can claim from us such legislation. It would reduce us to a vassalage but little less degrading than that of the slaves." But in no State can the progress of this great controversy be more satisfactorily observed than in Massachusetts. There the abolitionists were most uncompromising and determined, and so respectable were they in numbers and character that those who were opposed to their opinions and proceedings were not long afterward glad enough to get their votes in seasons of particular emergency. But Massachusetts respectability, taking its tone from Boston, as the tone of Boston was governed by its commercial interests, was then ready for almost unconditional surrender, of all which it should have held most dear, to the slave power. Edward Everett was Governor of the State, and went so far as to suggest that anti-slavery discussion "might be prosecuted as a misdemeanor at common law." This part of Governor Everett's message was referred to a committee of which Mr. George Lunt was chairman. Before this committee appeared in their own defence such abolitionists as Ellis Gray Loring, William Lloyd Garrison, Dr. Charles Follen, Samuel J. May, and William Goodell. It is almost impossible now to conceive of the indignities as possible to which these gentlemen were subjected by the chairman, Mr. Lunt. Dr. Follen, one of the mildest and most amiable of men, was peremptorily silenced. "You are here," said Mr. Lunt to Mr. May, "to exculpate yourselves if you can"—as if the remonstrants had been criminals at the bar of public justice. Such treatment excited great indignation among those who were present merely as spectators. Dr. William Ellery Channing—the story is still related in Boston—walked across the room to offer Mr. Garrison his hand, and to speak to him words of sympathy and encouragement. From that day the progress of anti-slavery opinions in Massachusetts went on almost without cessation. They colored and affected the action of political parties ; they broke up and scattered an organization which had held the State in fee for more than a generation ; they proved themselves superior to all the reports and resolutions which such men as Mr. Lunt could bring forward ; they won for their supporters all the distinction which place and popular confidence could confer, and reduced those who rejected them to the leanest of minorities. All things worked together for good. The murder of Lovejoy, at Alton in 1837, was a triumph of slavery which proved in the end one of the most fatal of its misfortunes. It sent Dr. Channing to Faneuil Hall to protest against such an outrage upon law and justice. It sent there Wendell Phillips to make his first speech, which rendered him at once famous. It created a public sympathy in Boston and throughout the State which was never lost, which the immense influence of Mr. Webster was unable to overcome, and which prepared the way, first for the Free Soil and then for the Republican Party. Boston conservatism occasionally made a good deal of noise afterward, but it never carried another election. "Politics," said Mr. Franklin Pierce about that time in the Senate, " are beginning to mingle with that question." And " he profoundly regretted that individuals of both parties were submitting to the catechism of the abolitionists." Mr. Pierce was right ; but there was a good deal more to come.

The intense hostility of a portion of the Northern people to the measures and methods of the early abolitionists did not and could not prevent a gradual change in the temper and the opinions of vast numbers of reflecting and conscientious men, who saw the sole remedy only in political action. The audacity of the slave power, never for a moment satisfied, gave its friends at the North no opportunity of appealing successfully to Northern interests. The most imprudent of mankind were always doing something which fanned the slumbering embers again into a blaze. They would not let well enough alone. They would not temporize even when to do so would have been greatly to their advantage. South Carolina, for instance, had been for years in the habit of imprisoning colored seamen during their detention at Charleston. Massachusetts appointed Samuel Hoar, of Concord, the agent of the State to prosecute suits to test the legality of these imprisonments. Mr. Hoar was not only a gentleman of great personal worth, but he belonged to one of the oldest families in the State, and for many years had been respected as a jurist of great ability and integrity. To what indignities he was subjected, and how he was expelled from the State, the history of those times will never fail to tell. One result of this was to make abolitionists of a great number of highly respectable people who otherwise might never have been moved from the path of the strictest conservatism. The admission of Texas as a slave State brought into the anti-slavery ranks, ill-defined as they were, great numbers of persons who otherwise might have kept silence forever. It caused a meeting of protest in Faneuil Hall, over which Charles Francis Adams presided. The resolutions were drawn up by Charles Sumner. They were pre-

sented by John G. Palfrey. Garrison and Phillips were there, and
for once the anti-slavery men of the non-political and the political
cal schools worked together. The matter was discussed in the
colleges and the law schools, in the factories and work-shops ;
it was then that the great political revolution in so many States
began. Above all, it sharply defined the line between those Whigs
and Democrats who, after a political wrong had been accomplished, were willing quietly to submit, and those who thought
that the wrong should be a fair warning against others of a similar character. If the motive of annexation was the preservation
of slavery, then there was all the more reason for watching
slavery closely.

The case of Mr. Giddings is an excellent illustration of the
folly by which the Whig Party alienated many of its best
friends. If he was anything, Mr. Giddings was every inch a
Whig. He clung to his political organization when many
another man would have left it in disgust. He was, while Mr.
John Quincy Adams survived, the steady and able ally of that
statesman in the House of Representatives. But neither this
nor his strong anti-slavery sentiments prevented him from
being a warm friend and supporter of Henry Clay. He clung
to his party until his party nominated General Taylor. This
was a supposed submission to the slave power, though it did
not turn out to be afterward, which, sent Mr. Giddings into the
Free Soil ranks in 1848. What men went with him, and what
came of that movement, even after it had to all appearance
utterly failed, is well enough known. No wonder Mr. Giddings
felt that the North should have different men in the public
councils, when with a large majority it could not shield him
from outrages in the House to which the lowest of men would
hardly have submitted outside of it.

The Democratic Party often exhibited as little wisdom. It
had not, for instance, a stronger and more able soldier than Mr.
John P. Hale, of New Hampshire. Personally very popular, he

was an excellent debater, never found wanting in an emergency, and one who was alike equal to attack or defence. He was, however, foremost in his denunciation of the plan for the annexation of Texas—a measure which he characterized as " eminently calculated to provoke the scorn of earth and the judgment of Heaven." He had already been nominated for the next Congress by the Democrats of his district, but another convention was called, and the name of Mr. Hale was taken from the ticket. It is to tell the whole historical story to say that this day's absurd action made Mr. Hale a Senator of the United States. This is the story everywhere. The Whig National Convention, which treated with such utter contempt the protests of anti-slavery Whigs, was the last which met with any prospect of good fortune before it. The day was pregnant with great events, and great political changes were at hand. The Barnburner revolt in New York assisted in forwarding the great reform. There were yet to be defeats, and men's minds were not entirely fixed ; but both great parties in 1848 sealed their political doom with suicidal hands. Mr. Allen, of Massachusetts, had said in the Whig National Convention, " It is evident the terms of union between the Whigs of the North and the Whigs of the South are the perpetual surrender by the former of the high offices and powers of the Government to their Southern confederates. To these terms, I think, sir, the free States will no longer submit." Mr. Wilson declared that he would " not be bound by the proceedings of the convention ;" and Mr. Stanley, of North Carolina, with far-seeing sagacity, retorted that he was " injuring no one but himself"—a declaration which in the light of subsequent events seems sufficiently amusing.

Before the dissatisfied delegates went home the Buffalo Convention was decided upon. The first State Convention of the new party in Massachusetts was held in Worcester, and was attended by men who have since been often enough heard of— by Henry Wilson, Charles Francis Adams, Charles Sumner, E.

Rockwood Hoar, to mention no others. The action of the Buffalo Convention in nominating Mr. Van Buren for President brought a great portion of the Democratic Party to the new organization, especially in Massachusetts, and in that State the party has never fairly recovered from the events of that campaign. The nomination of Charles Francis Adams for Vice-President was deemed a sufficient concession to the bolting Whigs. It was a ticket for an honest man to support, although no prospect of success was before it. The campaign started with great spirit in Ohio, being led by Chase, Giddings, Root, and other distinguished men. The new party went through a campaign which resulted in entire defeat and—in victory ! But it had cast two hundred and ninety-thousand votes for freedom ; it had defeated a candidate the avowed supporter of slavery ; and it had secured the election of another who, although a slaveholder, was at least not a trimmer and a doughface.

Here as well as anywhere may be considered the distinctive character of those who early engaged in this war against slavery extension. It need not be said that coalition was necessary, and coalition always implies the co-operation of those who find each other useful, but who may be governed by widely different motives. Those who had conscientiously entertained a hatred of slavery found an opportunity of alliance with others, whose hostility was at least recent, and who had managed to get along with the South so long as that section conceded to them a fair share in the Government. The Democratic wing of the Free Soil Party made great pretensions to anti-slavery sentiment. Among those who were loudest was John Van Buren, of New York. He went so far as to say at Utica, in the Barnburners' Convention, "We expect to make the Democratic Party of this State the great anti-slavery party of this State, and through it to make the Democratic Party of the United States the great anti-slavery party of the United States." Subsequent events showed that this meant very little save the desire for revenge on the part of a son who was irritated by what he regarded as the personal wrongs of a father. Not many years elapsed before John Van Buren was again in the Democratic Party, when it was even more thoroughly than before the servant of slavery, with the immoral aspects of the institution more fully developed. With him returned to their allegiance many thousands of Democrats. He was supple, clever, and adroit. As a platform speaker he had few equals ; but that he was altogether sincere perhaps it would be too much to say.

No man is personally identified more historically with the Republican Party than Henry Wilson. He had great virtues and great faults of character. His natural impulses were warm and generous. He had absolute physical courage, and when his passions were aroused he was a formidable enemy. He could put a personal injury in abeyance if he thought it for his advantage to do so ; but he had a long memory, and although he might forgive he never forgot. He had great skill in party manœuvre, and a perfect faith in party management. It was perhaps his real misfortune that his first political successes of any importance were secured by coalitions. It is true that many of these were originated by himself, but he was not, it must be said in his defense, the originator of the opportunity. He was perfectly frank in his avowal of what he thought to be not only the expediency but the virtue of joining in any political movement which would advance his own political opinions, without much regard for appearances. Others acquiesced in such bargains—Mr. Wilson went farther, for he believed in them. There was no nicety, no moral scrupulosity in his constitution. This made it easy for him to act with anybody or everybody ; and to this easy political virtue he owed his first election to the United States Senate. He joined the Know-Nothing Party without in the least accepting its particular tenets. He did not hesitate to receive Democratic votes. In Massachusetts the Whig Party was in his way, and in the way of the anti-slavery views which he undoubtedly entertained, and he determined upon its destruction. He never apologized for alliances which others thought to be immoral. He was a leader of those who regarded slavery as sinful and impolitic ; he himself undoubtedly shared in their opinions ; but he did not hesitate in an emergency to act with those whose views were widely different. After his success was definitely assured he became more independent, and, it must be added, more consistent. His capacity for public affairs was of a first-rate order, and he had entirely risen above the defects of his early education. He was a born political soldier, and did quite as much as any man to bring the Republican Party to compactness and coherence.

Mr. Charles Sumner was of a character widely different from that of his colleague. The latter, with all his merits, was ingrain a politician ; Mr. Sumner was perhaps the worst politician in the United States. While the struggle which resulted in making him a Senator of the United States was going on in the Massachusetts Legislature, he kept resolutely aloof from the contest, and neither by word nor by deed indicated his approval or disapproval of the coalition. Even when the prolonged contest resulted in his election, he left the city of Boston that he might avoid the congratulations of his supporters of either sort. He followed what he called " a line of reserve." In a letter to Mr. Wilson he thanked that gentleman for " the energy, determination, and fidelity" with which he had fought the battle, and said, " For weal or woe, you must take the responsibility of having placed me in the Senate of the United States." It is doubtful whether Mr. Sumner did entirely approve the means which were used to make him in the first instance a Senator ; but, like other anti-slavery Whigs and Democrats, he acquiesced. So sturdy a man as Robert Rantoul, Jr., accepted a seat in the Senate under precisely the same conditions, and he was elected to the House of Representatives in the same way. Even Horace Mann defended the coalition.

Mr. Sumner's career in the Senate was never in the least influenced by the necessity of conciliating Democrats at home; and long before his re-election anything like coalition had, by the march of events, been made unnecessary. Ultimately Mr. Sumner's hold upon the hearts of the people of Massachusetts became so strong that the efforts of a petty clique to unseat him, could not under any circumstances probably have been successful. He was regarded, especially after the felonious assault upon him in the Senate Chamber, as a martyr to the cause. He was a great man for great occasions; and by long familiarity with the business of the Senate he became much more practically useful than he was at first; but he could not be considered a popular member, and there were those who thought him somewhat arrogant. He never worked well in the traces of party, and there was something of the virtuoso in his character, which his less refined associates did not relish. His speeches were very carefully prepared, but they were often loaded with learning, and the more elaborate portions of them smelt of the lamp. His name, however, is inseparably and most honorably connected with the greatest of events, and he will doubtless be remembered long after he ceases to be read.

Charles Francis Adams had been among the earliest of the Conscience Whigs of Massachusetts. His distrust of the South and of the slaveholder was natural, for he had received a large inheritance of family grievances, real or supposed. None of them, however, prevented him from permitting his name to be used with that of Mr. Van Buren, and he accepted the nomination for the Vice-Presidency from the Buffalo Convention with perfect complacency. But if his passions were strong, his political tastes were occasionally fastidious, and probably he never thoroughly relished the Massachusetts Coalition. He exhibited on many occasions the same remarkable mixture of ardor and conservatism which characterized his illustrious father. He could lead sometimes with special ability, but he could not be easily nor often led. Party harness sat very easily upon his shoulders, and he could throw it off whenever he pleased. But of the new party he was an invaluable member, for his training for public affairs had been first-rate ; the historical associations of his name were interesting and attractive ; he was very wealthy ; and he was a master of political science. Opposed as he was to the coalition which elected Mr. Sumner, he shared that opposition with Richard H. Dana, Jr., Samuel Hoar, John G. Palfrey, and some other eminent Free Soilers. Ultimately, of course, these differences of opinion subsided ; but Mr. Adams has shown, with other members of the party, that the same freedom of judgment which had led to its formation still guided many of its choicest spirits. Of the brilliant career of Mr. Adams, subsequent to these events, it is unnecessary here to speak. The present time finds him a member of that Democratic Party which he has so often and so bitterly denounced. The fact is to be most pleasantly regarded as evidence of the perfect independence of his character.

All the temptations which led several prominent Whigs to repudiate the nomination of General Taylor in 1848 had no effect upon Mr. William H. Seward. His time had not yet come, but it was well known that his political opinions were of an anti-slavery color, and that he was particularly sensitive upon the point of surrendering fugitives from slavery. These views began to develop more definitely after his election to the United States Senate in 1849. In the debate upon the admission of California into the Union in 1850, he used the phrase " *higher law* than the Constitution," a part of which has become proverbial. He fought the compromises to the last. In his speech at Rochester in 1858 he had alluded to the " irrepressible conflict," and this phrase also has become famous, as well as the declaration that " the United States must and will become either entirely a slaveholding nation or entirely a free labor nation." In 1860 in the Senate he avowed that his vote should never be

given to sanction slavery in the common territories of the
United States, " or anywhere else in the world." His services
as Secretary of State during the Rebellion were of the first
order, and especially his management of our foreign relations.
Undoubtedly his wisdom and forethought saved us upon more
than one occasion from a foreign war. His adherence to office
under President Johnson did much to injure his popularity ;
and perhaps he was not sorry definitely to retire from public life
in 1869, and to find a new and rational pleasure in prolonged
foreign travel.    Mr. Seward was a man of fine literary tastes, of
no mean literary skill ; he had the faculty of acquiring and of
keeping friends ; and in the social circle he was devoted and
affectionate.    The disappointment of his public life, which considered altogether was eminently successful, was his failure to
secure the Presidency ; but it must have been an alleviation to
know that he shared this with so many eminent men.    His
public career was peculiarly consistent, and perhaps of all public characters of his time he was oftenest found upon the side
of the oppressed and the unfortunate, even in cases which had
no political significance.

The man who even before 1846, and in that year, argued that
slavery was local and dependent upon State law, was Salmon P.
Chase, of Ohio, and nothing could be more astonishing than the
changes which ultimately placed such a lawyer upon the bench
of the Supreme Court, and in the place just before occupied by
Chief-Justice Taney.    He was one of the few remarkable men
to whom the old Liberty Party was indebted for an existence, to
which the Republican Party also owes something.    He was the
first or among the first to propose the Free Soil movement and
the Buffalo Convention in 1848, and over this body he presided.
He too was sent to the United States Senate by a coalition of Free
Soil members and Democrats of the Ohio Legislature in 1849 ; but
the Ohio Democrats in their State Convention had already declared slavery to be a national evil, which rendered the coali-

tion at least not absurd and contradictory. Mr. Chase made haste to disavow all connection with the Democrats after the nomination of Mr. Pierce in 1852, upon a pro-slavery platform. With his record and strong opinions upon the subject of slavery he came naturally into the Republican Party, and into the Cabinet of President Lincoln as Secretary of the Treasury in 1861. As Chief-Justice of the United States, his great learning, his sense of equity, and his liberal views of important public questions won him a permanent reputation as a lawyer. He did not always agree with the policy of the Republican Party, and he was even talked of as a candidate of the Democrats for the Presidency—a nomination which was not accorded to him, but which it was understood that he was willing to accept under certain conditions. He is an excellent instance of what the reader of this chapter must have observed—the tendency, during stormy political seasons, of really able men to cut loose the bonds of party and to seek in new affiliations the accomplishment of cherished purposes and the vindication of profound convictions. Judge Chase, in his own State, was a man of unbounded popularity. This was never shaken by any course which he thought fit to pursue ; and to the last no man ever doubted his integrity.

Not as President, but as one of the leaders who made the Republican Party possible, the career of Abraham Lincoln before he was elected to the office in which he died a martyr to his principles, ought here to be alluded to. In Congress, which he entered in 1848, he doubted the constitutionality of slavery in the District of Columbia ; he suggested the expediency of abolishing the slave-trade there ; and he warmly advocated the Wilmot Proviso. When the project for the repeal of the Missouri Compromise was brought forward, he found his place in the great contest at once. His platform duels with Douglas in Illinois will never be forgotten, and his speech at Springfield utterly demolished the sophistry of the " great principle" which asserted that a man in Nebraska might not only govern himself, but also govern other persons without their consent. He too declared that no government could endure permanently which was " half slave and half free." How well he demeaned himself in his high office it is unnecessary to say. He grew larger and larger under the pressure of the terrible situation ; he was as tender as a woman, and as stern as a Roman ; he thought, planned, acted, always with perfect caution, with native sagacity, with a perfect appreciation of the situation. It was no accident, it was the impulse of character and the prompting of the heart which led Abraham Lincoln into the Republican Party, of which he was a defender and ornament. In the most doubtful days, if there be a party which is on the side of justice and humanity, a man with a heart is sure to find it ; and if there be another, its exact opposite, pledged to oppression, to selfishness, and to corruption, the man without a heart is sure to drift into it.

In this chapter many honored names have been necessarily omitted. The object has been to refer to only a few of the most prominent as examples of fidelity to great principles and to ideas worthy of the support of the American people. After all, more have been omitted than mentioned. We might have spoken of Horace Mann, the uncompromising philanthropist, the profound scholar, and the life-long advocate of popular education ; of John G. Palfrey, who was among the first of Massachusetts Whigs to risk all save the reward of a good conscience for the sake of the slave ; of the young and eloquent Burlingame, first known as a popular speaker, but who afterward developed into a most able diplomatist ; and we might have added something of the magnetic influence which drew the young men of the North about the banner of freedom, and awakened an enthusiasm which made the strict lines and the self-seeking policy of the old parties distasteful to their generous natures. Happy will the nation be should any such great emergency again arise, if once more the old honesty shall be awakened and the old enthusiasm stimulated !

# REPUBLICAN VICTORIES.

THE POPULAR AND ELECTORAL VOTE AT EACH
PRESIDENTIAL ELECTION SINCE THE
FORMATION OF THE

## REPUBLICAN PARTY.

## Reduction of the Public Debt.

## POPULAR VOTE OF 1856.

| STATES. | James Buchanan, Democratic. | | John C. Fremont, Republican. | | M. Fillmore, American. | | Total Vote. |
|---|---|---|---|---|---|---|---|
| | Vote. | Maj. | Vote. | Maj. | Vote. | Maj. | |
| 1 Alabama..... | 46,739 | 18,187 | ......... | ........ | 28,552 | ..... | 75,291 |
| 2 Arkansas.... | 21,910 | 11,123 | ......... | ........ | 10,787 | ..... | 32,697 |
| 3 California.... | 53,365 | *17,200 | 20,691 | ... .... | 36,165 | ..... | 110,221 |
| 4 Connecticut. | 34,995 | ....... | 42,715 | 5,105 | 2,615 | ..... | 80,325 |
| 5 Delaware.... | 8,004 | 1,521 | 308 | ........ | 6,175 | ..... | 14,487 |
| 6 Florida...... | 6,358 | 1,525 | ......... | ........ | 4,833 | .:. .. | 11,191 |
| 7 Georgia..... | 56,578 | 14,350 | ......... | ........ | 42,228 | ... .. | 98,806 |
| 8 Illinois...... | 105,348 | †9,159 | 96,189 | ........ | 37,444 | ..... | 238,981 |
| 9 Indiana...... | 118,670 | 1,909 | 94,375 | ........ | 22,386 | ..... | 235,431 |
| 10 Iowa........ | 36,170 | ....... | 43,954 | ‡7,784 | 9,180 | ..... | 89,304 |
| 11 Kentucky... | 74,642 | 6,912 | 314 | .... ... | 67,416 | ..... | 142,372 |
| 12 Louisiana... | 22,164 | 1,455 | ......... | ........ | 20,709 | . . .. | 42,873 |
| 13 Maine....... | 39,080 | ....... | 67,379 | 24,974 | 3,325 | ..... | 109,784 |
| 14 Maryland. . | 39,115 | ....... | 281 | ........ | 47,460 | 8,064 | 86,856 |
| 15 Massachus'ts | 39.240 | ....... | 108,190 | 49,324 | 19,626 | ..... | 167,056 |
| 16 Michigan.... | 52,136 | ....... | 71,762 | 17,966 | 1,660 | ..... | 125,558 |
| 17 Mississippi. | 35,446 | 11,251 | ......... | ........ | 24,195 | ..... | 59,641 |
| 18 Missouri..... | 58,164 | 9,640 | ......... | ........ | 48,524 | ..... | 106,688 |
| 19 N. H'pshire . | 32,789 | ....... | 38,345 | 5,134 | 422 | ..... | 71,556 |
| 20 New Jersey.. | 46,943 | *18,605 | 28,338 | ........ | 24,115 | ..... | 99,396 |
| 21 New York... | 195,878 | ....... | 276,007 | ‡80,129 | 121,604 | ..... | 596,487 |
| 22 N. Carolina.. | 48,246 | 11,360 | ......... | ........ | 36,886 | ..... | 85,132 |
| 23 Ohio........ | 170,874 | ....... | 187,497 | ‡16,623 | 28,126 | ..... | 386,497 |
| 24 P'nsylvania.. | 230,710 | 1,025 | 147,510 | ........ | 82,175 | ..... | 460,395 |
| 25 Rhode Island | 6,680 | ....... | 11,467 | 3,112 | 1,675 | .. :. | 19,822 |
| 26 S. Carolina.. | Electors | chosen | by the | Legis- | lature. | ... . | ....... |
| 27 Tennessee... | 73,638 | 7 460 | ......... | ........ | 66,178 | ..... | 139,816 |
| 28 Texas....... | 31,169 | 15,530 | ......... | ........ | 15,639 | ..... | 46,808 |
| 29 Vermont:.... | 10,569 | ....... | 39,561 | 28,447 | 545 | ..... | 50,675 |
| 30 Virginia..... | 89,706 | 29,105 | 291 | ........ | 60,310 | ..... | 150,307 |
| 31 Wisconsin .. | 52,843 | ....... | 66,090 | 12,668 | 579 | ..... | 119,512 |
| Total...... | 1,838,169 | 142,353 | 1,341,264 | 146,730 | 874,53 | 8,0644 | 4,053,967 |
| Buchanan's Plurality... | †496,905 | | | | | | |

\* Plurality over Fillmore.    † Plurality over Fremont.    ‡ Plurality over Buchanan.

## ELECTORAL VOTE OF 1856.

| STATES. | Buchanan | Fremont | Fillmore | Breckinridge | Dayton | Donelson | Total. |
|---|---|---|---|---|---|---|---|
| 1 Alabama | 9 | | | 9 | | | 9 |
| 2 Arkansas | 4 | | | 4 | | | 4 |
| 3 California | 4 | | | 4 | | | 4 |
| 4 Connectic't | | 6 | | | 6 | | 6 |
| 5 Delaware | 3 | | | 3 | | | 3 |
| 6 Florida | 3 | | | 3 | | | 3 |
| 7 Georgia | 10 | | | 10 | | | 10 |
| 8 Illinois | 11 | | | 11 | | | 11 |
| 9 Indiana | 13 | | | 13 | | | 13 |
| 10 Iowa | | 4 | | | 4 | | 4 |
| 11 Kentucky | 12 | | | 12 | | | 12 |
| 12 Louisiana | 6 | | | 6 | | | 6 |
| 13 Maine | | 8 | | | 8 | | 8 |
| 14 Maryland | | | 8 | | | 8 | 8 |
| 15 Mass'chu'ts | | 13 | | | 13 | | 13 |
| 16 Michigan | | 6 | | | 6 | | 6 |
| 17 Mississippi | 7 | | | 7 | | | 7 |
| 18 Missouri | 9 | | | 9 | | | 9 |
| 19 N. Hamps'e | | 5 | | | 5 | | 5 |
| 20 New Jersey | 7 | | | 7 | | | 7 |
| 21 New York | | 35 | | | 35 | | 35 |
| 22 N. Carolina | 10 | | | 10 | | | 10 |
| 23 Ohio | | 23 | | | 23 | | 23 |
| 24 Pennsylv'ia | 27 | | | 27 | | | 27 |
| 25 R Island | | 4 | | | 4 | | 4 |
| 26 S. Carolina | 8 | | | 8 | | | 8 |
| 27 Tennessee | 12 | | | 12 | | | 12 |
| 28 Texas | 4 | | | 4 | | | 4 |
| 29 Vermont | | 5 | | | 5 | | 5 |
| 30 Virginia | 15 | | | 15 | | | 15 |
| 31 Wisconsin | | 5 | | | 5 | | 5 |
| Total | 174 | 114 | 8 | 174 | 114 | 8 | 296 |

## POPULAR VOTE OF 1860.

| | STATES. | A. Lincoln, Republican. | | S. A. Douglas, Ind. Dem. | | J. C. Breckinridge, Democratic. | | John Bell, Const. Union. | | Total Vote. |
|---|---|---|---|---|---|---|---|---|---|---|
| | | Vote. | Maj. | Vote. | Maj. | Vote. | Maj. | Vote. | Maj. | |
| 1 | Alabama. | .......... | ....... | 13,651 | .... | 48,831 | 7,355 | 27,825 | ...... | 90,307 |
| 2 | Arkansas. | .......... | ....... | 5,227 | .... | 28,732 | 3,411 | 20,094 | ...... | 54,053 |
| 3 | California | 39,173 | *657 | 38,516 | .... | 34,334 | ...... | 6,817 | ...... | 118,840 |
| 4 | Conn'icut | 43,692 | 10,238 | 15,522 | .... | 14,641 | ...... | 3,291 | .. .... | 77,146 |
| 5 | Delaware. | 3,815 | ... .... | 1,023 | .... | 7,347 | †3,483 | 3,864 | ...... | 16,049 |
| 6 | Florida... | .......... | ... .... | 367 | .... | 8,543 | 2,739 | 5,437 | ...... | 14,347 |
| 7 | Georgia.. | .......... | ....... | 11,590 | .... | 51,889 | †9,003 | 42,886 | ...... | 106,365 |
| 8 | Illinois... | 172,161 | 5,629 | 160,215 | .... | 2,404 | ..... | 3,913 | ...... | 338,693 |
| 9 | Indiana .. | 139,033 | 5,923 | 115,509 | .... | 12,295 | ...... | 5,306 | ...... | 272,143 |
| 10 | Iowa..... | 70,409 | 12,487 | 55,111 | .... | 1,048 | ..... | 1,763 | ...... | 128,331 |
| 11 | Kentucky | 1,364 | ....... | 25,651 | .... | 53,143 | ..... | 66,058 | ‡12,915 | 146,216 |
| 12 | Louisiana | .......... | ....... | 7,625 | .... | 22,681 | †2,477 | 20,204 | ...... | 50,510 |
| 13 | Maine.... | 62,811 | 27,704 | 26,693 | .... | 6,368 | ...... | 2,046 | ...... | 97,918 |
| 14 | Maryland | 2,294 | ....... | 5,966 | .... | 42,482 | †722 | 41,760 | ...... | 92,502 |
| 15 | Mass..... | 106,533 | 43,891 | 34,372 | .... | 5,939 | ...... | 22,331 | ...... | 169,175 |
| 16 | Michigan. | 88,480 | 22,213 | 65,057 | .... | 805 | ..... | 405 | ...... | 154,747 |
| 17 | Minn'sota | 22,069 | 9,339 | 11,920 | .... | 748 | ..... | 62 | ...... | 34,799 |
| 18 | Mississ'pi | .......... | ....... | 3,283 | .... | 40,797 | 12,474 | 25,040 | ...... | 69,120 |
| 19 | Missouri.. | 17,028 | ....... | 58,801 | †429 | 31,317 | ...... | 58,372 | ...... | 165,518 |
| 20 | N. Hamp. | 37,519 | 9,085 | 25,881 | .... | 2,112 | ..... | 441 | ...... | 65,953 |
| 21 | N. Jersey. | 58,324 | ....... | 62,801 | 4,477 | ... •.... | ..... | ...... | ...... | 121,125 |
| 22 | New York | 362,646 | 50,136 | 312,510 | .... | ....... | ..... | ....... | ...... | 675,156 |
| 23 | N. Carol'a | .......... | ....... | 2,701 | .... | 48,339 | 648 | 44,990 | ...... | 96,030 |
| 24 | Ohio .... | 231,610 | 20,779 | 187,232 | .... | 11,405 | ..... | 12,194 | ...... | 442,441 |
| 25 | Oregon... | 5,270 | *1,319 | 3,951 | .... | 3,006 | ... .... | 183 | ...... | 12,410 |
| 26 | Penn..... | 268,030 | 59,618 | 16,765 | .... | 178,871 | ..... | 12,776 | ...... | 476,442 |
| 27 | R. Island. | 12,244 | 4,537 | 7,707 | .... | ..... | ..... | ..... | ..... | 19,951 |
| 28 | S. Carol'a | Electors | chosen | by the | Le- | gisla- | ture. | ...... | ..... | |
| 29 | Tennes'e | .......... | ....... | 11,350 | ..... | 64,709 | ..... | 69,274 | ‡4,565 | 145,333 |
| 30 | Texas.... | .... ..... | .. .... | ...... .... | .... | 47,548 | 32,110 | 15,438 | ...... | 62,986 |
| 31 | Vermont. | 33,808 | 24,772 | 6,849 | .... | 1,969 | ..... | 218 | ...... | 42,844 |
| 32 | Virginia.. | 1,929 | ........ | 16,290 | .... | 74,323 | ..... | 74,681 | ‡358 | 167,223 |
| 33 | Wiscon'n | 86,110 | 20,040 | 65,021 | .... | 888 | ..... | 161 | .. .... | 152,180 |
| | Total... | 1,866,352 | 326,391 | 1,375,157 | 4,477 | 847,514 | 58,737 | 587,830 | ....... | 4,676,853 |
| | Lincoln's | Plurality | *491,195 | | | | | | | |

* Plurality over Douglas.   † Plurality over Bell.   ‡ Plurality over Breckinridge.

## ELECTORAL VOTE OF 1860.

| STATES. | PRESIDENT. | | | | VICE-PRESIDENT. | | | | Total. |
|---|---|---|---|---|---|---|---|---|---|
| | A. Lincoln, of Ill. | J. C. Breckinridge, of Ky. | John Bell, of Tenn. | S. A. Douglas, of Ill. | H. Hamlin, of Maine. | Joseph Lane, of Oregon. | Edward Everett, of Mass. | H. V. Johnson, of Ga. | |
| 1 Alabama ......... | ..... | 9 | ..... | ..... | ..... | 9 | ..... | ..... | 9 |
| 2 Arkansas.......... | ..... | 4 | ..... | ..... | ..... | 4 | ..... | ..... | 4 |
| 3 California......... | 4 | ..... | ..... | .... | 4 | ..... | ..... | ..... | 4 |
| 4 Connecticut....... | 6 | ..... | ..... | ..... | 6 | ..... | ..... | ..... | 6 |
| 5 Delaware. ....... | ..... | 3 | ..... | .... | ..... | 3 | ..... | ..... | 3 |
| 6 Florida ........... | ..... | 3 | ..... | ..... | ..... | 3 | ..... | ..... | 3 |
| 7 Georgia........... | ..... | 10 | ..... | ..... | ..... | 10 | ..... | ..... | 10 |
| 8 Illinois............ | 11 | ..... | .. .. | ..... | 11 | ..... | ..... | ..... | 11 |
| 9 Indiana ........... | 13 | ..... | ..... | ..... | 13 | ..... | ..... | ..... | 13 |
| 10 Iowa.............. | 4 | ..... | ..... | ..... | 4 | .. .. | ..... | ..... | 4 |
| 11 Kentucky......... | ..... | .. .. | 12 | ..... | ..... | ..... | 12 | ..... | 12 |
| 12 Louisiana....... | ..... | 6 | ..... | ..... | ..... | 6 | ..... | ..... | 6 |
| 13 Maine ........... | 8 | ..... | ..... | ..... | 8 | ..... | ..... | ..... | 8 |
| 14 Maryland......... | ..... | 8 | ..... | ..... | ..... | 8 | ..... | ..... | 8 |
| 15 Massachusetts..... | 13 | ..... | ..... | ..... | 13 | ..... | ..... | ..... | 13 |
| 16 Michigan......... | 6 | ..... | ..... | ..... | 6 | ..... | ..... | ..... | 6 |
| 17 Minnesota ........ | 4 | ..... | ..... | ..... | 4 | ..... | ..... | ..... | 4 |
| 18 Mississippi....... | ..... | 7 | ..... | ..... | ..... | 7 | ..... | ..... | 7 |
| 19 Missouri.......... | ..... | ..... | ..... | 9 | ..... | ..... | .. .. | 9 | 9 |
| 20 New Hampshire... | 5 | ..... | ..... | ..... | 5 | ..... | ..... | .. .. | 5 |
| 21 New Jersey....... | 4 | ..... | ..... | 3 | 4 | ..... | ..... | 3 | 7 |
| 22 New York........ | 35 | ..... | ..... | ..... | 35 | ..... | ..... | ..... | 35 |
| 23 North Carolina.... | ..... | 10 | ..... | ..... | ..... | 10 | ..... | ..... | 10 |
| 24 Ohio ............. | 23 | ..... | ..... | ..... | 23 | .. .. | ..... | ..... | 23 |
| 25 Oregon... ....... | 3 | ..... | ..... | ..... | 3 | ..... | ..... | ..... | 3 |
| 26 Pennsylvania ..... | 27 | ..... | ..... | ..... | 27 | ..... | ..... | ..... | 27 |
| 27 Rhode Island..... | 4 | ..... | ..... | ..... | 4 | ..... | .. .. | ..... | 4 |
| 28 South Carolina.... | ..... | 8 | ..... | .. .. | ..... | 8 | ..... | ..... | 8 |
| 29 Tennessee........ | .. .. | ..... | 12 | ..... | ..... | ..... | 12 | ..... | 12 |
| 30 Texas ............ | ..... | 4 | ..... | ..... | ..... | 4 | ..... | ..... | 4 |
| 31 Vermont......... | 5 | ..... | ..... | ..... | 5 | ..... | ..... | ..... | 5 |
| 32 Virginia.......... | ..... | ..... | 15 | ..... | ..... | ..... | 15 | ..... | 15 |
| 33 Wisconsin ........ | 5 | ..... | ..... | .. .. | 5 | ..... | ..... | ..... | 5 |
| Total ........... | 180 | 72 | 39 | 12 | 180 | 72 | 39 | 12 | 303 |

## POPULAR VOTE OF 1864.

| STATES. | Abraham Lincoln, Republican. | | Geo. B. McClellan, Democratic. | | Total Vote. |
|---|---|---|---|---|---|
| | Vote. | Majority. | Vote. | Majority. | |
| 1 Alabama*............... | ......... | ......... | ......... | ......... | ......... |
| 2 Arkansas*............... | ......... | ......... | ......... | ......... | ......... |
| 3 California............... | 62,134 | 18,293 | 43,841 | ......... | 105,975 |
| 4 Connecticut... ......... | 44,691 | 2,406 | 42,285 | ......... | 86,976 |
| 5 Delaware............... | 8,155 | ......... | 8,767 | 612 | 16,922 |
| 6 Florida*............... | ......... | ......... | ......... | ......... | ......... |
| 7 Georgia*............... | ......... | ......... | ......... | ......... | ......... |
| 8 Illinois... ... ...... | 189,496 | 30,766 | 158,730 | ......... | 348,226 |
| 9 Indiana................. | 150,422 | 20,189 | 130,233 | ......... | 280,655 |
| 10 Iowa.................... | 89,075 | 39,479 | 49,596 | ......... | 138,671 |
| 11 Kansas................. | 16,441 | 12,750 | 3,691 | ......... | 20,132 |
| 12 Kentucky.............. | 27,786 | ......... | 64,301 | 36,515 | 92,087 |
| 13 Louisiana*............. | ......... | ......... | ......... | ......... | ......... |
| 14 Maine................. | 61,803 | 17,592 | 44,211 | ......... | 106,014 |
| 15 Maryland ............. | 40,153 | 7,414 | 32,739 | ......... | 72,892 |
| 16 Massachusetts. .. ...... | 126,742 | 77,997 | 48,745 | ......... | 175,487 |
| 17 Michigan............... | 91,521 | 16,917 | 74,604 | ......... | 166,125 |
| 18 Minnesota.............. | 25,060 | 7,685 | 17,375 | ......... | 42,435 |
| 19 Mississippi*............ | ......... | ......... | ......... | ......... | ......... |
| 20 Missouri............... | 72,750 | 41,072 | 31,678 | ......... | 104,428 |
| 21 Nevada................ | 9,826 | 3,232 | 6,594 | ......... | 16,420 |
| 22 New Hampshire........ | 36,400 | 3,529 | 32,871 | ......... | 69,271 |
| 23 New Jersey ........... | 60,723 | ......... | 68,024 | 7,301 | 128,747 |
| 24 New York .... . ..... | 368,735 | 6,749 | 361,986 | ......... | 730,721 |
| 25 North Carolina*........ | ......... | ......... | ......... | ......... | ......... |
| 26 Ohio.................. | 265,174 | 59,586 | 205,568 | ......... | 470,722 |
| 27 Oregon ............... | 9,888 | 1,431 | 8,457 | ......... | 18,345 |
| 28 Pennsylvania .. ....... | 296,391 | 20,075 | 276,316 | ......... | 572,707 |
| 29 Rhode Island .......... | 13,692 | 5,222 | 8,470 | ......... | 22,162 |
| 30 South Carolina*........ | ......... | ......... | ......... | ......... | ......... |
| 31 Tennessee*............ | ......... | ......... | ......... | ......... | ......... |
| 32 Texas*................ | ......... | ......... | ......... | ......... | ......... |
| 33 Vermont............... | 42,419 | 29,098 | 13,321 | ......... | 55,740 |
| 34 Virginia*.............. | ......... | ......... | ......... | ......... | ......... |
| 35 West Virginia........... | 23,152 | 12,714 | 10,438 | ......... | 33,590 |
| 36 Wisconsin ............. | 83,458 | 17,574 | 65,864 | ......... | 149,342 |
| Total ............... | 2,216,067 | 451,770 | 1,808,725 | 44,428 | 4,024,792 |
| Lincoln's Majority... . | ......... | 407,342 | | | |

The eleven States marked thus (*) did not vote.

## ELECTORAL VOTE OF 1864.

| | STATES. | PRESIDENT. | | | V. PRESIDE'T. | | | Total. | | STATES. | PRESIDENT. | | | V. PRESIDENT. | | | Total. |
|---|---|---|---|---|---|---|---|---|---|---|---|---|---|---|---|---|---|
| | | A. Lincoln, of Ill. | G. B. McClellan, of N.J. | Vacancies. | A. Johnson, of Tenn. | G. H. Pendleton, of O. | Vacancies. | | | | A. Lincoln, of Ill. | G. B. McClellan, of N.J. | Vacancies. | A. Johnson, of Tenn. | G. H. Pendleton, of O. | Vacancies. | |
| 1 | Alabama | .. | .. | 8 | .. | .. | 8 | 8 | 20 | Missouri | 11 | .. | .. | 11 | .. | .. | 11 |
| 2 | Arkansas | .. | .. | 5 | .. | .. | 5 | 5 | 21 | Nevada | 2 | .. | 1 | 2 | .. | 1 | 3 |
| 3 | California | 5 | .. | .. | 5 | .. | .. | 5 | 22 | N. Hampshire | 5 | .. | .. | 5 | .. | .. | 5 |
| 4 | Connecticut | 6 | .. | .. | 6 | .. | .. | 6 | 23 | New Jersey | .. | 7 | .. | .. | 7 | .. | 7 |
| 5 | Delaware | .. | 3 | .. | .. | 3 | .. | 3 | 24 | New York | 33 | .. | .. | 33 | .. | .. | 33 |
| 6 | Florida | .. | .. | 3 | .. | .. | 3 | 3 | 25 | N. Carolina | .. | .. | 9 | .. | .. | 9 | 9 |
| 7 | Georgia | .. | .. | 9 | .. | .. | 9 | 9 | 26 | Ohio | 21 | .. | .. | 21 | .. | .. | 21 |
| 8 | Illinois | 16 | .. | .. | 16 | .. | .. | 16 | 27 | Oregon | 3 | .. | .. | 3 | .. | .. | 3 |
| 9 | Indiana | 13 | .. | .. | 13 | .. | .. | 13 | 28 | Pennsylvania | 26 | .. | .. | 26 | .. | .. | 26 |
| 10 | Iowa | 8 | .. | .. | 8 | .. | .. | 8 | 29 | Rhode Island | 4 | .. | .. | 4 | .. | .. | 4 |
| 11 | Kansas | 3 | .. | .. | 3 | .. | .. | 3 | 30 | South Carolina | .. | .. | 6 | .. | .. | 6 | 6 |
| 12 | Kentucky | .. | 11 | .. | .. | 11 | .. | 11 | 31 | Tennessee | .. | .. | 10 | .. | .. | 10 | 10 |
| 13 | Louisiana | .. | .. | 7 | .. | .. | 7 | 7 | 32 | Texas | .. | .. | 6 | .. | .. | 6 | 6 |
| 14 | Maine | 7 | .. | .. | 7 | .. | .. | 7 | 33 | Vermont | 5 | .. | .. | 5 | .. | .. | 5 |
| 15 | Maryland | 7 | .. | .. | 7 | .. | .. | 7 | 34 | Virginia | .. | .. | 10 | .. | .. | 10 | 10 |
| 16 | Massachusetts | 12 | .. | .. | 12 | .. | .. | 12 | 35 | W. Virginia | 5 | .. | .. | 5 | .. | .. | 5 |
| 17 | Michigan | 8 | .. | .. | 8 | .. | .. | 8 | 36 | Wisconsin | 8 | .. | .. | 8 | .. | .. | 8 |
| 18 | Minnesota | 4 | .. | .. | 4 | .. | .. | 4 | | | | | | | | | |
| 19 | Mississippi | .. | .. | 7 | .. | .. | 7 | 7 | | Total | 212 | 21 | 81 | 212 | 21 | 81 | 314 |

## POPULAR VOTE OF 1868.

| STATES. | Ulysses S. Grant, Republican. | | Horatio Seymour, Democratic. | | Total Vote. |
|---|---|---|---|---|---|
| | Vote. | Majority. | Vote. | Majority. | |
| 1 Alabama......... | 76,366 | 4,278 | 72,088 | .......... | 148,454 |
| 2 Arkansas ....... | 22,112 | 3,034 | 19,078 | .......... | 41,190 |
| 3 California........ | 54,583 | 506 | 54,077 | .......... | 108,660 |
| 4 Connecticut..... | 50,995 | 3,043 | 47,952 | .......... | 98,947 |
| 5 Delaware ........ | 7,623 | .......... | 10,980 | 3,357 | 18,603 |
| 6 Florida........... | Electors | chosen by | the Legis- | lature. | ........ |
| 7 Georgia.......... | 57,134 | .......... | 102,722 | 45,588 | 159,856 |
| 8 Illinois.... ...... | 250,303 | 51,160 | 199,143 | .......... | 449,446 |
| 9 Indiana......... | 176,548 | 9,568 | 166,980 | .......... | 343,528 |
| 10 Iowa............. | 120,399 | 46,359 | 74,040 | .......... | 194,439 |
| 11 Kansas ... ...... | 31,048 | 17,058 | 13,990. | .......... | 45,038 |
| 12 Kentucky........ | 39,566 | .......... | 115,890 | 76,324 | 155,456 |
| 13 Louisiana........ | 33,263 | .......... | 80,225 | 46,962 | 113,488 |
| 14 Maine............ | 70,493 | 28,033 | 42,460 | .......... | 112,953 |
| 15 Maryland........ | 30,438 | .......... | 62,357 | 31,919 | 92,795 |
| 16 Massachusetts.... | 136,477 | 77,069 | 59,408 | .......... | 195,885 |
| 17 Michigan... .... | 128,550 | 31,481 | 97,069 | .......... | 225,619 |
| 18 Minnesota....... | 43,545 | 15,470 | 28,075 | .......... | 71,620 |
| 19 Mississippi..... | .......... | .......... | .......... | .......... | ........ |
| 20 Missouri......... | 86,860 | 21,232 | 65,628 | .......... | 152,488 |
| 21 Nebraska........ | 9,729 | 4,290 | 5,439 | .... ....... | 15,168 |
| 22 Nevada......... | 6,480 | 1,262 | 5,218 | .......... | 11,698 |
| 23 New Hampshire.. | 38,191 | 6,967 | 31,224 | .......... | 69,415 |
| 24 New Jersey...... | 80,131 | .......... | 83,001 | 2,870 | 162,132 |
| 25 New York....... | 419,883 | .......... | 429,883 | 10,000 | 849,766 |
| 26 North Carolina... | 96,769 | 12,168 | 84,601 | .......... | 181,370 |
| 27 Ohio............. | 280,223 | 41,617 | 238,606 | .......... | 518,829 |
| 28 Oregon.......... | 10,961 | .......... | 11,125 | 164 | 22,086 |
| 29 Pennsylvania .... | 342,280 | 28,898 | 313,382 | .......... | 655,652 |
| 30 Rhode Island .... | 12,993 | 6,445 | 6,548 | .......... | 19,541 |
| 31 South Carolina... | 62,301 | 17,064 | 45,237 | .......... | 107,538 |
| 32 Tennessee....... | 56,628 | 30,499. | 26,129 | .......... | 82,757 |
| 33 Texas............ | .......... | .......... | .......... | .......... | ........ |
| 34 Vermont........ | 44,167 | 32,122 | 12,045 | .......... | 56,212 |
| 35 Virginia. ....... | .......... | .......... | .......... | .......... | ........ |
| 36 West Virginia.... | 29,175 | 8,869 | 20,306 | .......... | 49,481 |
| 37 Wisconsin....... | 108,857 | 24,150 | 84,707 | .... ...... | 193,564 |
| Total.......... | 3,015,071 | 522,642 | 2,709,613 | 217,184 | 5,724,684 |
| Grant's Majority........... | | 305,458 | | | |

## ELECTORAL VOTE OF 1868.

| | STATES. | PRESIDENT. | | | V.-PRESIDENT. | | | Total. | STATES. | PRESIDENT. | | | V.-PRESIDENT. | | | Total. |
|---|---|---|---|---|---|---|---|---|---|---|---|---|---|---|---|---|
| | | U. S. Grant, of Ill. | H. Seymour, of N. Y. | Vacancies. | S. Colfax, of Ind. | F. P. Blair, of Mo. | Vacancies. | | | U. S. Grant, of Ill. | H. Seymour, of N. Y. | Vacancies. | S. Colfax, of Ind. | F. P. Blair, of Mo. | Vacancies. | |
| 1 | Alabama | 8 | | | 8 | | | 8 | 20 Missouri | 11 | | | 11 | | | 11 |
| 2 | Arkansas | 5 | | | 5 | | | 5 | 21 Nebraska | 3 | | | 3 | | | 3 |
| 3 | California | 5 | | | 5 | | | 5 | 22 Nevada | 3 | | | 3 | | | 3 |
| 4 | Connecticut | 6 | | | 6 | | | 6 | 23 N. Hampshire. | 5 | | | 5 | | | 5 |
| 5 | Delaware | | 3 | | | 3 | | 3 | 24 New Jersey | | 7 | | | 7 | | 7 |
| 6 | Florida | 3 | | | 3 | | | 3 | 25 New York | | 33 | | | 33 | | 33 |
| 7 | Georgia | | 9 | | | 9 | | 9 | 26 N. Carolina | 9 | | | 9 | | | 9 |
| 8 | Illinois | 16 | | | 16 | | | 16 | 27 Ohio | 21 | | | 21 | | | 21 |
| 9 | Indiana | 13 | | | 13 | | | 13 | 28 Oregon | | 3 | | | 3 | | 3 |
| 10 | Iowa | 8 | | | 8 | | | 8 | 29 Pennsylvania | 26 | | | 26 | | | 26 |
| 11 | Kansas | 3 | | | 3 | | | 3 | 30 Rhode Island | 4 | | | 4 | | | 4 |
| 12 | Kentucky | | 11 | | | 11 | | 11 | 31 South Carolina | 6 | | | 6 | | | 6 |
| 13 | Louisiana | | 7 | | | 7 | | 7 | 32 Tennessee | 10 | | | 10 | | | 10 |
| 14 | Maine | 7 | | | 7 | | | 7 | 33 Texas | | | 6 | | | 6 | 6 |
| 15 | Maryland | | 7 | | | 7 | | 7 | 34 Vermont | 5 | | | 5 | | | 5 |
| 16 | Massachusetts | 12 | | | 12 | | | 12 | 35 Virginia | | | 10 | | | 10 | 10 |
| 17 | Michigan | 8 | | | 8 | | | 8 | 36 West Virginia. | 5 | | | 5 | | | 5 |
| 18 | Minnesota | 4 | | | 4 | | | 4 | 37 Wisconsin | 8 | | | 8 | | | 8 |
| 19 | Mississippi | | | 7 | | | 7 | 7 | Total | 214 | 80 | 23 | 214 | 80 | 23 | 317 |

## POPULAR VOTE OF 1872.

| | STATES. | U. S. Grant, Republican. | | H. Greeley, Dem. & Lib. Rep. | | O'Conor, Dem. | Black, Temperance. | Total Vote. |
|---|---|---|---|---|---|---|---|---|
| | | Vote. | Maj. | Vote. | Maj. | Vote. | Vote. | |
| 1 | Alabama.. | 90,272 | 10,828 | 79,444 | ........ | ........ | ........ | 169,716 |
| 2 | Arkansas. | 41,373 | 3,446 | 37,927 | ........ | ........ | ........ | 79,300 |
| 3 | California. | 54,020 | 12,234 | 40,718 | ........ | 1,068 | ........ | 95,806 |
| 4 | Conn'icut. | 50,638 | 4,348 | 45,880 | ........ | 204 | 206 | 96,928 |
| 5 | Delaware. | 11,115 | 422 | 10,206 | ........ | 487 | ........ | 21,808 |
| 6 | Florida ... | 17,763 | 2,336 | 15,427 | ........ | ........ | ........ | 33,190 |
| 7 | Georgia... | 62,550 | ........ | 76,356 | 9,806 | 4,000 | ........ | 142,906 |
| 8 | Illinois ... | 241,944 | 53,948 | 184,938 | ........ | 3,058 | ........ | 429,940 |
| 9 | Indiana... | 186,147 | 21,098 | 163,632 | ........ | 1,417 | ........ | 351,196 |
| 10 | Iowa...... | 131,566 | 58,149 | 71,196 | ........ | 2,221 | ........ | 204,983 |
| 11 | Kansas ... | 67,048 | 33,482 | 32,970 | ........ | 596 | ........ | 100,614 |
| 12 | Kentucky. | 88,766 | ........ | 99,995 | 8,855 | 2,374 | ........ | 191,135 |
| 13 | Louisiana. | 71,663 | 14,634 | 57,029 | ........ | ........ | ........ | 128,692 |
| 14 | Maine .... | 61,422 | 32,335 | 29,087 | ........ | ........ | ........ | 90,509 |
| 15 | Maryland. | 66,760 | ........ | 67,687 | 908 | 19 | ........ | 134,466 |
| 16 | Mass ..... | 133,472 | 74,212 | 59,260 | ........ | ........ | ........ | 192,732 |
| 17 | Michigan.. | 138,455 | 55,968 | 78,355 | ........ | 2,861 | 1,271 | 220,942 |
| 18 | Minn'sota. | 55,117 | 20,694 | 34,423 | ........ | ........ | ........ | 89,540 |
| 19 | Mississ'pi. | 82,175 | 34,887 | 47,288 | ........ | ........ | ........ | 129,463 |
| 20 | Missouri.. | 119,196 | ........ | 151,434 | 29,809 | 2,429 | ... ... | 273,059 |
| 21 | Nebraska. | 18,329 | 10,517 | 7,812 | ........ | ........ | ........ | 26,141 |
| 22 | Nevada ... | 8,413 | 2,177 | 6,236 | ........ | ........ | ........ | 14,649 |
| 23 | N. Hamp.. | 37,168 | 5,444 | 31,424 | ........ | 100 | 200 | 68,892 |
| 24 | N. Jersey. | 91,656 | 14,570 | 76,456 | ........ | 630 | ........ | 168,742 |
| 25 | New York | 440,736 | 51,800 | 387,281 | ........ | 1,454 | 201 | 829,672 |
| 26 | N. Carol'a. | 94,769 | 24,675 | 70,094 | ........ | ........ | ........ | 164,863 |
| 27 | Ohio ...... | 281,852 | 84,268 | 244,321 | ........ | 1,163 | 2,100 | 529,436 |
| 28 | Oregon.... | 11,819 | 3,517 | 7,730 | ........ | 572 | ........ | 20,121 |
| 29 | Penn ..... | 349,589 | 135,918 | 212,041 | ........ | ........ | 1,630 | 563,260 |
| 30 | R. Island.. | 13,665 | 8,336 | 5,329 | ........ | ........ | ........ | 18,994 |
| 31 | S. Carol'a. | 72,290 | 49,400 | 22,703 | ........ | 187 | ........ | 95,180 |
| 32 | Tennes'e. | 85,655 | ........ | 94,391 | 8,736 | ........ | ........ | 180,046 |
| 33 | Texas .... | 47,406 | ........ | 66,500 | 16,595 | 2,499 | ........ | 116,405 |
| 34 | Vermont.. | 41,481 | 29,961 | 10,927 | ........ | 593 | ... .... | 53,001 |
| 35 | Virginia... | 93,468 | 1,772 | 91,654 | ........ | 42 | ........ | 185,164 |
| 36 | W. Virg'a. | 32,315 | 2,264 | 29,451 | ........ | 600 | ........ | 62,366 |
| 37 | Wisconsin | 104,997 | 17,686 | 86,477 | ........ | 834 | ........ | 192,308 |
| | Total.... | 3,597,070 | 825,326 | 2,834,079 | 74,709 | 29,408 | 5,608 | 6,466,165 |
| | Grant's Majority.... | | 727,975 | | | | | |

## ELECTORAL VOTE OF 1872.

| STATES. | Ulysses S. Grant, of Ill. | T. A. Hendricks, of Ind. | B. Gratz Brown, of Mo. | C. J. Jenkins, of Ga. | D. Davis, of Illinois. | Not Counted. | H. Wilson, of Mass. | B. G. Brown, of Mo. | G. W. Julian, of Ind. | A. H. Colquitt, of Ga. | J. M. Palmer, of Illinois. | T. E. Bramlette, of Ky. | W. S. Groesbeck, of Ohio. | W. B. Machen, of Ky. | N. P. Banks, of Mass. | Not Counted. | Total. |
|---|---|---|---|---|---|---|---|---|---|---|---|---|---|---|---|---|---|
| 1 Alabama | 10 | | | | | | 10 | | | | | | | | | | 10 |
| 2 Arkansas | | | | | | 6 | | | | | | | | | | 6 | 6 |
| 3 California | 6 | | | | | | 6 | | | | | | | | | | 6 |
| 4 Connecticut | 6 | | | | | | 6 | | | | | | | | | | 6 |
| 5 Delaware | 3 | | | | | | 3 | | | | | | | | | | 3 |
| 6 Florida | 4 | | | | | | 4 | | | | | | | | | | 4 |
| 7 Georgia | | | 6 | 2 | | 3 | | 5 | | 5 | | | | | 1 | | 11 |
| 8 Illinois | 21 | | | | | | 21 | | | | | | | | | | 21 |
| 9 Indiana | 15 | | | | | | 15 | | | | | | | | | | 15 |
| 10 Iowa | 11 | | | | | | 11 | | | | | | | | | | 11 |
| 11 Kansas | 5 | | | | | | 5 | | | | | | | | | | 5 |
| 12 Kentucky | | 8 | 4 | | | | | 8 | | | | 3 | | 1 | | | 12 |
| 13 Louisiana | | | | | | 8 | | | | | | | | | | 8 | 8 |
| 14 Maine | 7 | | | | | | 7 | | | | | | | | | | 7 |
| 15 Maryland | | 8 | | | | | | 8 | | | | | | | | | 8 |
| 16 Massachusetts | 13 | | | | | | 13 | | | | | | | | | | 13 |
| 17 Michigan | 11 | | | | | | 11 | | | | | | | | | | 11 |
| 18 Minnesota | 5 | | | | | | 5 | | | | | | | | | | 5 |
| 19 Mississippi | 8 | | | | | | 8 | | | | | | | | | | 8 |
| 20 Missouri | | 6 | 8 | | 1 | | | 6 | 5 | | 3 | | 1 | | | | 15 |
| 21 Nebraska | 3 | | | | | | 3 | | | | | | | | | | 3 |
| 22 Nevada | 3 | | | | | | 3 | | | | | | | | | | 3 |
| 23 New Hampshire | 5 | | | | | | 5 | | | | | | | | | | 5 |
| 24 New Jersey | 9 | | | | | | 9 | | | | | | | | | | 9 |
| 25 New York | 35 | | | | | | 35 | | | | | | | | | | 35 |
| 26 North Carolina | 10 | | | | | | 10 | | | | | | | | | | 10 |
| 27 Ohio | 22 | | | | | | 22 | | | | | | | | | | 22 |
| 28 Oregon | 3 | | | | | | 3 | | | | | | | | | | 3 |
| 29 Pennsylvania | 29 | | | | | | 29 | | | | | | | | | | 29 |
| 30 Rhode Island | 4 | | | | | | 4 | | | | | | | | | | 4 |
| 31 South Carolina | 7 | | | | | | 7 | | | | | | | | | | 7 |
| 32 Tennessee | | 12 | | | | | | 12 | | | | | | | | | 12 |
| 33 Texas | | 8 | | | | | | 8 | | | | | | | | | 8 |
| 34 Vermont | 5 | | | | | | 5 | | | | | | | | | | 5 |
| 35 Virginia | 11 | | | | | | 11 | | | | | | | | | | 11 |
| 36 West Virginia | 5 | | | | | | 5 | | | | | | | | | | 5 |
| 37 Wisconsin | 10 | | | | | | 10 | | | | | | | | | | 10 |
| Total | 286 | 42 | 18 | 2 | 1 | 17 | 286 | 47 | 5 | 5 | 3 | 3 | 1 | 1 | 1 | 14 | 366 |

## POPULAR VOTE OF 1876.

| STATES. | S. J. Tilden, Democratic. | | R. B. Hayes, Republican. | | Peter Cooper, Greenback. | G. C. Smith, Temperance. | Scattering. | Total Vote. |
|---|---|---|---|---|---|---|---|---|
| | Vote. | Maj. | Vote. | Maj. | | | | |
| 1 Alabama... | 102,002 | 33,772 | 68,230 | ...... | ...... | ...... | ...... | 170,232 |
| 2 Arkansas... | 58,071 | 19,113 | 38,669 | ...... | 289 | ...... | ...... | 97,029 |
| 3 California . | 76,465 | ...... | 79,269 | 2,738 | 47 | ...... | 19 | 155,800 |
| 4 Colorado... | Electors chosen | | by Legis- | lature. | | | | |
| 5 Connecticut | 61,934 | 1,712 | 59,034 | ...... | 774 | 378 | 36 | 122,156 |
| 6 Delaware... | 13,381 | 2,620 | 10,752 | ...... | ...... | ...... | ...... | 24,133 |
| 7 Florida .... | 22,923 | ...... | 23,849 | 926 | ...... | ...... | ...... | 46,772 |
| 8 Georgia .... | 130,088 | 79,642 | 50,446 | ...... | ...... | ...... | ...... | 180,534 |
| 9 Illinois...... | 258,601 | ...... | 278,232 | 1,971 | 17,233 | 141 | 286 | 554,493 |
| 10 Indiana.... | 213,526 | 5,515 | 208,011 | ...... | 9,533 | ...... | ...... | 431,070 |
| 11 Iowa....... | 112,099 | ...... | 171,327 | 50,191 | 9,001 | 36 | ...... | 292,463 |
| 12 Kansas..... | 37,902 | ...... | 78,322 | 32,511 | 7,776 | 110 | 23 | 124,133 |
| 13 Kentucky.. | 159,690 | 59,772 | 97,156 | ...... | 1,944 | 818 | ...... | 259,608 |
| 14 Louisiana.. | 70,508 | ...... | 75,135 | 4,627 | ...... | ...... | ...... | 145,643 |
| 15 Maine...... | 49,823 | ...... | 66,300 | 15,814 | 663 | ...... | ...... | 116,786 |
| 16 Maryland.. | 91,780 | 19,756 | 71,981 | ...... | 33 | 10 | ...... | 163,804 |
| 17 Massach'ets | 108,777 | ...... | 150,063 | 40,483 | 779 | 84 | ...... | 259,703 |
| 18 Michigan . | 141,095 | ...... | 166,534 | 15,542 | 9,060 | 766 | 71 | 317,526 |
| 19 Minnesota.. | 48,799 | ...... | 72,962 | 21,780 | 2,311 | 72 | ...... | 124,144 |
| 20 Mississippi. | 112,173 | 59,568 | 52,605 | ...... | ...... | ...... | ...... | 164,778 |
| 21 Missouri... | 203,077 | 54,380 | 145,029 | ...... | 3,498 | 64 | 97 | 351,765 |
| 22 Nebraska... | 17,554 | ...... | 31,916 | 10,326 | 2,320 | 1,599 | 117 | 53,506 |
| 23 Nevada .... | 9,308 | ...... | 10,383 | 1,075 | ...... | ...... | ...... | 19,691 |
| 24 N. H'pshire | 38,509 | ...... | 41,539 | 2,954 | 76 | ...... | ...... | 80,124 |
| 25 New Jersey | 115,962 | 11,690 | 103,517 | ...... | 712 | 43 | ...... | 220,234 |
| 26 New York. | 521,949 | 26,568 | 489,207 | ...... | 1,987 | 2,359 | 1,828 | 1,017,330 |
| 27 N. Carolina | 125,427 | 17,010 | 108,417 | ...... | ...... | ...... | ...... | 233,844 |
| 28 Ohio ... ... | 323,182 | ...... | 330,698 | 2,747 | 3,057 | 1,636 | 76 | 658,649 |
| 29 Oregon..... | 14,149 | ...... | 15,206 | 547 | 510 | ...... | ...... | 29,865 |
| 30 Pennsylv'a. | 366,158 | .. ... | 384,122 | 9,375 | 7,187 | 1,319 | 83 | 758,869 |
| 31 Rhode Isl'd | 10,712 | ...... | 15,787 | 4,947 | 68 | 60 | ...... | 26,627 |
| 32 S. Carolina. | 90,006 | ...... | 91,870 | 964 | ...... | ...... | ...... | 182,776 |
| 33 Tennessee.. | 133,166 | 43,600 | 89,566 | ...... | ...... | ...... | ...... | 222,732 |
| 34 Texas...... | 104,755 | 59,955 | 44,800 | ...... | ...... | ...... | ...... | 149,555 |
| 35 Vermont... | 20,254 | ...... | 44,092 | 23,838 | ...... | ...... | ...... | 64,346 |
| 36 Virginia.... | 139,670 | 44,112 | 95,558 | ...... | ...... | ...... | ...... | 235,228 |
| 37 W. Virginia | 56,455 | 12,384 | 42,698 | ...... | 1,373 | ...... | ...... | 100,526 |
| 38 Wisconsin.. | 123,927 | ...... | 130,668 | 5,205 | 1,509 | 27 | ...... | 256,131 |
| Total.... | 4,284,757 | 545,672 | 4,033,950 | 248,501 | 81,740 | 9,522 | 2,636 | 8,412,605 |
| Tilden's Majority..... | | 156,909 | | | | | | |

## ELECTORAL VOTE OF 1876.

| STATES. | PRESIDENT. | | VICE-PRESIDENT. | | Total. | STATES. | PRESIDENT. | | VICE-PRESIDENT. | | Total. |
|---|---|---|---|---|---|---|---|---|---|---|---|
| | R. B. Hayes, of Ohio. | S. J. Tilden, of N.Y. | W. A. Wheeler, of N.Y. | T. A. Hendricks, of Ind. | | | R. B. Hayes, of Ohio. | S. J. Tilden, of N.Y. | W. A. Wheeler, of N.Y. | T. A. Hendricks, of Ind. | |
| 1 Alabama.... | .... | 10 | .... | 10 | 10 | 21 Missouri.... | .... | 15 | .... | 15 | 15 |
| 2 Arkansas.... | .... | 6 | ... | 6 | 6 | 22 Nebraska .... | 3 | ... | 3 | ... | 3 |
| 3 California.... | 6 | .... | 6 | .... | 6 | 23 Nevada....... | 3 | ... | 3 | ... | 3 |
| 4 Colorado.... | 3 | ... | 3 | .... | 3 | 24 N. H'mpshire | 5 | ... | 5 | ... | 5 |
| 5 Connecticut.. | .... | 6 | .... | 6 | 6 | 25 New Jersey.. | .... | 9 | .... | 9 | 9 |
| 6 Delaware..... | .... | 3 | .... | 3 | 3 | 26 New York.... | .... | 35 | .... | 35 | 35 |
| 7 Florida*...... | 4 | ... | 4 | .... | 4 | 27 N. Carolina.. | .. | 10 | ... | 10 | 10 |
| 8 Georgia...... | .... | 11 | ... | 11 | 11 | 28 Ohio ......... | 22 | .... | 22 | ... | 22 |
| 9 Illinois....... | 21 | ... | 21 | .... | 21 | 29 Oregon*. .... | 3 | ... | 3 | ... | 3 |
| 10 Indiana...... | .... | 15 | .... | 15 | 15 | 30 Pennsylvania | 29 | .... | 29 | ... | 29 |
| 11 Iowa ........ | 11 | ... | 11 | .... | 11 | 31 Rhode Island. | 4 | ... | 4 | ... | 4 |
| 12 Kansas...... | 5 | . . | 5 | .... | 5 | 32 S. Carolina*.. | 7 | ... | 7 | ... | 7 |
| 13 Kentucky.... | .... | 12 | .... | 12 | 12 | 33 Tennessee.... | .... | 12 | .... | 12 | 12 |
| 14 Louisiana*... | 8 | ... | 8 | .... | 8 | 34 Texas....... | ... | 8 | ... | 8 | 8 |
| 15 Maine........ | 7 | .... | 7 | ... | 7 | 35 Vermont..... | 5 | ... | 5 | ... | 5 |
| 16 Maryland..... | .... | 8 | .... | 8 | 8 | 36 Virginia. .... | .. | 11 | ... | 11 | 11 |
| 17 Massach'setts | 13 | ... | 13 | .... | 13 | 37 W. Virginia.. | .... | 5 | ... | 5 | 5 |
| 18 Michigan .... | 11 | ... | 11 | .... | 11 | 38 Wisconsin.... | 10 | . . | 10 | ... | 10 |
| 19 Minnesota.... | 5 | . . | 5 | .... | 5 | | | | | | |
| 20 Mississippi... | .... | 8 | .... | 8 | 8 | Total....... | 185 | 184 | 185 | 184 | 369 |

.* From Florida two sets of certificates were received ; from Louisiana, three : from Oregon, two ; and from South Carolina, two. They were referred to an Electoral Commission, formed under the provisions of the Compromise Bill, approved January 29th, 1877 ; the Commission decided in favor of counting the Electoral Vote, as returned in the table.

## Number of Counties in each State and Territory in 1878.

| | | | | | | | | |
|---|---|---|---|---|---|---|---|---|
| 1 | Alabama ........ | 67 | 19 | Minnesota. | 71 | 37 | West Virginia...... | 54 |
| 2 | Arkansas........ | 74 | 20 | Mississippi. ....... | 75 | 38 | Wisconsin.......... | 60 |
| 3 | California........ | 52 | 21 | Missouri ........... | 115 | | | |
| 4 | Colorado ........ | 30 | 22 | Nebraska........... | 62 | | Total Counties... | 2290 |
| 5 | Connecticut..... | 8 | 23 | Nevada............. | 14 | | | |
| 6 | Delaware........ | 3 | 24 | New Hampshire.... | 10 | | TERRITORIES. | |
| 7 | Florida.......... | 39 | 25 | New Jersey........ | 21 | | | |
| 8 | Georgia......... | 137 | 26 | New York ......... | 60 | | | |
| 9 | Illinois.......... | 102 | 27 | North Carolina..... | 94 | 1 | Arizona........... | 6 |
| 10 | Indiana ......... | 92 | 28 | Ohio .............. | 88 | 2 | Dakota............ | 34 |
| 11 | Iowa ........... | 99 | 29 | Oregon............. | 23 | 3 | Idaho ...... ...... | 10 |
| 12 | Kansas.......... | 76 | 30 | Pennsylvania...... | 67 | 4 | Montana .......... | 10 |
| 13 | Kentucky ....... | 117 | 31 | Rhode Island...... | 5 | 5 | New Mexico....... | 12 |
| 14 | Louisiana ....... | 58 | 32 | South Carolina..... | 33 | 6 | Utah ...... ...... | 20 |
| 15 | Maine.... ..... | 16 | 33 | Tennessee.......... | 94 | 7 | Washington......... | 24 |
| 16 | Maryland. ...... | 23 | 34 | Texas.............. | 151 | 8 | Wyoming.......... | 5 |
| 17 | Massachusetts .. | 14 | 35 | Vermont... ...... | 14 | | | |
| 18 | Michigan........ | 76 | 36 | Virginia........... | 105 | | Total............ | 121 |

## REPUBLICAN FINANCIAL ACHIEVEMENTS.

OFFICIAL TREASURY STATEMENT, SHOWING THE ANNUAL REDUCTIONS IN THE **Principal, Interest,** AND **Per Capita** AMOUNT OF THE **Public Debt,** FROM 1865 TO 1880.

| | Total interest-bearing debt. | Annual interest charge. | Debt on which interest has ceased. | Debt bearing no interest. |
|---|---|---|---|---|
| 1865............... | 2,221,311,918 29 | 137,742,617 43 | 1,245,771 20 | 458,090,180 25 |
| 1865—Aug. 3d.... | 2,381,530,294 96 | 150,977,697 87 | 1,503,020 09 | 461,616,311 51 |
| 1866—July 1st.... | 2,332,331,207 60 | 146,068,196 29 | 935,092 05 | 439,969,874 04 |
| 1867.............. | 2,248,067,387 66 | 138,892,451 39 | 1,840,615 01 | 428,218,101 20 |
| 1868.............. | 2,202,088,727 69 | 128,459,598 14 | 1,197,340 89 | 408,401,782 61 |
| 1869.............. | 2,162,060,522 39 | 125,523,998 34 | 5,260,181 00 | 421,131,510 55 |
| 1870.............. | 2,046,455,722 89 | 118,784,960 34 | 3,708,641 00 | 430,508,064 42 |
| 1871.............. | 1,934,696,750 00 | 111,949,330 50 | 1,948,902 26 | 416,565,680 06 |
| 1872.............. | 1,814,794,100 00 | 103,988,463 00 | 7,926,796 26 | 430,530,431 52 |
| 1873.............. | 1,710,483,950 00 | 98,049,804 00 | 51,929,710 26 | 472,069,332 94 |
| 1874............. | 1,738,930,750 00 | 98,796,004 50 | 3,216,590 26 | 509,543,128 17 |
| 1875.............. | 1,722,676,300 00 | 96,855,690 50 | 11,425,820 26 | 498,182,411 69 |
| 1876.............. | 1,710,685,450 00 | 95,104,269 00 | 3,902,420 26 | 465,807,196 89 |
| 1877.............. | 1,711,888,500 00 | 93,160,643 50 | 16,648,860 26 | 476,764,031 84 |
| 1878.............. | 1,794,735,650 00 | 94,654,472 50 | 5,594,560 26 | 455,875,682 27 |
| 1879.............. | 1,797,643,700 00 | 83,773,778 50 | 37,015,630 26 | 410,835,741 78 |
| 1880.............. | 1,723,993,100 00 | 79,633,981 00 | 7,621,455 26 | 388,800,815 37 |

| | Outstanding principal. | Cash in the Treasury July 1. | Total debt, less cash in Treasury. | Population of the United States. | Debt per capita. | Interest per capita. |
|---|---|---|---|---|---|---|
| 1865.. | 2,680,647,869 74 | 5,832,012 98 | 2,674,815,856 76 | 34,748,000 | 76 98 | 3 97 |
| 1865— | 2,844,649,626 56 | 88,218,055 13 | 2,756,431,571 43 | 35,228,000 | 78 25 | 4 29 |
| 1866— | 2,773,236,173 69 | 137,200,009 85 | 2,636,036,163 84 | 35,469,000 | 74 32 | 4 12 |
| 1867.. | 2,678,126,103 87 | 169,974,892 18 | 2,508,151,211 69 | 36,211,000 | 69 26 | 3 84 |
| 1868.. | 2,611,687,851 19 | 130,834,437 96 | 2,480,853,413 23 | 36,973,000 | 67 10 | 3 48 |
| 1869.. | 2,588,452,213 94 | 155,680,340 85 | 2,432,771,873 09 | 37,756,000 | 64 43 | 3 32 |
| 1870.. | 2,480,672,427 81 | 149,502,471 60 | 2,331,169,956 21 | 38,558,371 | 60 46 | 3 08 |
| 1871.. | 2,353,211,332 32 | 106,217,263 65 | 2,246,994,068 67 | 39,555,000 | 56 81 | 2 83 |
| 1872.. | 2,253,251,328 78 | 103,470,798 43 | 2,149,780,530 35 | 40,604,000 | 52 95 | 2 56 |
| 1873.. | 2,234,482,993 20 | 129,020,932 45 | 2,105,462,060 75 | 41,704,000 | 50 49 | 2 35 |
| 1874.. | 2,251,690,468 43 | 147,541,314 74 | 2,104,149,153 69 | 42,856,000 | 49 10 | 2 31 |
| 1875.. | 2,232,284,531 95 | 142,243,361 82 | 2,090,041,170 13 | 44,060,000 | 47 44 | 2 19 |
| 1876.. | 2,180,395,067 15 | 119,469,726 70 | 2,060,925,340 45 | 45,316,000 | 45 48 | 2 10 |
| 1877.. | 2,205,301,392 10 | 186,025,960 73 | 2,019,275,431 37 | 46,624,000 | 43 31 | 2 00 |
| 1878.. | 2,256,205,892 53 | 256,823,612 08 | 1,999,382,280 45 | 47,983,000 | 41 67 | 1 97 |
| 1879.. | 2,245,495,072 04 | 249,080,167 01 | 1,996,414,905 03 | 49,395,000 | 40 42 | 1 69 |
| 1880.. | 2,120,415,370 63 | 201,088,622 88 | 1,919,326,747 75 | 50,858,000 | 37 74 | 1 56 |

LIFE OF

# JAMES A. GARFIELD

OF OHIO.

# LIFE OF

# JAMES A. GARFIELD.

---

## CHAPTER I.

### BIRTH AND ANCESTRY.

PROBABLY it was the rather German-looking face of General Garfield that led a German paper in St. Louis to trace for him a Teutonic ancestry, by an ingenious etymological study of his name. What his forefathers were in remote times nobody knows, for the household traditions, like those of most New England families, do not go beyond the Atlantic. The name seems to be broadly English enough, in spite of the possibility of its being a corruption of Garfelder, or Gerbefelder, to be followed back to an Anglo-Saxon source, and we shall doubtless hear before long of an abundance of remote English cousins ready to claim kinship with the Republican candidate. There is nothing like a nomination for the Presidency to broaden a man's family ties. But whether the original stock be Anglo-Saxon or Teutonic, the American offshoot is as free from any foreign grafts as the purest Puritan blood of New England.

On both his father's and his mother's side General Garfield comes of a long line of New England ancestry. The first of the American Garfields was Edward, who came from Chester, England, to Massachusetts Bay as early as 1630, settled at Watertown, and died June 14th, 1672, aged ninety-seven. His son, Edward, Jr., had two wives ; first Rebecca ——, the mother of all his children, and second, Joanna, the widow of Thomas Buckminster, of Muddy River (Brookline), and the maternal ancestor of Colonel Joseph Buckminster, of Barre, who commanded a regiment in the battle of Bunker Hill, where he acquired a reputation for prudence and bravery. Edward Garfield, Jr., died in 1672, and his inventory amounted to £457 : 3 : 6. He was one of the earliest proprietors of Watertown, and was selectman in 1638, 1655, and 1652.

His son, Captain Benjamin Garfield, born in 1643, admitted freeman in 1690, was representative of Watertown to the Great and General Court nine times between 1689 and 1717 ; and he held numerous municipal appointments. He had two wives, Mehitabel Hawkins and Elizabeth Bridge, and eight children ; by the second wife he had a son Thomas, born December 12th, 1680, who was a prominent and leading citizen of Weston. He married Mercy Bigelow, daughter of Joshua and Elizabeth (Flagg) Bigelow, and had twelve children. The third, Thomas, married Rebecca Johnson, of Lunenburg, and had the following children : Solomon, born July 18th, 1743, and married May 20th, 1766, to Sarah Stimson, of Sudbury— these were the great grandfather and grandmother of General James A. Garfield ; Rebecca, born September 23d, 1745, married, October 31st, 1765, David Fiske ; Abraham, born April 3d, 1748, died August 15th, 1775, in the Revolutionary army ; Hannah, born August 15th, 1750 ; Lucy, born March 3d, 1745. The General's great-grandfather Solomon Garfield, was married in 1766 to Sarah Stimson, a widow, with children by her first husband, and went to live in the town of Weston, Massachusetts. Abraham Garfield, a brother of Solomon, was in the fight at Concord Bridge, and was one of the signers of the affidavits sent to the Continental Congress at Philadelphia to prove that the British were the aggressors in that affair and fired twice before the patriots replied. It seems that the skirmish was regarded somewhat as if it had been a case of assault and battery, and the patriots were desirous of justifying themselves by showing that the other fellows began the fight. After the Revolutionary War closed there was a large emigration from Massachusetts into the wilderness of Central New York. Solomon Garfield packed his household goods upon a wagon, joined the "movers," and went to Otsego County. He bought wild land in the township of Worcester, and reared a family of five children—Thomas, Solomon, Hannah, Rebecca, and Lucy.

One of Solomon Garfield's sons, Thomas, was the grandfather of General Garfield. He grew up in Worcester, married Asenath Hill, worked hard on a stony farm, had four children—Polly, Betsey, Abram, and Thomas—and died at thirty (when his youngest son Abram was two years old) of small-pox, which he contracted during a journey he made to Albany with a load of produce. His son Abram, born in 1799, was bound out to James Stone, a relative on his mother's side. At the age of fifteen he left his guardian and went to Madrid, St. Lawrence County, New York, where he worked by the month on a farm for three years. Afterward, when eighteen years old, he made his way to Newburg, Ohio, where he got employment chopping and clearing land. His guardian's wife was an aunt of Eliza Ballou, the girl whom he was afterward to marry. The mother of Eliza moved from Richmond, New Hampshire, with her family, after the death of her husband, and her children and the Garfield children got their education in the same district school-house in Worcester Township.

Eliza Ballou's father was a cousin of Hosea Ballou, the founder of Universalism in this country. Eliza was born in 1801. The Ballous are of Huguenot orgin, and are directly descended from Maturin Ballou, who fled from France on the revocation of the Edict of Nantes, and with other French Protestants joined Roger Williams' colony in Rhode Island, the only American colony founded on the basis of full religious liberty. The gift of eloquence is undoubtedly derived by General Garfield from the Ballous, who were a race of preachers. When Eliza's oldest brother, James, was eighteen, he got what was called in New York at that time the " Ohio fever," and persuaded his mother to sell the scanty possessions of the family in Otsego County and move to the new State with the three younger children. They left Worcester in 1814, followed the Susquehana Valley down to Harrisburg, then turned westward across the mountains, and, crossing the Ohio River at Wheeling, reached Perry Township, about ten miles from Zanesville, Muskingum County, at the end of the sixth week.

In 1820, Abram Garfield, then lacking a few months of his majority, left Newburg, Ohio, to join his old Otsego neighbors near Zanesville. He was a tall, robust young fellow, of very much the same type as his famous son, but a handsomer man, according to the verdict of his wife. He had a sunny, genial temper, like most men of great physical strength, was a great favorite with his associates, and was a natural leader and master of the rude characters with whom he was thrown in his forest-clearing work and his later labors in building the Ohio Canal. His education was confined to a few terms in the Worcester district school, and the only two specimens of his writing extant show that it was not thorough enough to give him much knowledge of the science of orthography. He was fond of reading, but the hard life of a poor man in a new country gave him little time to read books, if he had had the money to buy them. The weekly newspapers and a few volumes borrowed from neighbors formed his intellectual diet. It was only natural that the stout, handsome young man should speedily fall in love with his old schoolmate, Eliza, at whose mother's home in Muskingum County he was warmly welcomed. She was a slender girl, short of stature, with blue eyes and fair hair like his own, active, healthy, industrious, trained in all household labors, expert at the spinning-wheel and the loom, and able, in spite of her delicate-looking frame, to lend a vigorous hand to help her brothers in the harvest-field, as girls used to do in the pioneer days. In a word, she was just the wife for a young fellow like Abram Garfield, who had his way to make in the world.

Short courtships and early marriages were the rule in those days. Life was too serious and laborious to spend much time in love-making. On the 3d of February, 1829, Abram Garfield and Eliza Ballou were married in the village of Zanesville by a Justice of the Peace named Richard H. Hogan. The bridegroom lacked nine months of being twenty-one years of age, and the bride was only eighteen. They went to Newburg, Cuyahoga County, Ohio—now a part of the City of Cleveland —and began life in a small log-house on a new farm of eighty acres. In January, 1821, their first child, Mehitabel, was born. In October, 1822, Thomas was born, and Mary, in October, 1824. In 1826 the family removed to New Philadelphia, Tuscarawas County, where the father had a contract to construct three miles of canal. Men who worked for him are still living, and remember his great strength and energy and his remarkable control over the force of workmen in his employ Three years were spent in New Philadelphia. In 1827 the fourth child, James B., was born: This was the only one of the children that the parents lost. He died in 1830, after the family returned to the lake country. In January, 1830, Abram went to Orange Township, Cuyahoga County, where lived Amos Boynton, his half-brother—the son of his mother by her second husband—and bought eighty acres of land at two dollars an acre. The country was nearly all wild, and the new farm had to be carved out of the forest. Boynton purchased at the same time a tract of the same size adjoining, and the two families lived together for a few weeks in a log-house built by the joint labors of the men. Soon a second cabin was reared across the road. The dwelling of the Garfields was built after the standard pattern of the houses of poor Ohio farmers in that day. Its walls were of logs, its roof was of shingles split with an axe, and its floor of rude thick planking split out of tree-trunks with a wedge and maul. It had only a single room, at one end of which was the big cavernous chimney, where the cooking was done, and at the other a bed. The younger children slept in a trundle-bed, which was pushed under the bedstead of their parents in the day-time to get it out of the way, for there was no room to spare ; the older ones climbed a ladder to the loft under the steep roof. In this house James A. Garfield was born, November 19th, 1831.

The father worked hard early and late to clear his land and plant and gather his crops. No man in all the region around could wield an axe like him. Fenced fields soon took the place of the forest ; an orchard was planted, a barn built, and the family was full of hope for the future when death removed its strong support. One day in May, 1833, a fire broke out in the woods, and Abram Garfield, after heating his blood and exerting his strength to keep the flames from his fences and fields, sat down to rest where a cold wind blew, and was seized with a violent sore throat. A country doctor put a blister on his neck, which seemed only to hasten his death. Just before he died, pointing to his children, he said to his wife, " Eliza, I have planted four saplings in these woods. I leave them to your care." He was buried in a corner of a wheat-field on his farm. James, the baby, was eighteen months old at the time. His mother remembers that the father, a few days before he died, was reading a volume of " Plutarch's Lives" and holding the boy on one knee. James had just begun to say " papa" and " mamma," and the two words were his whole vocabulary. Stopping his reading a moment to listen to the child's prattle, the father said, " Say Plutarch, James." The boy pronounced the

word plainly, and repeated it several times. " Eliza," said the
father, " this boy will be a great scholar some day."

The loss of the father threw the family into great distress.
They were in debt, and there seemed no way out of their
trouble but to give up the homestead. The neighbors advised
the mother to break up the family, find homes for the older
children, and get some sort of employment to support herself
and the baby ; but she determined to make an effort to keep the
household together. Thomas, the oldest boy, was ten years old,
and soon became the main stay of the family. He was a brave,
affectionate, industrious lad, stalwart of frame, and devoted to
his mother and the younger children. Fifty acres of the farm
were sold to pay the debts, and on the remaining thirty Mrs.
Garfield managed, by the hardest toil and the closest economy,
to rear her family. Thomas did not marry until he was thirty,
when James had got his education and begun his career, and
the load of poverty had been lifted from the mother. He now
lives in Michigan. The two sisters are married and live in Solon, Ohio.

Abram Garfield was a Whig in politics, and a great admirer
of Henry Clay. He joined the Disciples Church, with his wife,
soon after his marriage, and not long after the denomination
was formed, under the influence of the preaching of Alexander
Campbell.

## CHAPTER II.

### A TOILSOME BOYHOOD.

THE childhood of James A. Garfield was passed in almost
complete isolation from social influences save those which proceeded from the home of his mother and that of his Uncle
Boynton. The farms of the Garfields and Boyntons were partially separated from the settled country around by a large

tract of forest on one side and a deep rocky ravine on another.
About a mile away ran the Chagrin River through a wild gorge.
For many years after Abram Garfield and his half-brother
Boynton built their log cabins, the nearest house was seven
miles distant, and when the country became well settled the
rugged character of the surface around their farms kept neighbors at a distance too great for the children of the two families
to find associates among them, save at the district school. So
the cousins grew up together like brothers and sisters. Indeed
there was a double bond between the two families, for Mrs.
Boynton was a sister of Mrs. Garfield. Boynton had six children
—three boys and three girls—who with the four Garfield children made a harmonious group, which only separated when the
older boys went away to earn wages at wood-chopping or in the
hay-field.

The district school-house stood upon a corner of the Garfield
farm, and it was there, when nearly four years old, that James
conned his "Noah Webster's Spelling Book," and learned his
"a-b ab's." The teacher was a young man from New Hampshire, named Foster. A few weeks after the term began he
told Mrs. Garfield that "Jimmy" was the most uneasy boy in
the school ; it was impossible to make him keep still, he said,
but he learned very fast. By the next spring "Jimmy" read
tolerably well, and the schoolmaster gave him a Testament as a
reward for being the best scholar in his class.

James was put to farm work as soon as he was big enough to
be of any use. The family was very poor, and the mother
often worked in the fields with the boys. She spun the yarn
and wove the cloth for the children's clothes and her own,
sewed for the neighbors, knit stockings, cooked the simple
meals for the household in the big fireplace, over which hung
an iron crane for the pot-hooks, helped plant and hoe the corn
and gather the hay crop, and even assisted the oldest boy to
clear and fence land. In the midst of this toilsome life the

brave little woman found time to instil into the minds of her children the religious and moral maxims of her New England ancestry. Every day she read four chapters of the Bible—a practice she keeps up to this time, and has never interrupted for a single day save when lying upon a sick bed. The children lived in an atmosphere of religious thought and discussion. Uncle Boynton, who was a second father to the Garfield family, flavored all his talk with Bible quotations. He carried a Testament in his pocket wherever he went, and would sit on his plough-beam at the end of a furrow to take it out and read a chapter. It was a time of religious ferment in Northern Ohio. New sects filled the air with their doctrinal cries. The Disciples, a sect founded by the preaching of Alexander Campbell, an eloquent and devout man of Scotch descent, who ranged over Kentucky, Ohio, Virginia, and Pennsylvania, from his home at Bethany in the " Pan Handle," had made great progress. They assailed all creeds as made by men, and declared the Bible to be the only rule of life. Attacking all the older denominations, they were vigorously attacked in turn. James' mind was filled at an early day with the controversies this new sect excited. The guests at his mother's house were mostly travelling preachers, and the talk of the neighborhood, when not about the crops and farm labors, was usually on religious topics. Politics had only a secondary hold on the local mind. When a lad of seven or eight, James was asked one day whether he was a Whig or a Democrat. He replied : " I'm a Whig, but I've not been baptized," supposing the party names to have some connection with the denominational divisions of which he heard so much.

At the district school James was known as a fighting boy. He found that the larger boys were disposed to insult and abuse a little fellow who had no father nor big brother to protect him, and he resented such imposition with all the force of a sensitive nature backed by a hot temper, great physical cour-

age, and a strength unusual for his age. His big brother Thomas
had finished his schooling and was much away from home,
working by the day or month to earn money for the support of
the family. Many stories are told in Orange of the pluck
shown by the future Major-General in his encounters with the
rough country lads in defence of his boyish rights and honor.
They say he never began a fight and never cherished malice,
but when enraged by taunts or insults would attack boys
of twice his size with the fury and tenacity of a bull-dog. A
few years after the death of his father the house was enlarged
in a curious fashion. The log school-house was abandoned for
a new frame building, and the old structure was bought by
Thomas Garfield for a trifle, and he and James, with the help
of the Boynton boys, pulled it down and put it up again on a
site a few steps in the rear of the Garfield dwelling. Thus the
family had two rooms and were tolerably comfortable, as far as
household accommodations were concerned. In these two
log buildings they lived until James was fourteen, when the
boys built a small frame house for their mother. It was
painted red and had three rooms below and two under the roof.
The original cabin had settled so much and got so awry that it
threatened to tumble down. Every year they had to saw off
the bottom of the front door, which hung upon wooden hinges,
to keep it from " binding" upon the floor. The new house cost
about three hundred dollars. The boys hired a carpenter and
worked with him. James thus got to be quite expert with the
saw and plane, and was able afterward to earn wages as a carpenter's assistant.

For a long time there was no newspaper taken in the Garfield
household. The first one the General remembers, for which his
mother subscribed, was the *Protestant Unionist*, a Disciples
weekly, printed in Pittsburg. Few books were to be had in
the neighborhood, but such as could be borrowed were devoured by James with indiscriminate avidity. Everything was fish

that came to his net. He particularly delighted in the old
" English Reader," which was the only reading book at the
school for pupils of all ages. Many of the extracts it contained
sunk so deeply into his mind by repeated rehearsal that he can
repeat whole pages to-day without pausing for a word. A
book that made a strong impression upon him at an early age
was a romance called " Alonzo and Melissa, or the Cow Boys
of the Revolution." Another was a sea tale called " Tom Hal-
yard." One of his cousins came into possession of a copy of
" Robinson Crusoe" minus the last twenty pages. He read the
book again and again until it was worn out by constant use. A
neighbor's boy got a copy of " Josephus" and the two got permission to read it as a reading book in the school one winter.
His hunger for reading was insatiable, and he forgot nothing that
he read. Even the florid and bombastic preface to Kirkham's
Grammar was read so often that he can repeat it now from
beginning to end. He was a master of the spelling-book before he was ten years old, and was the champion of his school
in the spelling matches with the neighboring districts. He
studied Pike's and Adams' Arithmetics, and Woodbridge's
Geography.

There were no playthings nor picture-books in the Garfield
family. They were too poor to buy such things. Yet it must
not be thought that they were exceptionally poor. All the
farmers' families in Northern Ohio had a life of hardship and
sacrifice in those days, and the lot of the Garfields was only
harder than the rest because of the death of the father. As
soon as the boys got old enough to earn money the household
was in as comfortable circumstances as were other families living on small farms. There were no social castes in the community, and the hard struggles of the Garfields with poverty
never caused them to be ranked below their more fortunate
neighbors, as would be the case at this time. Laziness, drunk-
enness, and immorality were all that dishonored persons in that

day. Work of all kinds was honorable, and no menial spirit attached to it.

James often got employment in the haying and harvesting season from the farmers of Orange. When he was sixteen he walked ten miles to Aurora, in company with a boy older than himself, looking for work. They offered their services to a farmer who had a good deal of hay cut. "What wages do you expect?" asked the man. "Man's wages—a dollar a day," replied young Garfield. The farmer thought they were not old enough to earn full wages. "Then let us mow that field by the acre," said the young man. The farmer agreed; the customary price per acre was fifty cents. By four o'clock in the afternoon the hay was down and the boys earned a dollar apiece. Then the farmer engaged them for a fortnight. James's first steady wages were earned from a merchant who had an ashery where he leached ashes and made black salts, which were shipped by lake and canal to New York. He got nine dollars a month and his board, and stuck to the business for two months, at the end of which his hair below his cap was bleached and colored by the fumes until it assumed a lively red hue. Afterward he went to Newburg, where an uncle lived who had a piece of oak-timbered land to clear on the edge of Independence Township. James agreed to chop one hundred cords of wood at fifty cents a cord. He boarded with one of his sisters, who was married and lived near by. He was a good chopper, and easily cut two cords a day. Near him worked a German, who was neither quick nor expert. James found he could make two cuts through a log while the German was making one, and he was disposed to disparage the clumsy fellow, but at the end of a week he found the slow chopper had as many cords piled up as he. This set him to thinking and observing, and he noticed that the German never stopped as he did to look at the blue lake and the distant sails, or sat on his log to rest and meditate, but kept steadily at his work like a machine. The boy learned a lesson of persistence and application. It was the story of the hare and the tortoise in a new form.

The view of Lake Erie and the passing sails stirred afresh in him the ambition to be a sailor, which almost every sturdy farmer's boy feels who reads tales of sea fights and adventures in the quiet monotony of his inland home. He resolved to ship on one of the lake craft, and with this purpose walked to Cleveland and boarded a schooner lying at the wharf, and told the captain he wanted to hire out as a sailor. The captain, a brutal, drunken fellow, was amazed at the impudence of the green country lad, and answered him with a torrent of profanity. Escaping as quickly as he could from the vessel, the lad walked up the river along the docks. Soon he heard himself called by name from the deck of a canal-boat, and, turning around, recognized a cousin, Amos Letcher, who told him he commanded the craft, and proposed to engage him to drive horses on the tow-path. The would-be sailor thought that here was a chance to learn something of navigation in a humble way, preparatory to renewing his application for service on the lakes. He accepted the offer and the wages of " ten dollars a month and found," and next day the boat started for Pittsburg with a cargo of copper ore. It was called the Evening Star, was open amidships, and had a cabin at the bow for the horses and one at the stern for the men. At Akron it left the main line of the Ohio Canal, and following the Pennsylvania branch took the young driver through the heart of the district he was afterward to represent in Congress, past the towns of Ravenna, Warren, Niles, and Youngstown, to the Beaver River ; thence by slack water to the Ohio at Beaver village, where the boat was taken in tow by the stern-wheeler Michigan and pulled up to Pittsburg. Some of the stories told of Garfield's canal adventures are fictitious. That of his victory over the burly boatman at the mouth of the Beaver is true, and also that of his narrow escape from drowning. He fell over-board, in the darkness, into Breakneck Creek, near Kent, Ohio (then Franklin Mills), while pulling in the bowline, and was saved from going under the boat by a lucky twist in the rope which caught between two planks and held till he pulled himself hand over hand up to the deck. On the return trip the Evening Star stopped at Brier Hill on the Mahoning River, and loaded with coal at the mines of David Tod, afterward Governor of Ohio, and a warm friend of Garfield, the Major-General and member of Congress. The boating episode in Garfield's life lasted through the season of 1848. After the first trip to Pittsburg the boat went back and forth between Cleveland and Brier Hill with cargoes of coal and iron.

Late in the fall the young driver, who had risen to the post of steersman, was seized with a violent attack of ague, which kept him at home all winter and in bed most of the time. All his summer's earnings went for doctors' bills and medicines. When he recovered, his mother, who had never approved his canal adventure, dissuaded him from carrying out his project of shipping on the lakes. To master one passion she stimulated another—that of study. She brought to her help the district school-teacher, an excellent, thoughtful man named Samuel D. Bates, who fired the boy's mind with a desire for a good educa-tion, and doubtless changed the course of his life. He went to the Geauga Academy, at Chester, a village a few miles dis-tant, and began a new career.

During the boyhood period above described Garfield had no political impressions. He remembers attending but one political meeting ; that was in the Harrison campaign. Nor did he ex-perience any deep religious emotions. He went regularly when at home to the Disciples meetings, first at Bentleyville and later at the school-house near his home, where his Uncle Boynton had organized a congregation. There was no Sunday-school in the neighborhood. The polemics of religion interested him deeply at that time, but his heart was not touched. He was familiar with Bible texts, and was often a formidable disputant. One day, when about fifteen, he was digging potatoes for a farmer in Orange and carrying them in a basket from the patch to the cellar. Near the cellar-door sat a neighbor talking to the farmer's grown-up daughter about the merits of the sprinkling and immersion controversy, and arguing that sprinkling was baptism within the meaning of the Scriptures. James overheard him say that a drop was as good as a fountain. He stopped on his way to the field and began to quote this text from Hebrews : " Let us draw near with a true heart, in full assurance of faith, having our hearts sprinkled from an evil conscience." " Ah, you see," said the man, " it says ' sprinkled.' " " Wait for the rest of the text," replied James ; " ' and our bodies washed with pure water ! ' Now, how can you wash your body in a drop of water ?" Without waiting for a reply, he hastened off to the potato-field.

He repulsed all efforts to persuade him to join the church, and when pressed hard stayed away from meetings for several Sundays. Apparently, he wanted full freedom to reach conclusions about religion by his own mental processes. It was not until he was eighteen and had been two terms at the Chester school that he joined his uncle's congregation. He was baptized in March, 1850, in a little stream putting into the Chagrin River. His conversion was accomplished by a quiet, sweet-tempered man who held a series of meetings in the school-house near the Garfield homestead, and told in the plainest and most straightforward manner the story of the Gospel. A previous perusal of Pollock's " Course of Time" had made a deep impression upon him and turned his thoughts to religious subjects.

## CHAPTER III.

### BRAVE EFFORTS FOR AN EDUCATION.

THE country schoolmaster who helped Mrs. Garfield dissuade her son from going as a sailor on the lakes in the spring of 1849 was a student at Geauga Academy, a Free Will Baptist institution in the village of Chester, ten miles away from the home of the Garfields in Orange. The argument which finally turned the robust lad from his cherished plan of adventure was advanced by his mother, and was that, if he fitted himself for teaching by a few terms in school, he could teach winters and sail summers, and thus have employment the year round. In the month of March, with seventeen dollars in his pocket, got together by his mother and his brother Thomas, James went to Chester with his cousins, William and Henry Boynton. The boys took a stock of provisions along, and rented a room with two beds and a cook-stove in an old unpainted house where lived a poor widow woman, who undertook to prepare their meals and do their washing for an absurdly small sum. The academy was a two-story building, and the school, with about a hundred pupils of both sexes, drawn from the farming country around Chester, was in a flourishing condition. It had a library of perhaps one hundred and fifty volumes—more books than young Garfield had ever seen before. A venerable gentleman named Daniel Branch was principal of the school, and his wife was his chief assistant. Mrs. Branch had introduced an iconoclastic grammar, which assailed all other systems as funded on a false basis; maintained that *but* was a verb in the imperative mood, and meant *be out ;* that *and* was also a verb in the imperative mood, and meant *add ;* and tried in other ways to upset the accepted etymology. Garfield had been reared in "Kirkham" at the district school, and refused to accept the new system. The grammar classes that term were a continu-

ous battle between him and his teacher. At Chester he first
saw an algebra. What was of more importance, though he did
not know it at the time, he first saw his future wife. Lucretia
Rudolph, a quiet, studious girl in her seventeenth year, was
among the students. There was no association between the
two, however, save in classes. James was awkward and bash-
ful, and contemplated the girls at a distance as a superior order
of beings.

There was a literary society connected with the academy, and
James began to take part in the debates, but with a good deal
of diffidence. He read his first essay at one of the school exercises, and was glad that there was a short curtain across the
front of the platform which hid his trembling legs from the view
of the audience. Among the books he read was the autobiog-
raphy of Henry C. Wright, and he was greatly impressed by
the author's account of how he lived in Scotland on bread,
milk, and crackers, and how well he was, and how hard he
could study. James told his cousins that they were extravagant, and that another term they must board themselves and
adopt Henry C. Wright's diet. At the end of the term of
twelve weeks he went home to Orange, helped his brother
build a barn for their mother, and then worked for day wages
at haying and harvesting. With the money he earned he paid
off some arrears of doctors' bills left from his long illness.
When he returned to Chester in the fall he had one silver sixpence in his pocket. Going to church next day he dropped the
sixpence in the contribution-box.

He had made an arrangement with Heman Woodworth, a carpenter in the village, to live at his house and have lodging, board,
washing, fuel, and light for one dollar and six cents a week, and
this sum he expected to earn by helping the carpenter on Satur-
days and at odd hours on school days. The carpenter was building a two-story house, and James' first work was to get out siding at two cents a board. The first Saturday he planed fifty-one

boards, and so earned a dollar and two cents, the most money
he had ever got for a day's work. That term he paid his way,
bought a few books, and returned home with three dollars in
his pocket. He now thought himself competent to teach a
country school, but in two days' tramping through Cuyahoga
County failed to find employment. Some schools had already
engaged teachers, and where there was still a vacancy the trustees thought him too young. He returned home completely
discouraged and greatly humiliated by the rebuffs he had met
with. He made a resolution that he would never again ask for
a position of any sort, and the resolution was kept, for every
public place he has since had has come to him unsought.

Next morning, while still in the depths of despondency, he
heard a man call to his mother from the road, " Widow Gaffield " (a local corruption of the name Garfield), " where's your
boy Jim ? I wonder if he wouldn't like to teach our school at
the Ledge." James went out and found a neighbor from a
district a mile away, where the school had been broken up for
two winters by the rowdyism of the big boys. He said he
would like to try the school, but before deciding must consult
his uncle, Amos Boynton. That evening there was a family
council. Uncle Amos pondered over the matter and finally
said, " You go and try it. You will go into that school as
the boy, ' Jim Gaffield' ; see that you come out as Mr. Garfield,
the school master." The young man mastered the school, after
a hard tussle in the school-room with the bully of the district,
who resented a flogging and tried to brain the teacher with a
billet of wood. No problem in his after life ever took so much
absorbing thought and study as that of making the Ledge
school successful. He devised all sorts of plans for making
study interesting to the children ; joined in the out-door sports
of the big boys, read aloud evenings to the parents where he
boarded, and won the hearts of old and young. Before spring
he got the name of the best schoolmaster who ever taught at

the Ledge. His wages were twelve dollars a month and board, and he " boarded around " in the families of the pupils.

He had forty-eight dollars in the spring—more money than had ever been in his possession before. Before returning to Chester he joined the Disciples Church, and his religious experience, together with his new interest in teaching, caused him·to abandon his boyhood ambition of becoming a sailor. During his third term at the academy he and his cousin Henry boarded themselves and put in practice Henry C. Wright's cheap dietary scheme. At the end of six weeks the boys found their expenses for food had been just thirty-one cents per week apiece. Henry thought they were living too poorly for good health, and they agreed to increase their outlay to fifty cents a week apiece. James had up to this time looked upon a college course as wholly beyond his reach, but he met a college graduate who told him he was mistaken in supposing that only the sons of rich parents were able to take such a course. A poor boy could get through, he said, but it would take a long time and very hard work. The usual time was four years in preparatory studies and four in the regular college course. James thought that by working part of the time to earn money he could get through in twelve years. He then resolved to bend all his energies to the one purpose of getting a college education.

From this resolution he never swerved a hair's-breadth. Until it was accomplished it was the one overmastering idea of his life. The tenacity and single-heartedness with which he clung to it and the sacrifices he made to realize it unquestionably exerted a powerful influence in moulding and solidifying his character. He began to study Latin, philosophy, and botany. When the spring term ended he went home again and worked through the summer at haying and carpentering. Next fall he was back at Chester for a fourth term, and in the winter he got a village school to teach in Warrensville, at sixteen dollars a

month and board.   One of the boys wanted to study geometry.
The teacher had never got so far in mathematics, but he bought
a text-book, studied nights, kept ahead of his pupil, and took
him through without his once suspecting that the master was
not an expert in the science.   In the spring he went with his
mother to visit relatives in Muskingum County, riding for the
first time on a railroad train.   The Cleveland and Columbus
Railroad was just open, and the travellers went by it to
Columbus, where they saw the State Capitol and the Legislature, and from whence they proceeded by stage to Zanesville,
and then floated eighteen miles in a skiff down the Muskingum
River to their destination.   James taught a spring school in a
log building on Back Run, in Harrison Township.   There was
coal in a bank near the school-house, and the teacher and his
boys dug the fuel for their fire.

Returning to Orange in the summer, he decided to go on
with his education at a new school just established by the
Disciples at Hiram, Portage County, a petty cross-roads
village, twelve miles from a town and a railroad.   His religious feeling naturally called him to the young institution of
his own denomination.   In August, 1851, he arrived at Hiram,
and found a plain brick building standing in the midst of a
corn-field, with perhaps a dozen farm-houses near enough for
boarding places for the students.   It was a lonely, isolated
place on a high ridge dividing the waters flowing into Lake
Erie from those running southward to the Ohio.   He lived in a
room with four other pupils, studied harder than ever, having
now his college project fully anchored in his mind, got through
his six books of Cæsar that term, and made good progress in
Greek.   In the winter he again taught school at Warrensville,
and earned eighteen dollars a month.   Next spring he was back
at Hiram, and during the summer vacation he helped build a
house in the village, planing all the siding and shingling the
roof.

He met at Hiram a woman who exercised a strong influence on his intellectual life—Miss Almeda A. Booth, a teacher in the school. She was nine years older than the young student, possessed a mind of remarkable range and grasp, and a character of unusual sweetness, purity, and strength. She became his guide and companion in his studies, his mental and moral heroine, and his unselfish, devoted friend. The friendship between them continued until she died a few years ago, when he delivered an oration on her life and character before the pupils of the Hiram Eclectic Institute. Young Garfield was again thrown into class associations at Hiram with Lucretia Rudolph, whose father had settled there to educate his four children. A strong, mutual attachment grew out of this association, and the young people entered into an engagement to marry as soon as James should graduate at college and establish himself in life.

At the beginning of his second year at Hiram, Garfield was made a tutor in place of one of the teachers who fell ill, and thenceforward he taught and studied at the same time, working tremendously to fit himself for college. His future wife recited to him two years in Greek, and when he went to college she went to teach in the Cleveland schools, and to wait patiently the realization of their hopes. When he went to Hiram he had studied Latin only six weeks and had just begun Greek, and was therefore just in a condition to fairly begin the four years' preparatory course ordinarily taken by students before entering college in the Freshman class. Yet in three years' time he fitted himself to enter the Junior class, two years further along, and at the same time earned his own living, thus crowding six years' study into three, and teaching for his support at the same time. To accomplish this, he shut the whole world out from his mind save that little portion of it within the range of his studies, knowing nothing of politics or the news of the day, reading no light literature, and engaging in no social recreations that took his time from his books.

In the spring of 1854, he wrote to the Presidents of Yale, Brown, and Williams, telling what books he had studied, and asking what class he could enter if he passed a satisfactory examination in them. All three wrote that he could enter the Junior year. President Hopkins, of Willams, added this sentence to the business part of his letter : " If you come here, we shall do what we can for you." This seemed like a kindly hand held out, and it decided him to go to Williams. He had been urged to go to the Disciples' College, in Bethany, Virginia, founded by Alexander Campbell, but with a wisdom hardly to be expected in a country lad devotedly attached to the sect represented by the Bethany school, he sought the wider culture and broader opportunities of a New England college.

## CHAPTER IV.

### TWO YEARS AT COLLEGE.

WHEN Garfield reached Williams College, in June, 1854, he had about three hundred dollars which he had saved while teaching in the Hiram school. With this money he hoped to manage to get through a year. A few weeks remained of the closing school year, and he attended the recitations of the Sophomore class in order to get familiar with the methods of the professors before testing his ability to pass the examinations for the Junior year. He had a keen sense of his want of the advantages of society and general culture which the students with whom he came in contact had enjoyed all their lives, but his homely manners and Western garb did not subject him to any slights or mortifications. The spirit of the college was generous and manly. No student was estimated by the clothes he wore ; no one was snubbed because he was poor. The in-tellectual force, originality, and immense powers of study possessed by the new comer from Ohio were soon recognized by his classmates, and he enjoyed as much respect, cordiality, and companionship as if he had been the son of a millionaire. The beauty of the scenery around Williamstown made a strong impression upon his fancy. He had never seen mountains before. The spurs of the Green Hills which reach down from Vermont and enclose the little college town in their arms were to the young man from the monotonous landscapes of the Western Reserve a wonderful revelation of grandeur and beauty. He climbed Greylock and explored all the glens and valleys of the neighborhood.

The examination for entering the Junior class was passed without trouble. Although self-taught, save for the help of his friend and companion in his studies, Miss Booth, his knowledge of the books prescribed was thorough. A long summer vacation followed his examination, and this time he employed in the college library, the first large collection of books he had ever seen. His absorption in the double work of teaching and fitting himself for college had hitherto left him little time for general reading, and the library opened a new world of profit and delight. He had never read a line of Shakespeare save a few extracts in the school reading-books. From the whole range of fiction he had voluntarily shut himself off at eighteen, when he joined the church, having serious views of the business of life, and imbibing the notion, then almost universal among religious people in the country districts of the West, that novel-reading was a waste of time, and therefore a sinful, worldly sort of intellectual amusement. When turned loose in the college library, with weeks of leisure to range at will over its shelves, he began with Shakespeare, which he read through from cover to cover. Then he went to English history and poetry. Of the poets, Tennyson pleased him best, which is not to be wondered at, for the influence of the laureate was then at its height. He learned whole poems by heart and can repeat them now.

After he had been six or eight months at college, and had devoured an immense amount of serious reading, he began to suffer from intellectual dyspepsia. He found his mind was not assimilating what he read, and would often refuse to be held down to the printed page. Then he revised his notions about books of fiction and concluded that romance is as valuable a part of intellectual food as salad of a dinner. He prescribed for himself one novel a month, and on this medicine his mind speedily recuperated and got back all its old elasticity. Cooper's " Leatherstocking Tales " were the first novels he read, and afterward Walter Scott. An English class-mate introduced him to the works of Dickens and Thackeray. He formed a habit in those days of making notes while he read of everything he did not clearly understand, such as historical references, mythological allusions, technical terms, etc. These notes he would take time to look up afterward in the library, so as to leave nothing obscure in his mind concerning the books he read. The thoroughness he displayed in his work in after-life was thus begun at that early period, and applied to every subject he took hold of. The ground his mind traversed he carefully cleared and ploughed before leaving it for fresh fields.

Garfield studied Latin and Greek, and took up German as an elective study. One year at college completed his classical studies, on which he was far advanced before he came to Williams. German he carried on successfully until he could read Goethe and Schiller readily and acquired considerable fluency in the conversational use of the language. He entered with zeal into the literary work of the school, joined the Philologian Society, was a vigorous debater, and in his last year was one of the editors of the *Williams Quarterly*, a college periodical of a high order of merit. To this magazine he was a frequent contributor in prose, and once wrote a poem. The influence of the mind and character of Dr. Hopkins was powerfully felt in shaping the direction of his thought and his views of life. He often says that the good President rose like a sun before him, and enlightened his whole mental and moral nature. His preaching and teaching were a constant inspiration to the young Ohio student, and he became the centre of his college life—the object of his reverence and hero-worship.

At the end of the fall term of 1854 came a winter vacation of two months, which Garfield employed in teaching a writing-school at North Pownal, Vermont. He wrote a bold, hand-some, legible hand, not at all like that in vogue nowadays in the systems taught in the commercial colleges, but a hand that was strongly individual and was the envy of the boys and girls who tried to imitate it in his Vermont class. It is said that a year or two before Garfield taught his writing-class in the North Pownal school-house, Chester A. Arthur taught the district school in the same building.

At the end of the college year, in June, Garfield went back to Ohio and visited his mother, who was then living with a daughter in Solon. His money was exhausted, and he had to adopt one of two plans, either to borrow enough to take him through to graduation at the end of the next year, or to go to teaching in order to earn the money, and thus break the contin-uity of his college course. He then hit upon the plan of insur-ing his life, and assigning the policy as security for a loan. His brother Thomas undertook to furnish the funds in instalments, but becomng embarrassed was not able to do so, and a neigh-bor, Dr. Robinson, assumed the obligation. Garfield gave his notes for the loan, and regarded the transaction as on a fair business basis, knowing that if he lived he would repay the money and that if he died his creditor would be secure.

His second winter vacation Garfield spent in Poestenkill, New York, a country neighborhood about six miles from Troy, where

a Disciple minister from Ohio, named Streeter, was preaching,
and where he soon organized a writing-school to employ his
time and bring him in a little money. Occasionally Garfield
preached in his friend's church. During a visit to Troy he
became acquainted with the teachers and directors of the public
schools of that city, and was one day surprised by the offer of a
position in them at a salary far beyond his expectations of what
he could earn after his graduation and return to Ohio. It was
a turning-point in his life. If he accepted, he could soon pay
his debts, marry the girl to whom he was engaged, and live a life
of comfort in an attractive Eastern city ; but he could not finish
his college course, and he would have to sever the ties with
friends in Ohio and with the struggling school at Hiram, to
which he was deeply attached. Had he taken the position, his
whole subsequent career would no doubt have been different.
While in church at Chicago just before the nomination last
June, he recognized in the congregation the man who made him
the offer in Troy. The two had not met since that time. " Do
you remember what you said on that occasion ?" asked his old
friend. " No ; I cannot recall the conversation." " We were
walking on a hill called Mount Olympus when I made you my
proposition. After a few moments silence you said : ' You are
not Satan, and I am not Jesus, but we are upon a mountain and
you have tempted me powerfully. I think I must say, get thee
behind me. I am poor, and the salary would soon pay my debts
and place me in a position of independence ; but there are two
objections. I could not accomplish my resolution to complete
a college course, and should be crippled intellectually for life.
Then my roots are all fixed in Ohio, where people know me and
I know them, and this transplanting might not succeed as well
in the long run as to go back home and work for smaller pay.' "

Study at Williams was easy for Garfield. He had been used
to much harder work at Hiram, where he had crowded a six
years' course into three, and taught at the same time. Now he

had the stimulus of a large class, an advantage he had never enjoyed before. His lessons were always perfectly learned, and he found a good deal of time for courses of reading that involved as much brain-work as the college text-books.

During his last term at Williams he made his first political speech, an address before a meeting gathered in one of the class-rooms to support the nomination of John C. Fremont. Although he had passed his majority nearly four years before, he had never voted. The old parties did not interest him ; he believed them both corrupted with the sin of slavery ; but when a new party arose to combat the designs of the slave power it enlisted his earnest sympathies. His mind was free from all bias concerning the parties and statesmen of the past, and could equally admire Clay or Jackson, Webster or Benton. He is the first man nominated for the Presidency whose political convictions and activities began with the birth of the Republican Party.

He graduated August, 1856, with a class honor established by President Hopkins and highly esteemed in the college—that of Metaphysics—reading an essay on "The Seen and the Unseen." It is singular how, at different times in the course of his education, he was thought to have a special aptitude for some single line of intellectual work, and how at a later period his talents seemed to lie just as strongly in some other line. At one time it was mathematics, at another the classics, at another rhetoric, and finally he excelled in metaphysics. The truth was that he had a remarkably vigorous and well-rounded brain, capable of doing effective work in any direction his will might dictate. The class of 1856 contained among its forty-two members a number of men who have since won distinction. Three became general officers in the volunteer army during the rebellion—Garfield, Daviess, and Thompson. Two, Bolter and Shattuck, were captains, and were killed in battle ; Eldridge, who now lives in Chicago, was a colonel ; so was Ferris Jacobs, of Delhi, N. Y. Rockwell is a quartermaster in the Regular Army. Gilfillan is Treasurer of the United States. Hill was Assistant Attorney General and is now a lawyer in Boston. Knox is a leading lawyer in New York. Newcombe is a professor in the University of the City of New York. In the class ahead of Garfield was Hitchcock, lately Senator from Nebraska, and Ingalls, now a Senator from Kansas. To furnish two United States Senators from one class and a Senator-elect and Presidential nominee from the next following class, is an honor which has probably never before fallen to any college. Ingalls was the poet of the school in his day, and many of his associates believed him destined to take rank in the future close up to Tennyson. Many years later, after he came to the Senate, Garfield met him at a dinner-party and brought the blushes to the Kansas statesman's face by reciting from memory two or three of his college productions.

---

## CHAPTER V.

### TEACHER AND PRINCIPAL AT HIRAM.

BEFORE Garfield graduated at Williams College the trustees of the Hiram Eclectic Institute elected him teacher of ancient languages, and the post was ready for him as soon as he got back to Ohio. It was not a professorship, because the institution was not a college, and did not become one until 1867, long after his connection with it ceased. A year later, when only twenty-six years old, he was placed at the head of the school, with the title of Chairman of the Board of Instruction, the Board waiting another year before conferring upon him the full honors of the Principalship. He continued to hold the position of Principal until he went into the army, in 1861. He was nominal Principal two years longer, the Board hoping he would return and manage the school after the war ended. When he went to Congress he was made Advising Principal and lecturer, and his name was borne upon the catalogues in this capacity until 1864. He is still one of the trustees.

Before he went to college, Garfield had begun to preach a little in the country churches around Hiram, and when he returned he began to fill the pulpit in the Disciples' Church in Hiram with considerable regularity. In his denomination no ordination is required to become a minister. Any brother having the ability to discourse on religious topics to a congregation is welcomed to the pulpit. His fame as a lay preacher extended throughout the counties of Portage, Summit, Trumbull, and Geauga, and he was often invited to preach in the towns of that region. He felt no special call to the ministry—if he gave up teaching he had already determined to go to the law —but he was an earnest supporter of the Christian sect with which he had connected himself, and was eager to advance its interests ; besides, it helped the school for the young Principal to make acquaintances in the surrounding country. Almost every sermon delivered away from home brought new pupils at the beginning of the next term.

His method of conducting recitations in the school embodied a series of technical questions for text-book answers, the assignment of topics, calls upon the students for their opinions and finally his own discussion of the subject-matter, which was always thorough, luminous, and singularly interesting. His memory was wonderful, and his thoughts would range over his reading and reflections to gather fresh material to illustrate and broaden the lessons beyond the range of the text-book. He was a famous teacher of English grammar ; if he had any specialty, this was it, but he seemed to teach all branches equally well—mathematics, classics, philosophy, history, etc. He had a code of rules for the school, but his own presence and personal force were more potent than all the regulations which could be devised. The students obeyed him because they loved him and respected him. He was cordial and companionable with them all, and made such careful studies of the pupils' characters that he knew what forces to bring to bear in each individual case to secure application to study and to awaken ambition for a noble life. Inspired by his wonderful influence, which seemed to reach to the fibres of every pupil's heart, the school became like a great harmonious family in which he was the wise, affectionate elder brother. One of his former pupils says of his peculiarities as a teacher :

" No matter how old the pupils were, Garfield always called us by our first names, and kept himself on the most familiar terms with all. He played with us freely, scuffled with us sometimes, walked with us in walking to and fro, and we treated him out of the class-room just about as we did one another. Yet he was a most strict disciplinarian, and enforced the rules like a martinet. He combined an affectionate and confiding manner with respect for order in a most successful manner. If he wanted to speak to a pupil, either for reproof or approbation, he would generally manage to get one arm around him and draw him close up to him. He had a peculiar way of shaking hands, too, giving a twist to your arm and drawing you right up to him. This sympathetic manner has helped him to advancement. When I was janitor he used sometimes to stop me and ask my opinion about this and that, as if seriously advising with me. I can see that my opinion could not have been of any value, and that he probably asked me partly to increase my self-respect and partly to show me that he felt an interest in me. I certainly was his friend all the firmer for it.

" I remember once asking him what was the best way to pursue a certain study, and he said : ' Use several text-books. Get the views of different authors as you advance. In that way you can plough a broader furrow. I always study in that way.' He tried hard to teach us to observe carefully and accurately.

He broke out one day in the midst of a lesson with, ' Henry, how many posts are there under the building down-stairs ?' Henry expressed his opinion, and the question went around the class, hardly one getting it right. Then it was : ' How many boot-scrapers are there at the door ?' ' How many windows in the building ?' ' How many trees in the field ?' What were the color of different rooms and the peculiarities of any familiar objects. He was the keenest observer I ever saw. I think he noticed and numbered every button on our coats. A friend of mine was walking with him through Cleveland one day, when Garfield stopped and darted down a cellar-way, asking his companion to follow, and briefly pausing to explain himself. The sign ' Saws and Files ' was over the door, and in the depths was heard a regular clicking sound. ' I think the fellow is cutting files,' said he, ' and I have never seen a file cut.' Down they went, and, sure enough, there was a man recutting an old file, and they stayed ten minutes and found out all about the process. Garfield would never go by anything without understanding it.

" Mr. Garfield was very fond of lecturing to the school. He ·spoke two or three times a week, on all manner of topics, generally scientific, though sometimes literary or historical. He spoke with great freedom, never writing out what he had to say, and I now think that his lectures were a rapid compilation of his current reading, and that he threw it into this form partly for the purpose of impressing it on his own mind. His facility of speech was learned when he was a pupil there. The societies had a rule that every student should take his stand on the platform and speak for five minutes on any topic suggested at the moment by the audience. It was a very trying ordeal. Garfield broke down badly the first two times he tried to speak, but persisted, and was at last, when he went to Williams, one of the best of the five-minute speakers. When he returned as Principal his readiness was striking and remarkable.

" At the time I was at school at Hiram, Principal Garfield was a great reader, not omnivorous, but methodical and in certain lines. He was the most industrious man I ever knew or heard of. At one time he delivered lectures on geology, held public debates on Spiritualism, preached on Sunday, conducted the recitations of five or six classes every day, attended to all the financial affairs of the school, was an active member of the Legislature, and studied law to be admitted to the Bar. He has often said that he never could have performed this labor if it had not been for the assistance of two gifted and earnest women—Mrs. Garfield herself, his early schoolmate, who had followed her husband in his studies, and Miss Almeda A. Booth, a member of the faculty. The latter was a graduate of Oberlin, and had been a teacher of young Garfield when he was a pupil, and now that he had returned as head of the faculty she continued to serve him in a sort of motherly way as tutor and guide. When Garfield had speeches to make in the Legislature or on the stump, or lectures to deliver, these two ladies ransacked the library by day and collected facts and marked books for his digestion and use in the preparation of the discourses at night. Mr. Garfield always acknowledged his great obligation to Miss Almeda Booth, and at her death, recently, he delivered one of the most touching and eloquent addresses of his life."

The attendance at the school ranged from a hundred and eighty to two hundred, and the salaries of teachers and Principal, not being fixed, but depending upon the revenue of the institution, fluctuated somewhat. The spring and fall terms were the fullest, because many of the pupils went out in the winter to teach country schools. Mr. Garfield's salary averaged about eight hundred dollars a year, a comfortable little income for rural Ohio in the times before the war.

He cast his first vote in 1856 for John C. Fremont, his own political career thus beginning with the first national campaign of the Republican Party. Before leaving Willams College he made a speech to the students on the question of slavery in the Territories, and during the fall, after he returned to Hiram, he spoke in the Disciples' Church in reply to Alphonso Hart, of Ravenna, who had delivered a Democratic address there a few nights before. Then a joint debate was arranged at Garretsville, between Hart and Garfield which attracted a good deal of local attention and is well remembered to this day by the older farmers of Portage County. This debate launched Garfield as a political speaker. His reputation as a stump orator widened steadily from that debate until it embraced first the State of Ohio and then the Nation.

A year after he took charge of the Hiram school Garfield married Lucretia Rudolph, his fellow-student and pupil in former years, to whom he had engaged himself before he went to Williams College. Their love had stood the test of time and absence, and now that he had made his place in the world and felt that he could support a family, there was nothing to hinder its consummation. The marriage took place at the house of the bride's parents, November 11th, 1858.

Miss Rudolph was a girl of unusual culture. A good scholar in Latin, Greek, and German, and also in mathematics and philosophy, she met the young teacher on his own intellectual plane. They read the same books and delighted in the same studies. Yet with all this learning, she was still a quiet, trusting, affectionate country girl who had but one hero in life, her lover and husband, but one ambition—to hold fast his love, and make for him a happy home. She was of medium stature, with dark hazel eyes, wavy brown hair, a rounded form, and an expression about her mouth denoting a calm, sweet temper, combined with a strong will. The marriage was a happy one. Indeed, it could hardly have been otherwise, for there was congeniality of taste, a high ideal of a pure home life, identity of religious belief, a great love of study and culture, and a long-standing affection to base it on.

## CHAPTER VI.

### IN THE STATE SENATE.

THE years of Garfield's Principalship of the Hiram Eclectic Institute were years of great intellectual activity. He delivered three lectures a week to the students, following usually the line of his reading. It was his habit to make skeleton notes of what he read, and by the aid of these notes to talk for half an hour upon the theme of the book, giving the ideas of the author and then his own comments. He delivered lectures before literary societies in the neighboring towns. One was on the "Character and Writings of Sir Walter Scott," another on the "Character of the German People," another on "Carlyle's Frederick the Great." He became greatly interested in the science of geology, and held a debate with William Denton on the question of whether all life upon the earth was developed by processes of law or had been introduced by successive creative acts. Denton held the development theory ; Garfield that of intelligent providential action. The discussion lasted five days and evenings, embraced twenty speeches on the part of each of the disputants, and was remarkable as a sustained and severe intellectual effort. It brought Garfield many invitations to deliver courses of lectures on geology. He prepared a course and gave it at a number of places in Northern Ohio. His labors upon the stump, beginning in 1856, with perhaps a score of speeches for Fremont and Dayton in country school-houses and town-halls in the region around Hiram, were extended in 1857 and 1858 over a wider area of territory, and in 1859 he began to speak at county mass-meetings. His first appearance at a big meeting was at Akron, where his name was put upon the bills below that of Salmon P. Chase. There the young teacher met for the first time the great anti-slavery leader whom he had honored and admired from his boyhood, and a friendship sprang up between the two which endured until Chase's death. All this time, while infusing new vigor into the Hiram school, delving in the fields of literature and science, and fighting on the stump the battles of the young Republican Party against slavery, Garfield did a great deal of pulpit work. Of his career as a lay preacher something will be said in another chapter. He often filled the pulpit in the Disciples' Church at Hiram, and for some time was the regular minister in Solon and Newburg, going on Saturday to one or the other of these places, and returning to Hiram for school duties Monday morning. Such an amount of work would have broken down any man not gifted with a remarkably vigorous brain and a remarkably vigorous body, but hard work in many lines at once seemed to be natural to him. He slept well, ate heartily, and was never overtasked by anything which could be done in the working hours of the twenty-four. Repose seemed not to be necessary to his organization. His mind never lay fallow.

In 1859, he was chosen by the faculty of Williams College to deliver the Master's Oration on Commencement Day, and taking his wife with him, he went down the St. Lawrence River to Quebec, and then crossed the New England States to Williamstown—making the first pleasure trip of his life. Before leaving home he had been solicited to be a candidate for the Legislature from Portage County, but declined. He thought at the time that the State Senate might have tempted him. The Senatorship from the district composed of Portage and Summit counties was conceded to Portage, and the politicians had generally agreed upon an old citizen of Ravenna, Mr. Prentiss, for the place. When Garfield returned from his Eastern trip, he learned that Mr. Prentiss had died during his absence and was met at Mantua station by some friends who desired him to be a candidate. He told them he would have to talk with the faculty at Hiram before he could give them an answer. The

teachers advised him to take the nomination, and said they
thought they could get along without him in the school during
the few weeks he would be in Columbus.  So he wrote to his
political friends that if they desired to nominate him without
any seeking or effort on his part, he would not refuse.  There
were a number of candidates, but Garfield was nominated at
the third ballot, and the district being heavily Republican, was
elected without trouble, although some fault was found with
him because of his refusal to pledge himself to this or that
measure and his declaration of a purpose to act independently
according to his own convictions of duty.

In January, 1860, he went to Columbus, and took his seat in
the State Senate.  Soon a warm friendship sprang up between
him and Jacob D. Cox, afterward Major-General, Governor,
and Secretary of the Interior.  The two roomed together,
studied together, read together, and worked together on measures of legislation.  They were called the Damon and Pythias
of the legislature.  He found himself with very little knowledge
of the machinery of the State Government, and to supply his
deficiency he adopted a plan that was characteristically original.
" If I trace a dollar," he said to his friend Cox, " from the pocket
of a taxpayer up to the State Treasury, and then out to its ultimate destination in the payment of State expenditures, and fa-
miliarize myself with all the statutes governing every transfer
of the money, I think I shall know pretty well how the State
machine works."  This plan he carried out, and at the end of
his investigation had thoroughly mastered the subject.  The
campaign of 1860 made him widely known throughout the
State.  Before the legislature adjourned a meeting was held in
Columbus to ratify the nomination of William Denison for Governor.  Chase, Giddings, Hassaurek, and Garfield were the
speakers.  Garfield spoke last.  He had just been reading a
poem by Charles Mackay, who had lately visited this country,
describing the progress southward of a Mississippi River steam-

er from St. Louis to New Orleans. With his remarkable memory, Garfield had the poem at his tongue's end, and a happy thought struck him to compare the progress of the Democratic Party from its old anti-slavery ideas toward absolute subserviency to the South to the voyage of the steamer as described by Mackay. The verses lent themselves marvellously to the comparison, especially one about driving a drove of squealing, grunting hogs across a plank upon the boat. The plank, in the illustration, was the Dred Scott decision and the hogs the unwilling Northern Democrats. The speech was a great hit, and made the young orator famous throughout the State. Invitations came to speak in Cincinnati and in most of the large towns. From a local stumper at school-house and township meetings, Garfield developed into one of the most popular campaign orators in the State.

He found time to read law assiduously while he was in the legislature. In 1858, he made up his mind that his future career should be at the Bar. Teaching seemed rather an episode than a permanent vocation, and he did not feel the inner call to devote himself to preaching, although he was a successful pulpit orator, and was a devoted believer in Christianity. He therefore entered his name as a law student in the office of Williamson & Riddle, in Cleveland, and got from Mr. Riddle a list of the books to be studied. His method of study was to read a chapter, close the book, and write a synopsis of it; then re-read the chapter and compare the synopsis with it. In this way the contents of the books became firmly fixed in his mind. In 1861 he applied to the Supreme Court in Columbus for admission to the Bar, was examined by a committee composed of Thomas M. Key, a distinguished lawyer of Cincinnati, and Robert Harrison, afterward a member of the Supreme Court Commission, and admitted. His intention was to open an office in Cleveland, but the breaking out of the war changed his plans.

During his two winters at Columbus, Garfield was chairman of the Committee on Colleges and Universities, and made a number of thoughtful reports. He introduced a bill for a geological survey of the State which the war pushed aside for a time, but which was afterward passed. In the winter of 1861 he offered a resolution inviting the Legislatures of Kentucky and Tennessee to visit Columbus as the guests of the Ohio Legislature, the purpose being to strengthen the bonds of the Union in view of the gathering storm of secession. The resolution was adopted, the invitation accepted, and Garfield went to Louisville as chairman of the Reception Committee, and made a notable speech there at a banquet. He was severely criticised at home for his course in this matter, but the visit of the two legislatures unquestionably exerted an important influence in strengthening the Union feeling in Kentucky and Tennessee.

Garfield and Cox were among the first to foresee that the end of secession would be war. After a long talk one night, they came to the conclusion that war was inevitable, and mutually pledged themselves to each other to enter the struggle and offer their lives to their country. This resolution was taken in no light mood. Both had homes and families. Governor Cox has often said since that the moment when he clasped hands with his friend and agreed to enter the army was the most solemn moment of his life. The comrades began at once to read military works and study the profession of arms. They introduced a bill offering the United States Government three millions of dollars for the war. Garfield offered a bill punishing treason against the State, and supported it with an exhaustive report and speech on the question of the possibility of treason being committed against a State, which carried the bill through. After McClellan came to Columbus to take command of the State troops, Garfield was sent to Springfield, Illinois, to procure five thousand stand of arms, a portion of those saved by General Lyon, and removed from the St. Louis arsenal. He suc-

ceeded in his mission, shipped the guns, and saw them safely
delivered at Columbus. He was sent to Cleveland by Governor
Denison soon after the fall of Fort Sumter to organize the Seventh and Eighth Regiments of Ohio infantry. The Governor
offered him the colonelcy of one of the new regiments, but he
declined because he did not think himself fit for such a post as
long as he was without military experience. If a West Pointer
could be got to take command, he would be glad, he said, of a
subordinate position. Finally, the Governor appointed him lieutenant-colonel and sent him to the Western Reserve to raise a
regiment, with the understanding that a West Pointer should
be found for its colonel if possible. Garfield suggested Captain (now General) Hazen, a Portage County man, then serving in the Regular Army, and Governor Dennison asked the
War Department to detail him, but General Scott would not
consent. So the Forty-second Regiment went into camp without
any colonel, and it was only then that Garfield yielded to the
solicitations of its officers and of the Governor, and consented
to take command.

## CHAPTER VII.

### FIGHTING FOR THE UNION.

THIS and the following chapter, relating to General Garfield's
military career, are copied without change from Whitelaw
Reid's " Ohio in the War," a comprehensive history, published
in 1867, of the part played by Ohio regiments and Ohio men in
suppressing the rebellion. Mr. Reid, now the distinguished
editor of the New York *Tribune*, was one of the most intrepid
and impartial of the war correspondents—those staff officers
of the people, sent with the armies of the Union to share their
dangers and hardships and describe their marches and battles
through the medium of the daily press. His account of

General Garfield's part in the war is peculiarly valuable, inasmuch as it was written long before there could be any political motive for exaggerating his heroism and military genius, as one of a series of criticisms, conspicuous for good judgment and fairness, upon the men from Ohio who won distinction in the national armies.

When the time came for appointing the officers for the Ohio troops, the legislature was still in session. Garfield at once avowed his intention of entering the service. But he displayed at the outset his signal want of tact and of skill in advancing his own interests. Of the three leading radical Senators, Garfield had the most personal popularity. Cox was at that time, perhaps, a more compact and pointed speaker—he had matured earlier, as (to change the figure) he was to culminate sooner. But he had never aroused the warm regard which Garfield's whole-hearted, generous disposition always excited. Yet Cox had the sagacity to see how his interests were to be advanced. He abandoned the Senate chamber ; installed himself as an assistant in the Governor's office, made his skill felt in the rush of business, and soon convinced the appointing power of his special aptitude for military affairs. In natural sequence he was presently appointed a brigadier-general. Garfield was sent off on a mission to some Western States to see about arms for the Ohio volunteers, and on his return he was offered the lieutenant-colonelcy of one of the reserve regiments, but his making haste slowly was not to injure his future career.

On the 14th of August, 1861, some months after the adjournment of the legislature, and after the successful close of McClellan's West Virginia campaign, the ex-Senator was finally appointed by Governor Denison Lieutenant-Colonel of the Forty-second Ohio Regiment not yet organized, a company for which had been recruited among the pupils of the Hiram Eclectic Institute.

It was understood that if he had cared to push the matter,

Garfield might have been colonel; but with a modesty quite unusual in those days of the war, he preferred to start low, and rise as he learned. Five weeks were spent in diligently drilling the regiment, and finally, about the time its organization was complete, the lieutenant-colonel was, without his own solicitation, promoted to the colonelcy.

It was not until the 14th of December that orders for the field were received. The regiment was then sent to Catlettsburg, Kentucky, and the colonel was directed to report in person to General Buell. That astute officer, though as opposite as the poles to Garfield in his political convictions, soon perceived the military worth of the young colonel. On the 17th of December he assigned Colonel Garfield to the command of the Seventeenth Brigade, and ordered him to drive the rebel forces under Humphrey Marshall out of the Sandy Valley, in Eastern Kentucky.

Up to this date no active operations had been attempted in the great department that lay south of the Ohio River. The spell of Bull Run still hung over our armies. Save the campaigns in Western Virginia, and the unfortunate attack by General Grant at Belmont, not a single engagement had occurred over all the region between the Alleghanies and the Mississippi. General Buell was preparing to advance upon the rebel position at Bowling Green, when he suddenly found himself hampered by two co-operating forces skilfully planted within striking distance of his flank. General Zollicoffer was advancing from Cumberland Gap to Ward Mill Spring; and Humphrey Marshall, moving down the Sandy Valley, was threatening to overrun Eastern Kentucky. Till these could be driven back, an advance upon Bowling Green would be perilous, if not actually impossible. To General George H. Thomas, then just raised from his colonelcy of regulars to a brigadier-generalship of volunteers, was committed the task of repulsing Zollicoffer ; to the untried colonel of the raw Forty-second Ohio, the task of repulsing Humphrey Marshall, and on their success the whole army of the department waited.

Colonel Garfield thus found himself, before he had ever seen a gun fired in action, in command of four regiments of infantry, and some eight companies of cavalry,* charged with the work of driving out of his native State the officer reputed the ablest of those, not educated to war, whom Kentucky had given to the Rebellion. Marshall had under his command nearly five thousand men, stationed at the village of Paintville, sixty miles up the Sandy Valley. He was expected by the rebel authorities to advance toward Lexington, unite with Zollicoffer, and establish the authority of the Provisional Government at the State capital. These hopes were fed by the recollection of his great intellectual abilities, and the soldierly reputation he had borne ever since he led the famous charge of the Kentucky Volunteers at Buena Vista.

Colonel Garfield joined the bulk of his brigade at the mouth of the Big Sandy, and moved with it directly up the valley. Meantime he ordered the small force at Paris to march overland and effect a junction with him a little below Paintville. The force with which he was able to move numbered about twenty-two hundred.

Marshall heard of the advance, through the sympathizing citizens, and fell back to protect his trains. As Garfield approached, January 7th, 1862, he ascertained the position of his enemy's cavalry, and sent some of his own mounted forces to make a reconnoissance in force of the positions which he still supposed Marshall's main body to occupy. He speedily discovered Marshall's retreat ; then hastily sent word back to his cavalry not to attack the enemy's cavalry until he had time to plant his

---

* The brigade was composed of the Fortieth and Forty-second Ohio, the Fourteenth and Twenty-second Kentucky Infantry, six companies of the First Kentucky Cavalry, and two companies of McLaughlin's (Ohio) Cavalry.

force on its line of retreat. Unfortunately, the circuitous route delayed the courier, and before Garfield's order could be delivered the attack had been made, and Marshall's cavalry had been driven back in considerable confusion. When, pushing on with the main column, he reached the road on which he had hoped to intercept their retreat, he found it strewn with overcoats, blankets, and cavalry equipments— proofs that they had already passed in their rout. Colonel Garfield pushed the pursuit with his cavalry till the infantry outposts were reached ; then, drawing back, encamped with his whole force at Paintville. Here, next morning, he was joined by the troops that had marched from Paris, so that his effective force was now raised to about thirty-four hundred men.

After waiting a day for rations, which were taken through with the utmost difficulty, on the 9th of January Garfield advanced upon Marshall's new position near Prestonburg. Before nightfall he had driven in the enemy's pickets, and had sent orders back to Paintville to forward the few troops—less than one thousand in all—who had not been supplied with rations in time to move with the rest of the column. The men slept on their arms, under a soaking rain. By four o'clock in the morning of January 10th, they were in motion.

Marshall was believed to be stationed on Abbott's Creek. Garfield's plan, therefore, was to get over upon Middle Creek, and so plant himself on the enemy's rear. But in fact Marshall's force was upon the heights of Middle Creek itself, only two miles from Prestonburg, So, when Garfield, advancing cautiously westward up the creek, had consumed some hours in these movements, he came upon a semi-circular hill, scarcely one thousand yards in front of which was Marshall's position, between the forks of the creek. The expected reinforcements from Paintville had not yet arrived, and, conscious of his comparative weakness, Colonel Garfield determined first to develop the enemy's position more carefully. A small body of picked men, sent dashing up the road, drew a fire both from the head of the gorge through which the road lead and from the heights on its left. Two columns were then moved forward, one on either side of the creek, and the rebels speedily opened upon them with musketry and artillery. The fight became somewhat severe at times, but was, on the whole, desultory. Garfield reinforced both of his columns, but the action soon developed itself mainly on the left, where Marshall speedily concentrated his whole force. Meantime Garfield's reserve was now also under fire from the commanding position held by the enemy's artillery. He was entirely without artillery to reply ; but the men stationed themselves behind trees and rocks, and kept up a brisk though irregular fusilade.

At last, about four o'clock in the afternoon, the reinforcements from Paintville arrived. As we now know, these still left Marshall's strength superior to that of his young assailant ; but the troops looked upon their opportune arrival as settling the contest. Unbounded enthusiasm was aroused, and the approaching column was received with prolonged cheering. Garfield now promptly formed his whole reserve for attacking the enemy's right and carrying his guns. The troops were moving rapidly up in the fast-gathering darkness, when Marshall hastily abandoned his position, fired his camp equipage and stores, and began a retreat which was not ended till he had reached Abingdon, Virginia. Night checked the pursuit. Next day it was continued for some distance, and some prisoners were taken ; but a further advance in that direction was quite impossible without more transportation, and, indeed, would have been foreign to the purpose for which General Buell had ordered the expedition.

Speaking of these movements on the Sandy, after he had gained more experience of war, Garfield said : " It was a very rash and imprudent affair on my part. If I had been an officer of more experience I probably should not have made the attack. As it was, having gone into the army with the notion that fighting was our business, I didn't know any better."

A fresh peril, however, now beset the little force. An un_ usually violent rain-storm broke out, the mountain gorges were all flooded, and the Sandy rose to such a height that steam boat-men pronounced it impossible to ascend the stream with sup-plies. The troops were almost out of rations, and the rough, mountainous country was incapable of supporting them. Colonel Garfield had gone down the river to its mouth. He ordered the Sandy Valley, a small steamer which had been in the quartermaster's service, to take on a load of supplies and start up. The captain declared it was impossible. Efforts were made to get other vessels, but without success.

Finally Colonel Garfield ordered the captain and crew on board, stationed a competent army officer on deck to see that the captain did his duty, and himself took the wheel. The captain still protested that no boat could possibly stem the rag-ing current, but Garfield turned her head up the stream and began the perilous trip. The water in the usually shallow river was sixty feet deep, and the tree-tops along the bank were almost submerged. The little vessel trembled from stem to stern at every motion of the engines ; the waters whirled her about as if she were a skiff ; and the utmost speed that steam could give her was three miles an hour. When night fell the captain of the boat begged permission to tie up. To at-tempt ascending that flood in the dark he declared was mad-ness. But Colonel Garfield kept his place at the wheel. Finally, in one of the sudden bends of the river, they drove, with a full head of steam, into the quicksand of the bank. Every effort to back off was in vain. Mattocks were procured and excavations were made around the imbedded bow. Still she stuck. Garfield at last ordered a boat to be lowered to take a line across to the opposite bank. The crew protested against venturing out in the flood. The Colonel leaped into the boat himself and steered it over. The force of the current carried them far below the point they sought to reach ; but they finally succeeded in making fast to a tree and rigging a windlass with rails sufficiently powerful to draw the vessel off and get her once more afloat.

It was on Saturday that the boat left the mouth of the Sandy. All night, all day Sunday, and all through Sunday night they kept up their struggle with the current, Garfield leaving the wheel only eight hours out of the whole time, and that during the day. By nine o'clock Monday morning they reached the camp, and were received with tumultuous cheering. Garfield himself could scarcely escape being borne to headquarters on the shoulders of the delighted men.

Through the months of January, February, and March, several small encounters with guerrillas in the mountains occurred, generally favorable to the Union arms, and finally resulting in the expulsion of the bands of marauders from the State. Just on the border, however, at the rough pass across the mountains, known as Pound Gap, eighty miles north of Cumberland Gap, Humphrey Marshall still kept up a post of observation, held by a force of about five hundred men. On the 14th of March, Garfield started with five hundred infantry and a couple of hundred cavalry against this detachment. The distance was forty miles, and the roads were at their worst, but by the evening of the next day he had reached the foot of the mountain, two miles north of the Gap. Next morning he sent the cavalry directly up the Gap road, to attract the enemy's attention, while he led the infantry along an unfrequented footpath up the side of the mountain. A heavy snow-storm helped to conceal the movements. While the enemy watched the cavalry, Garfield had led the infantry, undiscovered, to within a quarter of a mile of their camp. Then he ordered an attack. The enemy were taken by surprise and a few volleys dispersed them. They retreated in confusion down the eastern slope of the mountain, followed for several miles into Virginia by the cavalry. Considerable quantities of stores were captured. The troops rested for the night in the sixty comfortable log huts which the enemy had built, and the next morning burned them down, together with every thing else left by the enemy which they could not carry away.

Six days afterward an order was received to leave a small garrison at Piketon, and to transfer the rest of the command rapidly to Louisville.

These operations in the Sandy Valley had been conducted with such energy and skill as to receive the special commendation of the commanding general and of the Government. General Buell had been moved to words of unwonted praise.

The following is the text of General Buell's congratulatory order :

" HEADQUARTERS DEPARTMENT OF THE OHIO, } 
LOUISVILLE, KENTUCKY, January 20, 1862. }

" *General Orders No. 40.*

" The general commanding takes occasion to thank General Garfield and his troops for their successful campaign against the rebel force under General Marshall on the Big Sandy, and their gallant conduct in battle. They have overcome formidable difficulties in the character of the country, the condition of the roads, and the inclemency of the season ; and, without artillery, have, in several engagements, terminating in the battle on Middle Creek on the 10th inst., driven the enemy from intrenched positions, and forced him back into the mountains, with the loss of a large amount of baggage and stores, and many of his men killed or captured.

" These services have called into action the highest qualities of a soldier—fortitude, perseverance, courage."

The War Department had conferred the grade of brigadier-general, the commission bearing the date of the battle of Middle Creek. And the country, without understanding very well the details of the campaign—of which, indeed, no satisfactory account was published at the time—fully appreciated the satisfactory result. The discomfiture of Humphrey Marshall was a source of special chagrin to the rebel sympathizers of Kentucky, and of amazement and admiration throughout the loyal West, and Garfield took rank in the public estimation among the most promising of the younger volunteer generals.

Later criticism will confirm the general verdict then passed upon the Sandy Valley campaign. It was the first of the brilliant series of successes that made the spring of 1862 so memorable. Mill Springs, Fort Henry, Fort Donelson, Nashville, Island No. 10, Memphis, followed in quick succession; but it was Garfield's honor that he opened this season of victories. His plans, as we have seen, were based on sound military principles; the energy which he threw into their execution was thoroughly admirable, and his management of the raw volunteers was such that they acquired the fullest confidence in their commander, and endured the hardships of the campaign with a fortitude not often shown in the first field-service of new troops. But the operations were on a small scale, and their chief significance lay in the capacity they developed, rather than in their intrinsic importance.

## CHAPTER VIII.

### MAJOR-GENERAL AND CHIEF OF STAFF.

On his arrival at Louisville, from the Sandy Valley, General Garfield found that the Army of the Ohio was already beyond Nashville, on its march to Grant's aid at Pittsburg Landing. He hastened after it, reported to General Buell about thirty miles south of Columbia, and, under his order, at once assumed command of the Twentieth Brigade, then a part of the division under General Thomas J. Wood. He reached the field of Pittsburg Landing about one o'clock on the second day of the battle, and participated in its closing scenes.

The next day he moved with Sherman's advance, and had a sharp encounter with the enemy's rear-guard, a few miles beyond the battle-field. His brigade bore its full share in the tedious siege operations before Corinth, and was among the earliest in entering the abandoned town after General Beauregard's evacuation.

Then, when General Buell, turning eastward, sought to prepare for a new aggressive campaign with his inadequate forces, General Garfield was assigned to the task of rebuilding the bridges and reopening the Memphis and Charleston Railroad eastward from Corinth to Decatur. Crossing the Tennessee here, he advanced to Huntsville, where he remained during the rest of his service in that campaign. He was presently put at the head of the court-martial for the trial of General Turchin, whose conduct at Athens had been the occasion of a parting howl against General Mitchel, and had been one of the earliest subjects forced upon the attention of General Buell on his arrival.\* His manifest capacity for such work led to his subsequent detail on several other courts-martial.

The old tendency to fever and ague, contracted in the days of his tow-path service on the Ohio Canal, was now aggravated in the malarious climate of the South, and General Garfield was finally sent home on sick-leave about the first of August. Near

---

\* This case attracted great attention at the time, and General Turchin was vehemently championed by the newspapers, particularly those of Chicago. The charges against him were neglect of duty, to the prejudice of good order and discipline, in permitting the wanton and disgraceful pillage of the town of Athens, Alabama ; conduct unbecoming an officer and a gentleman, in failing to pay a hotel bill in the town ; and insubordination, in disobeying the orders against the molestation of peaceful citizens in person and property. Some of the specifications particularized very shameful conduct. The court found him guilty (except as to the hotel-bill story), and sentenced him to dismissal from the army. Six of its members recommended him to clemency on account of mitigating circumstances, but the sentence was executed.

the same time the Secretary of War, who seems at this early day to have formed the high estimate of Garfield which he continued to entertain throughout the war, sent orders to him to proceed to Cumberland Gap, and relieve General George W. Morgan of his command. But when they were received he was too ill to leave his bed. A month later the Secretary ordered him to report in person at Washington, as soon as his health would permit.

On his arrival it was found that the estimate placed upon his knowledge of law, his judgment, and his loyalty had led to his selection as one of the first members of the court-martial for the noted trial of Fitz John Porter. In the duties connected with this detail most of the autumn was consumed. General Garfield was understood to be one of the clearest and firmest in the conviction that General Porter had wilfully permitted Pope's defeat at the second Bull Run, and that no less punishment than dismissal from the service would be at all adequate to his offence.

The intimacy that sprang up during the trial between General Garfield and General Hunter, the President of the court-martial, led to an application for him for service in South Carolina, whither Hunter was about to start. Garfield's anti-slavery views had been greatly strengthened by his experience thus far during the war, and the South Carolina appointment, under a commander so radical as Hunter, was on this account peculiarly gratifying. But in the midst of his plans and preparations, the old army in which he had served plunged into the battle of Stone River. A part of the bitter loss that followed was the loss of Garesche, the lamented Chief of Staff to the commanding general. Garfield was at once selected to take his place ; the appointment to South Carolina was revoked ; and early in January he was ordered out to General Rosecrans.

The Chief of Staff should bear the same relation to his general that a Minister of State does to his sovereign. What this last relation is the most brilliant of recent historians shall tell us : " The difference between a servant and a Minister of State lies in this : that the servant obeys the orders given him, without troubling himself concerning the question whether his master is right or wrong ; while a Minister of State declines to be the instrument for giving effect to measures which he deems to be hurtful to his country. The Chancellor of the Russian Empire was sagacious and polite. . . . That the Czar was wrong in these transactions against Turkey no man knew better. . . . But, unhappily for the Czar and for his Empire, the Minister did not enjoy so commanding a station as to be able to put restraint upon his sovereign, nor even, perhaps, to offer him counsel in his angry mood."* We are now to see that in some respects our Chief of Staff came to a similar experience.

From the day of his appointment, General Garfield became the intimate associate and confidential adviser of his chief. But he did not occupy so commanding a station as to be able to put restraint upon him.

The time of the general's arrival marks the beginning of that period of quarrels with the War Department in which General Rosecrans frittered away his influence and paved the road for his removal. We have seen in tracing the career of that great strategist and gallant soldier, how unwise he always was in caring for his own interests, and how imprudent was the most of his intercourse with his superiors. Yet he was nearly always right in his demands. General Garfield earnestly sympathized with his appeals for more cavalry † and for revolving arms. But he did all that lay in his power to soften the tone of asperity which his chief adopted in his dispatches to Washington. Sometimes he took the responsibility of totally

* Kinglake's " Crimean War," vol. i. chap. xvi.
† A demand which General Buell had made, quite as emphatically as his successor, and with an accurate prediction of the evils that would flow from its absence.

suppressing an angry message. Oftener he attempted to soften the phraseology. But in all of this there was a limit beyond which he could not go ; and when Rosecrans had pronounced certain statements of the department " a profound, grievous, cruel, and ungenerous official and personal wrong," the good offices of the Chief of Staff were no longer efficacious—the breach was irreparable. Thenceforward he could only strive to make victories in the field atone for the errors in council.

He regarded the army as vitally defective. We have already pointed out, in tracing the actions of its chief, the great mistake of retaining as commanders of the wings such incapables as A. M. McCook and T. L. Crittenden. Almost the first recommendation made by General Garfield was for their displacement. It is gratifying now to know that he was so little moved by popular prejudice, and so well able to perceive real ability beneath concealing misfortunes, that he urged upon Rosecrans to replace them by Irvin McDowell and Don Carlos Buell. With George H. Thomas already in command, with men like these as his associates, and with the energy and genius of Rosecrans to lead them, the Army of the Cumberland would have been the best officered army in the service of the nation. But Rosecrans was unwilling to adopt the suggestion—for a reason creditable to his kindness of heart, but not to his military character. Crittenden and McCook ought to be removed —of that he had no doubt, but—" he hated to injure two such good fellows." And so the " two good fellows " went on until Chickamauga.*

* To the above statement it should be added that General Garfield made the recommendation for the removal of Crittenden and McCook in the course of a discussion of the battle of Stone River, in which Rosecrans explicitly said that these officers had shown themselves incompetent in that engagement. Garfield did not take the ground that Buell and McDowell had approved themselves equal to the high commands they had formerly held, but, discussing this, he argued at length their masterly qualifications for im-

From the 4th of January to 24th of June General Rosecrans
lay at Murfreesboro. Through five months of this delay
General Garfield was with him. The War Department demanded an advance, and, when the spring opened, urged it
with unusual vehemence. General Rosecrans delayed, waiting
for cavalry, for re-inforcements, for Grant's movements before
Vicksburg, for the movements of the enemy, for the operations
of his generals. The Chief of Staff at first approved the delays,
till the army should be strengthened and massed, but long before the delaying officers were ready he was urging movement
with all of his power. He had established a secret service
system, then perhaps the most perfect in any of the Union
armies. From the intelligence it furnished he felt sure that
Bragg's force had been considerably reduced, and was now
greatly inferior to that of Rosecrans. As he subsequently said,
he refused to believe that this army, which defeated a superior
foe at Stone River, could not now move upon an inferior one
with reasonable prospects of success.

Finally, General Rosecrans formally asked his corps, division,
and calvary generals as to the propriety of a movement. With
singular unanimity, though for diverse reasons, they opposed it.
Out of seventeen generals, not one was in favor of an immediate
advance, and not one was even willing to put himself on record
as in favor of an early advance.

General Garfield collated the seventeen letters sent in from
the generals in reply to the questions of their commander, and
fairly reported their substance, coupled with a cogent argument
against them and in favor of an immediate movement. This
report we venture to pronounce the ablest military document
known to have been submitted by a Chief of Staff to his

portant subordinate positions, as well as the fact that this offer
of an opportunity to come out from the cloud under which they
rested would insure their gratitude and incite them to their very
best efforts.

superior during the war. General Garfield stood absolutely
alone, every general commanding troops having, as we have
seen, either openly opposed or failed to approve an advance.
But his statements were so clear and his arguments so forcible
that he carried conviction.

Twelve days after the reception of this report the army moved
—to the great dissatisfaction of its leading generals. One of
the three corps commanders, Major-General Thomas L. Crittenden, approached the Chief of Staff at the headquarters on
the morning of the advance : " It is understood, sir," he said,
" by the general officers of the army, that this movement is
your work. I wish you to understand that it is a rash and fatal
move, for which you will be held responsible."

This rash and fatal move was the Tullahoma campaign—a
campaign perfect in its conception, excellent in its general execution, and only hindered from resulting in the complete destruction of the opposing army by the delays which had too
long postponed its commencement. It might even yet have destroyed Bragg but for the terrible season of rains which set in
on the morning of the advance, and continued uninterruptedly
for the greater part of a month. With a week's earlier start it
would have ended the career of Bragg's army in the war.

There now sprang up renewed differences between General
Rosecrans and the War Department. In the general policy that
controlled the movements of the army Garfield heartily sympathized ; he had, in fact, aided to give shape to that policy.
But he had deplored his chief's testy manner of conducting his
defence to the complaints of the War Department, and did his
best to soften the asperities of the correspondence.

At last came the battle of Chickamauga. Such by this time
had come to be Garfield's influence, that he was nearly always
consulted and often followed. He wrote every order issued
that day—one only excepted. This he did rarely as an amanu-
ensis, but rather on the suggestions of his own judgment, after-

ward submitting what he had prepared to Rosecrans for approval or change. The one order which he did not write was
the fatal order to Wood which lost the battle. The meaning
was correct ; the words, however, did not clearly represent
what Rosecrans meant, and the division commander in question
so interpreted them as to destroy the right wing.

The general commanding and his Chief of Staff were caught
in the tide of the disaster and borne back toward Chattanooga.
The Chief of Staff was sent to communicate with Thomas,
while the general proceeded to prepare for the reception of the
routed army.

Such at least were the statements of the reports, and, in a
technical sense, they were true. It should never be forgotten,
however, in Garfield's praise, that it was on his own earnest
representations that he was sent—that, in fact, he rather procured permission to go to Thomas and so back into the battle,
than received orders to do so. He refused to believe that
Thomas was routed or the battle lost. He found the road en-
vironed with dangers ; some of his escort were killed, and they
all narrowly escaped death or capture. But he bore to Thomas
the first news that officer had received of the disaster on the
right, and gave the information on which he was able to extricate
his command. At seven o'clock that evening, under the personal supervision of General Gordon Granger and himself, a
shotted salute from a battery of six Napoleon guns was fired into
the woods after the last of the retreating assailants. They
were the last shots of the battle of Chickamauga, and what was
left of the Union Army was master of the field. For the time
the enemy evidently regarded himself as repulsed ; and Garfield said that night, and has always since maintained, that
there was no necessity for the immediate retreat on Rossville.

Practically, this was the close of General Garfield's military
career. A year before, while he was absent in the army, and
without any solicitation on his part, he had been elected to

Congress from the old Giddings district, in which he resided. He was now, after a few weeks' service with Rosecrans at Chattanooga, sent on to Washington as the bearer of despatches. He there learned of his promotion to a major-generalship of volunteers, "for gallant and meritorious conduct at the battle of Chickamauga." He might have retained this position in the army ; and the military capacity he had displayed, the high favor in which he was held by the Government, and the certainty of his assignment to important commands, seemed to augur a brilliant future. He was a poor man, too, and the major-general's salary was more than double- that of the Congressman. But on mature reflection he decided that the circumstances under which the people had elected him to Congress bound him up to an effort to obey their wishes. He was furthermore urged to enter Congress by the officers of the army, who looked to him for aid in procuring such military legislation as the country and the army required. Under the belief that the path of usefulness to the country lay in the direction in which his constituents pointed, he sacrificed what seemed to be his personal interests, and on the 5th of December, 1863, resigned his commission, after nearly three years' service.

General Garfield's military career was not of a nature to subject him to trials on a large scale. He approved himself a good independent commander in the small operations in the Sandy Valley. His campaign there opened our series of successes in the West ; and, though fought against superior forces, began with us the habit of victory. After that he was only a subordinate, but he always enjoyed the confidence of his immediate superiors, and of the department. As a chief of staff he was unrivalled. There, as elsewhere, he was ready to accept the gravest responsibilities in following his convictions. The bent of his mind was aggressive ; his judgment of purely military matters was good ; his papers on the Tullahoma campaign will stand a monument of his courage and his far-reaching, soldierly sagacity ; and his conduct at Chickamauga will never be forgotten by a nation of brave men.

---

## CHAPTER IX.

### GARFIELD AT CHICKAMAUGA.

THE foregoing chapter closes the extract from Whitelaw Reid's history of " Ohio in the War." As an appropriate pendant, the following letter from W. F. G. Shanks, which recently appeared in the New York *Tribune*, is added. Mr. Shanks was at the battle of Chickamauga as a correspondent of the New York *Herald :*

A good deal of surprised comment was made, during the sessions of the Chicago Convention, at the statesmanlike utterances and attitude of General Garfield before it, as though such might not have been expected. His moderation, his candor, his evident sincerity and earnestness, and his conciliatory and politic utterances are not new to the style and manner of the man. He has distinguished himself in the display of the same argumentative and diplomatic qualities on more than one occasion. In fact, General Garfield's military record is that of one who was at once warrior and statesman, equally brave in the field and sagacious in counsels affecting the policy, if not the military conduct, of the war.

One of the first incidents of his military career to bring him into general notice was not a feat of war, but of argument. In January, 1863, he became the Chief of Staff to Major General William S. Rosecrans, then in command of the Army of the Cumberland. How he came to be selected by Rosecrans the present writer does not remember, but it was soon after the battle of Stone River, in which the former chief was killed. Garfield was looked upon as about the only mature member of the staff, Rosecrans having a partiality for young and gallant spirits like Captain Charles Thompson, Major Bond, Colonel Mickler, Captain Hunter Brooke, Major Horace Porter, subsequently on Grant's staff, and Major Morton McMichael. Not that Garfield was much older than these, but he had a mature look always, and his mood was ever serious, as if there was in the peril of the Nation something more of personal concern and personal interest to him than to most of his associates. It was while Garfield was acting in this capacity under Rosecrans that Clement C. Vallandigham, of Ohio, banished to the South for his treasonable sentiments, was brought to Murfreesboro, Tenn., where the army lay, to be sent by a flag of truce, into the rebel lines, a few miles distant, at Tullahoma. When brought into camp, Vallandigham was taken, in the usual course of business, to Rosecrans's headquarters, and he and Garfield being acquaintances, it was natural that they should fall into conversation, and equally natural that the conversation should be in regard to the policy and conduct of the war in a political sense. The conversation was reported by a correspondent of the Cincinnati *Gazette*, who was present, and was copied into almost every paper of the country, both loyal and rebel, as a fine illustration of sound and argumentative views on both sides. The comments of the loyal papers were highly complimentary to General Garfield, and this brought him into particular notice. His last words with Vallandigham on the next morning, just as the latter was about to be escorted into the rebel lines, at once finely illustrated Garfield's quickness and neatness at repartee and that familiarity on his part with Shakespeare without which no education can be said to be complete. Vallandigham, on his appearance in the room at a very early hour of the morning, with an affectation of unconcern and light-heartedness which he could not have felt, threw himself into a tragic air, and in a mock heroic vein exclaimed, from *Romeo and Juliet ;*

> " Night's candles are burnt out, and jocund day
> Stands tiptoe on the misty mountain-tops."

Here he hesitated, when Garfield quickly but quietly finished the speech by adding, in a half aside, to the aide-de-camp in charge of the flag of truce escort, waiting to convey Vallandigham to the rebel lines :

" I must begone and live, or stay and die."

Vallandigham, however, overheard and caught the hidden meaning of the citation, and blushed scarlet as he made its application.

Later on, in the campaign of the Army of the Cumberland against Bragg at Chattanooga, Garfield again encountered a prominent Southern gentleman in argument as to the policy of the war. What Garfield said was a powerful plea, in advance, for the policy subsequently adopted of freeing and arming the slaves of the South. This was published in the Cincinnati *Gazette* about the last of August, 1863, and would be well worth reproducing as an illustration of the clear, forcible, and logical views of the then comparatively young politician on the great questions of the time. Like the interview with Vallandigham, the conversation was quoted all over the North and served to bring Garfield into further notice.

The first martial achievement of Garfield which attracted general attention was his conduct at Chickamauga, on the second day of that battle, September 20th, 1863. His conspicuous bravery on that occasion won for him the rank of major-general. As Chief of Staff, it was his duty to remain with General Rosecrans, and it happened that the latter had established his headquarters for the day in the rear of the right wing and centre, leaving General George H. Thomas to look personally to the direction of the left wing. McCook and Crittenden were commanders of the other two corps. Soon after the fog, which for the most of the morning enveloped the field and made manœuvring almost impossible, the rebels, under Longstreet, who had come from Lee's Virginia army to take part in this great contest, made a grand assault on the right and centre.  A division of Crittenden's corps was moving to the left at this juncture, and the gap in the line had not been filled by other troops when the attack was made.  The rebels penetrated far to the rear of the Union line at this point, and turned and drove back the right of Thomas's forces and the left of the other two corps. The latter were eventually routed, driven across a ridge of hills to roads leading into Chattanooga, toward which they retreated in dreadful disorder and panic.  Thomas, however, held his ground, withdrawing his right only a little.  In the tumult of the defeat of the right and centre, McCook, Crittenden, and Rosecrans, with their staff officers, were driven beyond the ridge named, and they too started for Chattanooga, not knowing how Thomas had fared.  Garfield followed his commander about half way to Chattanooga, but refused to go any farther, and accompanied only by his orderly and Captain William B. Gaw, of the Engineers, who offered to act as his guide, he rode through Rossville Gap in the mountain range, and pushed southward again in search of General Thomas, the firing of whose guns, indicating that there was a brisk fight still going on, could be distinctly heard.  Garfield on this occasion literally followed the Napoleonic maxim for the guidance of his generals : '' March in the direction of the heaviest firing.''

At the time he made this attempt the road by which Garfield expected to reach General Thomas was under cover of the sharp-shooters and advance guards of the rebels, who were pushing forward to secure possession of the road and thereby cut off Thomas's line of retreat.  Garfield did not know of their presence there until admonished of it by the sharp fire of the enemy. The horses of both Garfield and Gaw were shot at the first fire, and Garfield's orderly was wounded.  They were compelled to swerve from the beaten road and take to the fields and mountain-side.  Gaw was perfectly familiar with the topography, and following his guidance Garfield ran the gauntlet of the rebel line and finally reached General Thomas in safety.

He reached the " Rock of Chickamauga " just after the repulse of the enemy in a formidable assault all along Thomas's line, which the rebels enveloped on both flanks. He found Thomas and his staff, General Gordon Granger, General James B. Steedman, General Wood, and others grouped in a hollow of an open field, a depression just sufficient to protect them from the rebel fire. It is all a myth about General Thomas standing on a big rock, his breast thrown out in defiant attitude, with a look of scorn on his face. There were no rocks on the field ; none nearer than Lookout Mountain, ten miles away. The fact was that Thomas was very glad of the security afforded by the depression in the field, and his look was one of much concern and anxiety, and everybody knew that he was heartily wishing it was nightfall, that he might slip away and get back to Chattanooga. The historic scene was sketched shortly after, and a very accurate painting of it, by Walker, hangs on the walls of General J. Watts DePeyster, in this city. There were several dead trees still standing, and numbers of those present in the group did not disdain their shelter, so near were the rebel marksmen, posted high in the branches of trees for the purpose of firing on the group.

When Garfield reached Thomas, he at once gave the latter a brief account of the disaster to the right and centre, and heard from General Thomas a statement of his own situation and intention. This conversation was cut short by another assault of the rebel lines. It was made with great force and in great desperation, the rebels evidently foreseeing that if repulsed they could not get their troops in position for still another attack before the sun went down. The fire lasted furiously for half an hour, when the rebels again broke and abandoned the assault. During all this fight General Garfield quietly sat on the ground, behind one of the dead trees alluded to, and coolly indited a dispatch to General Rosecrans, detailing the situation. While he sat there, and during the heaviest of the firing, a white dove, after hovering around and above for several minutes, finally settled on the topmost perch of the tree above Garfield's head. Here it remained during the heat of the fight, and when the musketry ceased it flew away to the North. Garfield's attention and that of General Wood was called to the bird. The latter said nothing, but went on writing. Wood simply said in reply: " Good omen of peace." Garfield having finished his dispatch, sent it by an officer, and himself remained on the field with General Thomas until the retreat was effected the same night to Chattanooga.

---

## CHAPTER X.

### FIRST TERM IN CONGRESS.

In the summer of 1862, when everybody supposed the war was going to end in a few months, a number of officers who had gained distinction in the field were taken up at home and elected to Congress. Among them was General Garfield, who was nominated by the Republicans of Joshua R. Giddings's old district while with his brigade in Kentucky. He had no knowledge of any such movement in his behalf, and when he accepted the nomination, he did so in the belief that the rebellion would be subdued before he would be called upon to take his seat in the House in December, 1863. His nomination was partly the result of his military fame and partly of a desire on the part of the friends of Giddings to defeat his successor, John Hutchins, who had pushed him out of Congress four years before. Garfield's popularity made him the most available man in the district for this purpose. He was elected by a large majority.

He continued his military service up to the day of the meeting of Congress. Even then he seriously thought of resigning his position as a Representative rather than his Major-General's commission, and would have done so had not Lincoln urged him to enter Congress. He has often expressed regret that he did not fight the war through. Had he done so, he would no doubt have ranked at its close among the foremost of the victorious Generals of the Republic, for he displayed in his Sandy Valley campaign and at the battle of Chickamauga the highest qualities of generalship. A brilliant opening awated him in the Army of the Cumberland. General Thomas wanted him to take command of a corps. President Lincoln told him he greatly needed the influence in the House of one who had had practical military experience to push through the needed war legislation. He yielded, and on the 5th of December, 1863, gave up his generalship and took his seat in the House.

He was appointed on the Military Committee, under the chairmanship of General Schenck, and was of great service in carrying through the measures which recruited the armies during the closing years of the war. Schenck had just come out of the army with a shattered right arm and a Major-General's epaulets. The two Ohio soldiers became fast friends and coworkers. They took lodgings in the same house, ate at the same table, and devoted their combined energies to carrying through Congress such practical legislation as their experience in the field had shown was needed to fill up the wasted ranks and increase the efficiency of the forces engaged in the suppression of the rebellion. Garfield opposed the continuance of the commutation law, which allowed men drafted to escape service by paying three hundred dollars, or by pleading a variety of disabilities. A draft of 200,000 had produced only 13,000 men for actual service. President Lincoln went to the Capitol and told the Military Committee that this law must be repealed or the armies drawn back and placed upon the defensive. The political campaign of 1864 was at hand, and members of Congress were afraid of the effect of a vigorous draft upon the fortunes of the Republican Party. One of the committee reminded Lincoln that his own re-election was pending, and that of all the members of the House, and that the unpopularity of a draft which could not be evaded might defeat them all. Lincoln replied, with a solemnity of manner unusual with him : " It is not necessary that I should be re elected, or that the members of this Congress should be re-elected, but it is necessary that the rebellion should be suppressed, and the Union restored. Give me the men I ask, and I will end the war with another year ; refuse, and I must withdraw our armies from Atlanta and from the march to Richmond." General Garfield warmly supported the President ; the timidity of Congress was overcome ; the draft was vigorously enforced, and the rebellion was crushed within the time Lincoln promised.

General Garfield soon took rank in the House as a ready and forcible debater, a hard worker, and a diligent, practical legislator. His superior knowledge used to offend some of his less learned colleagues at first. They thought him bookish and pedantic, until they found how solid and useful was his store of knowledge, and how pertinent to the business in hand were the drafts he made upon it. His genial personal ways soon made him many warm friends in Congress. The men of brains in both houses and in the departments were not long in discovering that here was a fresh, strong intellectual force that was destined to make its mark upon the politics of the country. They sought his acquaintance, and before he had been long in Washington he had the advantage of the best society of the capital.

In the summer of 1864, a breach occurred between the President and some of the most radical of the Republican leaders in Congress over the question of the reconstruction of the States of Arkansas and Louisiana. Congress passed a bill providing for the organization of loyal governments within the Union lines of these States, but Lincoln vetoed it and appointed military Governors. Senator Ben Wade, of Ohio, and Representative Henry Winter Davis, of Maryland, united, in a letter to the New York *Tribune*, sharply criticising the President for defeating the will of Congress. This letter became known as the Wade-Davis manifesto, and created a great sensation in political circles. The story got about in the Nineteenth District that General Garfield had expressed sympathy with the position of Wade and Davis. His constituents condemned the document, and were strongly disposed to set him aside and nominate another man for Congress. When the convention met the feeling against Garfield was so pronounced that he regarded his re-nomination as hopeless. He was called upon to explain his course. He went upon the platform and everybody expected something in the nature of an apology, but he boldly defended his position, approved the manifesto, justified Wade, and said he had nothing to retract and could not change his honest convictions for the sake of a seat in Congress. He had great respect, he said, for the opinions of his constituents, but greater regard for his own. If he could serve them as an independent Representative, acting on his own judgment and conscience, he would be glad to do so, but if not, he did not want their nomination ; he would prefer to be an independent private citizen. Probably no man ever talked in that way before or since to a body of men who held his political fate in their hands. Leaving the platform, he strode out of the hall and down the stairs, supposing that he had effectually cut his own throat. Scarcely had he disappeared when one of the youngest delegates sprang up and said : " The man who has the courage to face a convention like that deserves a nomination. I move that General Garfield be nominated by acclamation." The motion was carried with a shout which reached the ears of the Congressman and arrested him on the sidewalk as he was returning to the hotel. He was re-elected by a majority of over 12,000.

## CHAPTER XI.

### IN CONGRESS—1865 TO 1867.

AT the beginning of the Thirty-ninth Congress in December, 1865, General Garfield asked Speaker Colfax to transfer him from the Committee on Military Affairs to that of Ways and Means, saying that in the near future financial questions would occupy the attention of the country and he desired to be in a position to study them carefully in advance. The Military Committee having on its hands the work of reorganizing the Regular Army on a peace basis, was the more important of the two at the time, but Garfield foresaw the storm of agitation and delusion concerning the debt and the currency which was soon to break upon the country, and wisely prepared to meet it. He began a long and severe course of study, ransacking the Congressional Library for works that threw light on the experience of other countries, and that gave the ideas of the thinkers and statesmen of all nations on these subjects. As he read he made copious notes, which were of great service to him in after years. Most of all he studied the history of the long suspension of specie payments in Great Britain during and after the Napoleonic wars. He used to sit at his library-table until long after midnight, surrounded by volumes of Parliamentary reports and debates. In them he found every dishonest theory and wild delusion respecting the public debt and paper money which was afterward advanced in this country as new and beneficial discoveries. The Bullion Report of Horner and Huskisson was like a flood of light to him. He used to characterize it as the bulwark of sound currency ideas for this whole century. It demonstrated by facts too plain for controversy that gold had not risen during the suspension, but was still the measure of values, though out of use as currency, and that it was paper which went up and down. In Sir Robert Peel's manly avowal in 1820 that Horner had been right in 1810 and he wrong, and in his subsequent sturdy defence of specie payments, he found much instructive material which he afterward used to good effect in the battles he led against inflation and repudiation.

Then he went back to study the history of the Continental currency, and still further back to the French assignats and the George Law scheme, and afterward passed down the line of early American statesmen, gathering their wisdom to reinforce his belief that the precious metals were the only trustworthy standards of value. All this time there was not a ripple of financial agitation in Congress. The public mind was wholly occupied with the new Constitutional Amendments and the legislation for reconstructing the Rebel States. In the passage of those amendments and that legislation he bore a prominent part, but he never relaxed his financial studies. They gave him the firm basis of fact and conviction which was like a rock under his feet in all the turbulent agitation of the following years. He forged from them a sharp sword to slash the wind-bag paper-money schemes of demagogues and fanatics, and to cut to pieces the many projects which arose for repudiating the obligations of the nation to its creditors.

His membership of the Ways and Means opened up a line of congenial work in connection with the tariff and the system of internal revenue taxation. These two sources of income, gauged to the needs of the war, had to be changed to conform to the conditions of peace. In the course of this work and of the investigations which accompanied it, he reached a conclusion upon the tariff question from which he has never departed since—namely, that whatever may be the truth or falsity of abstract theories about free trade, the interests of the United States require a moderate protective system. He made a speech in which he expressed his views on this subject very clearly. Subsequent experience and study has shown him no occasion for modifying those views. In March, 1866, he made his first speech on the currency question, and took strong ground in favor of a speedy return to specie payments. " On the one side," he said, " it is proposed to return to solid and honest values ; on the other to float on the boundless and shoreless sea of paper money, with all its dishonesty and broken pledges. I, for one, am unwilling that my name shall be linked to the fate of a paper currency. I believe that any party which commits itself to paper money will go down amid the general disaster, covered with the curses of a ruined people." In that speech he traced the history of suspension in England and drew from it a warning for this country which few were disposed to heed at the time.

General Garfield's third nominaton, in 1866 was not accomplished without resistance. Some of the iron-workers in the southern part of his district were dissatisfied because he was not willing to go to the extreme length of an almost prohibitive tariff on their products. They brought forward as their candidate the old member John Hutchins, whose place Garfield had taken four years before, and made an active canvass of the district, flooding it with circulars attacking Garfield's record in Congress, and charging him, without evidence, with being a free trader. They elected a small minority of the delegates to the nominating convention, but their strength was not great enough to make a showing against a movement to renominate Garfield by acclamation. In after-years, when the crash of 1873 had shown the folly of over-stimulating manufactures by exorbitant tariffs, these same iron-masters became convinced that he was their best friend.

In the summer of 1867 General Garfield went to Europe, and made a rapid tour through Great Britain and the Continent. His health failed under the pressure of too much brain-work, and he took this means of recuperating. This was the only year since he entered public life that he had been absent from a political campaign. He returned late in the fall to find that Pendletonism—a demand for the payment of the bonded debt in irredeemable greenback notes—had run rampant in Ohio, and had taken possession of the Republican Party as well as of the Democracy. A reception was given him at Jefferson, in his district, which assumed the form of a public meeting. He was told that he had better say nothing about his financial views, for his constituents had made up their minds that the bonds ought to be redeemed in greenbacks. He made a speech in which he told his friends plainly that they were deluded, that there could be no honest money not redeemable in coin and no honest payment of the debt could be made save in coin, and that as long as he was their representative he should stand on that ground, whatever might be their views. The speech produced a deep impression throughout the district. The next June the National Republican Convention took sound ground upon the debt and currency questions, and most Republicans who had been carried away by Pendletonism grew ashamed of their folly.

In the Fortieth Congress General Garfield was put back upon the Military Committee and made its chairman. The work was hardly to his taste but there was plenty of it to do, and he engaged in it with his usual energy. It consisted mainly in tying up the loose threads of the war, examining the claims for pay and bounty of irregular military organizations and of officers and men in whose records there were technical errors. General Garfield set on foot a thorough examination of the condition of the army, the organization and efficiency of the staff and line, and sought to correct by legislation the errors of routine and tradition, and to modernize the service. He prepared a report which has since been a standard work in military circles.

The time for taking the decennial census was at hand, and on his motion a special committee was raised to prepare the needed legislation. Although second on the committee, he was its acting chairman. The committee devoted six weeks to the study of the subject, and prepared a bill which considerably enlarged the field of statistics to be covered by the census, and sought to make the returns far more valuable than before to the political economist and the sociologist. The bill passed the House but failed in the Senate, and the census of 1870 was taken under the old law. Ten years later, however, the Garfield bill was revived, and with a few modifications made by the Commissioner of the Census, became the law for the census of 1880.

General Garfield got a bill through for the establishment of a National Bureau of Education, in response to a report of the National Teachers' Association. This bureau is his own creation, and he had to defend it for many years against the assaults of the weak-government people, who did not want any new function added to the Federal Government. At last, however, its utility was so fully demonstrated that the attacks ceased.

In 1868 Garfield was renominated without opposition, and chosen a fourth time to represent his district.

----

## CHAPTER XII.

### IN CONGRESS—1869–1875.

On the organization of the Forty-first Congress, in December, 1869, General Garfield was made chairman of the Committee on Banking and Currency. The inflation movement was rapidly gathering force in the country, and men of both parties in Congress were swept into it by fear of their constituents. A cry was set up that times were getting hard because there was not money enough to do the business of the people. The West, particularly, clamored for more currency. The necessary shrinkage from war prices was taken as a proof of a dearth of circulating medium. False tabular statements were circulated, making a contrast between the amount of currency in circulation in 1865 and 1869. General Garfield led the opposition to inflation. Seeing that what the people needed to lead them to right conclusions was information, he studied the situation with great care and his speeches bristled with facts which could not be controverted. Finally, after a long fight in his committee with the men who wanted to throw out a flood of new greenbacks, he brought in and carried through Congress, a bill allowing an addition of fifty-four millions to the national bank circulation and giving preference in the assignment of the new issue to the States which had less than their quota of the old circulation. This measure was a stunning blow to the inflation movement. The new issue was not all taken up for four years, and during all that time it was a sufficient answer to all demands for "more money" to call attention to the fact that there was currency waiting in the Treasury for any one who would organize a bank. Soon after the fifty-four millions were applied for national banking was made perfectly free. Then the inflationists were forced to change their ground, assault the banks, and claim that it was greenbacks which were to bless the country, and make people rich, and no other kind of paper money. The New York gold panic came during General Garfield's chairmanship of the Banking Committee. Under orders of the House, he conducted with great sagacity and thoroughness an investigation which exposed all the secrets of the gold gamblers' plot which culminated in "Black Friday". He made a report which was a complete history of the affair, and the lesson he drew from it was that the only certain remedy against the recurrence of such transactions was to be found in the resumption of specie payments. Pushing his researches into financial subjects, and defending on all occasions the principle that the only safe and sound currency was one based upon coin, he became the recognized leader of the honest-money party in the House and the most potent single factor in the opposition to inflation.   He helped work up the bill to strengthen the public credit, which failed to get through during the closing days of Johnson's administration, but was passed as soon as Grant came in and was the first measure to which the new President put his signature.   This bill committed Congress fully to the payment of the public debt in coin and was the fortress around which the financial battle raged in subsequent years.   Thaddeus Stevens, deluded in his old age by the sophistries concerning the greenbacks, deserted the hard-money side in the struggle over the bill, declared that the bonds were payable in greenbacks, and denied that he had taken other ground in his advocacy of the original five-twenty bond bill in 1862.   General Garfield made an analysis of the history of the law and showed that in the debate over the bill Stevens said six times that the bonds were payable in coin ; that everybody so understood the contract at the time ; that the Secretary of the Treasury so advertised the bonds ; that the people bought them with the promise that they were to be so paid.   Garfield's speech furnished the rallying ground for the opponents of the greenback theory.   Day after day the New York *Tribune* kept a paragraph standing in its editorial columns challenging a refutation of the facts he had presented. From the strong bulwark of those facts a successful appeal was made to the conscience of the American people.

In December, 1871, General Garfield was placed at the head of the important Committee on Appropriations, a position which made him the leader of the majority side of the House.   With his old habit of doing everything he undertook with the utmost thoroughness, he made a laborious study of the whole history of appropriation bills in this country and of the English budget system.   Especially did he seek to discover the philosophic law back of all legislation, if one existed, governing the return of a nation from the high plane of war expenditures to the normal level of peace. He found that the experience of both England and this country, in the past, showed that it took a period after the close of a war about twice as long as the war itself to get upon a peace basis of expenditures.

He made a speech in which he predicted that by the end of 1876 Congress would reach the limit of the lowest possible reduction of expenditures, and that from that time forward there would be a gradual increase under the conditions of peace, in a ratio which he stated in proportion to the growth of population and the settlement of new territory. About a year ago, in an article on " Appropriations and Missappropriations," in the *North American Review*, he quoted his prediction of 1871, and showed that it had come true within a few months of the time then fixed, and within a small percentage of the increase after that date which he had stated. That speech of 1871 was the first regular budget speech, explaining thoroughly the needs of all departments of the Government, and the means for meeting them, which had ever been made in the House. Thereafter, General Garfield made such a speech regularly every year on introducing the General Appropriation Bill, and his successors in the chairmanship of the committee have continued the custom.

General Garfield found a great deal of looseness and confusion in the practice concerning estimates and appropriations. Unexpended balances were lying in the Treasury, amounting to $130,000,000, beyond the supervision of Congress and subject to the drafts of Government officers. There were besides what were called permanent appropriations, which ran on from year to year without any legislation. Garfield instituted a sweeping reform. He got laws passed covering all old balances back into the Treasury, making all appropriations expire at the end of the fiscal year for which made, unless needed to carry out contracts, and covering in all appropriations at the end of every second year. At the same time he required the Executive Departments to itemize their estimates of the money needed to run the Government much more fully than had been done before, so that Congress could know just how every dollar it voted was to be expended.

All this time he was a rigid but intelligent economist. He was often forced to make himself unpopular by opposing the measures of his fellow-members involving unwise expenditures of public money. He was the faithful guardian of the Treasury, but he pursued no penny-wise policy. The needs of the country and the requirements of an efficient administration were fully appreciated, and the irresponsible efforts of the Democrats to cripple the Government by a reckless cutting down of its supplies were successfully resisted. The total expenses of the Government were steadily reduced under his management but no branch of the public service had its efficiency impaired by such reduction.

The four years of his chairmanship of appropriations were years of close and unremitting labor. He worked habitually fifteen hours a day. In addition to the demands of his own department of legislation, he took part in all the general work of the House, bore a leading part in all the debates involving the principles of the Republican Party, fought without cessation a brave battle against inflation and repudiation, and omitted no opportunity to aid in educating the public mind to a comprehension of the importance of returning to specie payments.

## CHAPTER XIII.

### A CAMPAIGN OF SLANDER.

FIVE times had General Garfield been chosen to represent the old Giddings district without serious opposition in his own party, and without a breath of suspicion being cast upon his personal integrity. With one exception, all his nominations had been made by acclamation. In his sixth canvass, however, a storm of calumny broke upon him. A concerted attack was made upon him for the purpose, if possible, of defeating him in the Convention, and failing in that, to beat him at the polls. He was charged with bribery and corruption in connection with the Crédit Mobilier affair and the De Golyer pavement contract, and with responsibility for the Salary Grab. A few Liberal Republicans of 1872 led the attack and the Democrats supported them. The district was soon broadcast with printed sheets traducing him. An extra sheet of the New York *Sun*, devoted to assailing and misrepresenting his record, was printed and sent in enormous numbers to the district. So many copies were received in the town of Painesville alone that a dray was loaded with them. Wherever Garfield went on his canvass of his district, he found the sheets in everybody's hand. He met the charges in a bold, straightforward way, published a pamphlet, reviewing the testimony against him, showed that the only evidence connecting him with the Crédit Mobilier stock was the unsupported and self-contradicted testimony of Oakes Ames, who had himself sworn at the beginning of the investigation that Garfield had none of the stock ; that in the pavement business he had earned and received a fee, as any other lawyer might have done, in a matter which was not before Congress nor likely to come there ; and that he opposed the Salary Grab persistently, and only voted at the last for the appropriation bill containing it when the alternative was its passage or an extra session, with all its expense and its disturbance to business ; and that he had refused to receive the extra pay, and had so fixed it in the Treasury that neither himself nor his heirs could ever draw it.

In the Convention, General Garfield was nominated by a majority of three to one, and the opposition to him did not bring forward a candidate, but merely cast blank votes. His enemies then took their charges before the people. They nominated a second Republican candidate—a Methodist presiding elder, well-known and highly esteemed throughout the district, hoping to defeat the regular nominee. General Garfield met the charges against him before the jury of his constituents. He visited all parts of the district, speaking day and night at township meetings. The verdict of the election was a complete vindication of his character and actions. It was the year of the great Republican back-set. The Republicans lost every Northern State, from Massachusetts to Illinois. Governor Noyes, their soldier-candidate for re-election in Ohio, was beaten. Congressional districts that had gone Republican ever since the party was formed deserted to the Democracy. The adjoining district to Garfield's, which had given unbroken Republican majorities of from 4000 to 7000, elected a Democrat. All the general influences which produced this reaction were, of course, at work in Garfield's district, in addition to the personal charges against him and the special efforts made to defeat him. He held his district, however. It is important to notice the figures of the vote, for it has been claimed that the district rebuked him by cutting down his majority heavily. The fact is, his majority was greater than that of the State ticket, greater than Governor Noyes's. The total Republican vote fell off, but not so much as in many other districts. Nothing was accomplished by the campaign of mud-slinging. The honest, intelligent farmers of the Nineteenth District heard the evidence on both sides and refused to believe that they had been represented for twelve years by a rascal. They declined to withdraw their confidence from General Garfield. The vote, as contrasted with that of 1872, was as follows :

In 1872, Garfield's vote for Congress was 19,189 ; opposition vote, 8254, Garfield's majority, 10,935. State ticket : Republican candidate for Secretary of State, 19,202 ; Democratic candidate, 8313. Republican majority, 10,889. In 1874, Garfield's vote for Congress was 12,591 ; opposition vote, 6245, Garfield's majority, 6346 ; Noyes's (Rep.) vote for Governor, 12,543 ; Allen's (Dem.) vote for Governor, 6021 ; Noyes's majority 6524 ; Garfield's vote more than Noyes's, 47. Garfield's falling off from 1872, 6598 ; Noyes's falling off from vote for State ticket in 1872, 6659. Garfield's decrease less than Noyes's, 61.

These figures are a perfect refutation of the charge that General Garfield's district gave any credence to the slanders so widely circulated against him. His constituents fully vindicated him, and in 1876 and 1878 nominated him by acclamation and elected him by increased majorities.

* * *

## CHAPTER XIV.

### LEADING THE MINORITY.

THE result of the elections of 1874 was to give the Democrats control of the House which met in December, 1875. Hitherto the legislative work of General Garfield had been constructive. The impress of his thought, study, and genius had been given to all the measures for closing the war, restoring popular government in the South, conferring suffrage and citizenship on the emancipated slaves, reorganizing the army, funding the national debt, and placing the currency on a sound basis. Now he was

called upon to defend this work against the assaults of the party
which step by step had opposed its accomplishment, and which
by the aid of the solid support of the late rebel element had
gained power in Congress.    One of the first movements of the
Democrats was for universal amnesty.    Mr. Blaine offered an
amendment to their bill excluding Jefferson Davis.    Then followed the famous debate about the treatment of prisoners of
war, opened by Blaine's dashing attack on Hill, continued by
Hill's reply defending the South, and charging that Confederates had been starved in Northern prisons, and closing with
Garfield's response to Hill.    Garfield, by a brilliant stroke of
parliamentary strategy, forced a Democrat to testify to the falsity of Hill's charge.    He said that the Elmira, New York, district, where was located during the war the principal prison for
captured rebels, was represented in the House by a Democrat.
He did not know him, but he was willing to rest his case wholly
on his testimony.    He called upon the member from Elmira to
inform the House whether the good people of his city had permitted the captured Confederate soldiers in their midst to suffer
for want of food.    The gentleman thus appealed to rose
promptly and said that to his knowledge the prisoners had received exactly the same rations as the Union soldiers guarding
them.    While this statement was being made, a telegraphic dispatch was handed to General Garfield.    Holding it up he said,
" The lightnings of heaven are aiding me in this controversy."
The dispatch was from General Elwell, of Cleveland, who had
been the quartermaster at the Elmira prison, and who telegraphed that the rations issued to the rebel prisoners were in
quantity and quality exactly the same as those issued to their
guards.    Garfield's speech killed the Democrats' bill.    They
withdrew it rather than risk a vote.

Mr. Blaine's transfer to the Senate soon after this debate left
Garfield the recognized leader of the Republicans in the House.
Mr. Kerr, the Democratic Speaker, died in the midst of his term,

and in the election for his successor General Garfield received the unanimous Republican vote. All his party associates turned to him with one accord as the man best fitted by experience, talent, and judgment to lead them. Soon after, in August, 1876, came the dispute with Lamar, in which Garfield's ability as an orator and a party chief shone with new brilliancy. Lamar was the greatest orator the Democrats had, and was selected by them to make a key-note campaign speech. In order to prevent, if possible, an effective reply, this effort was postponed to the end of the session. Four days before the adjournment Lamar got the floor and delivered the speech so long prepared. It was a sharp attack upon the Republican party, an appeal for sympathy for the " oppressed South," and an argument to show that peace and prosperity could come only through Democratic rule. General Garfield took notes of the speech. All his colleagues insisted that he alone was competent to break the force of Lamar's masterly effort. This speech is usually accounted the greatest of his life. It created a furor in the House. All business was suspended for ten minutes after he finished, so great was the excitement. One hundred thousand copies of the speech were subscribed for at once by members who wanted to circulate it in their districts, and during the campaign over a million copies were distributed. It contributed powerfully to the success of the Republican party in the Presidential campaign of that year.

After the election arose the dispute about the count of the votes of South Carolina, Florida, and Louisiana. President Grant telegraphed to General Garfield under date of November 10th, as follows : " I would be gratified if you would go to New Orleans and remain until the vote of Louisiana is counted. Governor Kellogg requests that reliable witnesses be sent to see that the canvass of the vote is a fair one. U. S. GRANT."

Garfield went to Washington, consulted with the President, and then proceeded to New Orleans in company with John Sherman, Stanley Matthews, and a number of other prominent Republicans. The Democratic National Committee had already dispatched a committee there to look after the interests of their party. Neither in the newspapers at the time, nor in the subsequent report of the Potter Committee, was there any charge of unfairness brought against General Garfield on account of his actions in Louisiana. The special work was assigned him of taking up the official testimony in relation to the Parish of West Feliciana and reporting upon it. So conscientious was he in the matter that he was not content with the written testimony, but sent for the witnesses themselves and examined them personally, in order to satisfy himself of their credibility. He wrote a full account of the conduct of the campaign and election in West Feliciana which was embodied in Sherman's letter to President Grant. While on his way to Washington, returning from New Orleans, he was again chosen by the unanimous vote of the Republicans of the House as their candidate for Speaker.

General Garfield opposed the Electoral Commission bill. In common with many of the best constitutional lawyers in the country, he held that the terms of the Constitution and the practice of the first forty years after its adoption made it the duty of the Vice-President to count the Electoral votes, Congress being present as official witnesses, and not as participants in the transaction. He did not object to a commission as a mere committee to examine and report upon the facts, but he maintained that it could have no judicial authority. In support of his position he made a strong legal argument to the House. In spite of his opposition to the commission scheme, when the bill passed he was selected as a member of the tribunal. The Republicans of the House were to have two members. They met in caucus, and were about to ballot, when Mr. McCreary, of Iowa, said that there was one name on which they were all agreed, and which need not be submitted to the formality of a vote—that of James A. Garfield. Garfield was chosen by acclamation. The second Commissioner was George F. Hoar, of Massachusetts, who afterward presided over the Chicago Convention, which nominated General Garfield for the Presidency.

As a member of the Electoral Commission, General Garfield delivered two opinions, in which he brought out with great clearness the point that the Constitution places in the hands of the Legislatures of the States the power of determining how their Electors shall be chosen, and that Congress had no right to go behind the final decision of a State. If there was nothing in the Constitution or laws of a State touching the matter, its legislature could appoint Electors, as Vermont had done after her admission to the Union. This position, although in accord with the unbroken practice and the long line of constitutional authorities from the foundation of the Government, was antagonized by the Democrats, who tried to make Congress a great returning board, to canvass the returns of the election and take testimony as to the fairness of the action of local boards and State authorities.

Immediately after President Hayes's inauguration the Republicans in the Ohio Legislature desired to elect General Garfield to the United States Senate in place of John Sherman, who had resigned his seat to enter the Cabinet. Mr. Hayes made a personal appeal to him to decline to be a candidate and remain in the House to lead the Republicans in support of the Administration. General Garfield acceded, in the belief that his services would be of more value to the party in the House than in the Senate, and withdrew his name from the canvass, greatly to the disappointment of his friends in Ohio, who had already obtained pledges of the support of a large majority of the Republican members of the Legislature.

When Congress met in December, 1877, the reaction against Hayes, on account of his Southern policy, was in full force, and there was imminent danger of a split in the Republican Party on this question which would cripple if not destroy it. General Garfield threw himself into the breach as a pacificator, to keep the party together. He saw that if Republicans quarrelled among themselves in the face of a united enemy, they could have no hope of future success. He prevented by his influence the holding of caucuses which would develop antagonisms and lead to bitter debates, and by his "Louisiana Pacification Speech," threw oil on the troubled waters. With rare sagacity and judgment, he succeeded in preventing a public outbreak of the feeling against the adminstration until the Potter Committee was raised by the Democrats to reopen the Electoral dispute and try the President's title. That committee united the Republicans like a closed fist. They rallied as one man to the defence of the President's right to be President. Mr. Hayes's subsequent conduct in upholding the election laws by his vetoes and in courageously asserting Republican doctrine in regard to the supremacy of the national authority, cemented the party by the strong tie of principle and all old controversies within itself were soon forgotten.

In the session of 1878, General Garfield led the long struggle in defence of the resumption act, which was assailed by the Democrats with a vigor born of desperation. His speech in support of the law was accepted by Republicans throughout the country as the financial gospel of the time. He also made a remarkable speech on the tariff question, in opposition to Wood's bill, which sought to break down the protective system.

During the extra session of 1879, forced by the Democrats, for the purpose of bringing the issue of the repeal of the Federal election laws prominently before the country, General Garfield led the Republican minority with consummate tact and judgment. The plan of the Democrats was to open the debate with a general attack on the Republican Party in order to throw their adversaries upon the defensive as apologists for the course of their party. McMahon, of Ohio, was selected to make the opening speech. Garfield did not wait for him to make his argument, but securing the floor ahead of him, delivered his famous " Revolution in Congress " speech, in which he attacked the Democrats with such vigor and exposed with so much force their scheme for withholding appropriations for the support of the Government, to compel the President to sign their political measures, that they were thrown into confusion, and instead of taking the offensive, were obliged to resort to a weak, defensive campaign. Driven from position to position by successive vetoes and by the persistent assaults of the Republican minority, they ended with a ridiculous fiasco. Instead of refusing $45,000,000 of appropriations, as they threatened at the beginning, they ended by appropriating $44,600,000 of the amount, leaving only $400,000 unprovided for.

Last winter the Democrats recommenced the fight, but in a feeble, disheartened way. They set out to refuse all pay to the United States Marshals unless the President would let them wipe out the election laws. General Garfield met them with a powerful speech on " Nullification in Congress," in which he showed that while it was clearly the foremost duty of the law-makers in Congress to obey the laws, the Democrats had become leaders in an attempt to disobey them and break them down.

General Garfield's last work in Congress was a report on the Tucker Tariff Bill. An attempt was made by an advertising agency in New York last spring to prejudice the press of the country against him by making him appear as the friend of the paper-makers' monopoly, because he opposed the repeal of the tariff on paper pulp. The paper-makers wanted the duty abolished and managed to make the news-papers believe that it alone was the cause of the high price of paper. General Garfield investigated the matter with his accustomed thoroughness, and found that when it cost seven cents to make a pound of paper, the value of the pulp was only one cent, and as the duty was twenty per cent., the difference it made in the cost of a pound of paper, was only four-tenths of a cent. The manufacturers had nearly doubled the price of paper and were pretending that this trifling duty was the cause of their exorbitant demands. General Garfield favored the reduction of the pulp tariff to ten per cent, but was not willing to break down an important industry and depart from the protective system in the case of a single article by repealing it altogether.

In January, 1880, General Garfield was chosen to the Senate by the Legislature of Ohio for the term of six years beginning March 4th, 1881. He received the unanimous vote of the Republican caucus, an honor never before conferred upon a citizen of Ohio by any party. The Republicans of his State with one accord demanded his promotion to the upper house of Congress, as a fitting reward for his long and faithful service in the lower branch, but the Republicans of the nation soon after selected him for a still greater promotion, and made him their candidate for the Presidency.

## CHAPTER XV.

### NOMINATED FOR PRESIDENT.

GENERAL GARFIELD went to the Republican National Convention at Chicago as a delegate at large from the State of Ohio. His great experience and prominence in national politics made him very naturally the leader of the delegation. Ohio had agreed to present the name of General Sherman to the convention as its candidate for President. General Garfield entered heartily into the Sherman movement, and labored earnestly for the success of the candidate of his State. His speech, presenting Sherman's name was universally applauded as a model of dignified oratory, and as a timely effort to prevent the sharp differences of feeling in the convention from weakening the party in the approaching campaign.   His wise utterances in favor of harmony were in such decided contrast to the heated declamation indulged in by many partisans of other candidates that the convention instinctively turned to him as the peacemaker who could bring harmony out of the troubled sea of contention.   His short speeches on questions arising before the convention during its long and turbulent session were all couched in the same vein of wise moderation, while adhering firmly to the principle of district representation and the right of every individual delegate to cast his own vote.

When the balloting began, a single delegate from Pennsylvania voted for Garfield.   No attention was paid to this vote, which was thought to be a mere eccentricity on the part of the man who cast it.   Later on a second Pennsylvania delegate joined the solitary Garfield man.   So the balloting continued, the fight being a triangular one, between Grant, Blaine and Sherman, with Washburne, Edmunds, and Windom in the field, ready for possible compromises.   General Garfield's plan, as the leader of the Sherman forces, was to keep his candidate steadily in the field, in the belief that in the end the Blaine men, seeing the impossiblity of the success of their favorite, would come to Sherman and thus secure his nomination.   After a whole day's voting, however, it became plain that a union of the Blaine and Sherman forces in favor of Sherman could not be effected, and that an attempt in that direction would throw enough additional votes to Grant to give him the victory.   Some unsuccessful efforts were made on the second day's voting to rally on Edmunds and Washburne.   Finally, on the 34th ballot, the Wisconsin men determined to make an effort in an entirely new direction to break the dead-lock.   They threw their 17 votes for Garfield.   General Garfield sprang to his feet and ·

protested against this proceeding, making the point of order that nobody had a right to vote for any member of the convention without his consent, and that consent, he said, "I refuse to give." The chairman declared that the point of order was not well taken, and ordered the Wisconsin vote to be counted. On the next ballot nearly the whole Indiana delegation swung over to Garfield, and a few scattering votes were changed to him from other States, making a total of fifty votes cast for him in all. Now it became plain that, by a happy inspiration, a way out of the difficulty had been found. On the 36th ballot, State after State swung over to Garfield amid intense excitement, and he was nominated by the following vote : Garfield, 399 ; Grant, 306 ; Sherman, 3 ; Washburne, 5. The nomination was accepted on all hands as an exceedingly fortunate one, and both the friends and opponents of General Garfield vied with each other in the enthusiasm with which they endorsed it. Congratulations poured in from all parts of the country, and on his way from Chicago to his farm in Ohio, General Garfield was the recipient of a popular ovation, which repeated itself at every town and railroad station.

---

## CHAPTER· XVI.

### GENERAL GARFIELD AS AN ORATOR.

GENERAL GARFIELD's reputation as a stump-speaker was, as we have seen in a preceding chapter, an affair of steady growth, beginning in the immediate vicinity of his home in Hiram, spreading in a few years to the neighboring counties, extending in 1860 to the State of Ohio, and afterward widening so as to embrace the whole country. At present there is probably no living political orator whose efforts before large audiences are so effective. He appeals directly to the reason of men, and only after he has carried his hearers along on a strong tide of argument to irresistible conclusions, does he address himself to their feelings. The emotions he arouses are all the more intense, from the fact that he has first convinced the mind that they are just and timely. He has a powerful voice, great personal magnetism, and a style of address that wins confidence at the outset, and he is a master of the art of binding together facts and logic into a solid sheaf of argument. At times he seems to lift his audience up and shake it with strong emotion, so powerful is his eloquence ; but he loves best to reason with his hearers, calmly but emphatically. He never reads a speech from manuscript ; he never writes one to commit to memory. His method of preparation is first to study his subject with great care, and then make a few head notes. With these notes to refer to, he speaks extemporaneously, and so well thought out is his matter that when reported verbatim it reads as if carefully written out in advance.

During the war General Garfield made but one speech—a Fourth of July oration delivered to five thousand soldiers from an army wagon in Alabama. In the campaign of 1864 he made a series of addresses in Ohio, Indiana, and Illinois, speaking sixty-five times and travelling 7,500 miles. The same year, before Congress adjourned, he went over to the eastern shore of Maryland, on the invitation of Postmaster-General Creswell, and spoke in Chestertown. This was the only time he ever met with a demonstration of mob spirit. Some rebel sympathizers in the crowd threw rotten eggs at him. He broke off the current of his discourse to say to them : "I have just come from fighting brave rebels at Chickamauga ; I shall not flinch before cowardly rebels like you." Then he went on with his speech and was not again assailed. Every year from 1864 to 1879 save one he spoke almost every day while the campaign lasted, either in his own or other States. In 1865 he took the lead of his party in advocating manhood suffrage in Ohio. A sentence from an address on this subject, delivered at Ravenna on July 4th, was kept standing as a motto in many of the Republican papers. It was, " Suffrage and safety, like liberty and union, are one and indivisible."

He has always regarded the stump as a great educating influence, and has felt a conscientious duty to offer to his audience the whole truth and the best thoughts he could command on the subject in hand. He is scrupulously careful in his statement of facts, and never gives as a fact what is only an opinion, or garbles an authority to gain support for an argument. His first speech in every campaign has for many years past been issued as a national campaign document.

Five years ago he began to go to the Maine canvass, and has kept up the custom regularly ever since. He has made three stumping tours of Michigan, one of New Hampshire, one of New Jersey, one of New York, one of Kansas, three of Indiana, two of Illinois, and he has also spoken in Wisconsin, Iowa, Pennsylvania, and other States. In Ohio there is scarcely a county where his voice has not repeatedly been heard before large assemblies. In 1868 he held a joint debate at Newark, O., with General George W. Morgan. In 1878 he carried on two joint discussions in Ohio with the present Senator Pendleton. In the first of these encounters, Pendleton supposed Garfield was going to make the same speech he had been making elsewhere in the canvass, and to this he thought his own stock speech for the campaign a sufficient reply, but Garfield surprised him by making an entirely fresh extemporaneous speech, consisting of a tremendous attack on the Democratic Party. Pendleton had nothing prepared to meet this, and was forced to make his old speech, which was an arraignment of the Republican Party. As Garfield had half an hour to close the debate, he was able to refute all of Pendleton's points, leaving his own to stand unanswered. His remarkable power of thinking on his legs was admirably exemplified on this occasion.

Outside of his political work, General Garfield has been a frequent platform speaker on topics connected with education, finance, and social science. In 1878 he delivered a notable address in Fanueil Hall, Boston on "Honest Money." In 1874 he delivered six lectures on social science at Hiram College. In 1869 he spoke on the value of statistics before the American Social Science Association in New York. In late years he has been an occasional contributor to the pages of the *Atlantic Monthly* and the *North American Review.*

A striking instance of General Garfield's power over a vast, excited multitude is related by a correspondent of the *Cincinnati Gazette :*

"I shall never forget the first time I saw General Garfield. It was the morning after President Lincoln's assassination. The country was excited to its utmost tension, and New York city seemed ready for the scenes of the French Revolution. The intelligence of Lincoln's murder had been flashed by the wires over the whole land. The newspaper head-lines of the transaction were set up in the largest type, and the high crime was on every one's tongue. Fear took possession of men's minds as to the fate of the Government, for in a few hours the news came on that Seward's throat was cut and that attempts had been made upon the lives of others of the Government officers. Posters were stuck up everywhere, in great black letters, calling upon the loyal citizens of New York, Brooklyn, Jersey City and neighboring places, to meet around the Wall Street Exchange and give expression to their sentiments. It was a dark and terrible hour. What might come next no one could tell, and men spoke with bated breath. The wrath of the workingmen was simply uncontrollable, and revolvers and knives were in the hands of thousands of Lincoln's friends, ready at the first opportunity to take the law into their own hands and avenge the death of the martyred President upon any and all who dared to utter a word against him.

" Eleven o'clock A.M. was the hour set for the rendezvous. Fifty thousand people crowded around the Exchange Building, cramming and jamming the streets, and wedged in tight as men could stand together. With a few to whom a special favor was extended, I went over from Brooklyn, at 9 A.M., and, even then, with the utmost difficulty, found way to the reception room for the speakers in the front of the Exchange Building, and looking out upon the high and massive balcony, whose front was protected by a heavy iron railing. We sat in solemnity and silence, waiting for General Butler, who, it was announced, had started from Washington and was either already in the city or expected every moment. Nearly a hundred generals, judges, statesmen, lawyers, editors, clergymen, and others, were in that room waiting Butler's arrival. We stepped out to the balcony to watch the fearfully solemn and swaying mass of people. Not a hurrah was heard, but for the most part dead silence, or a deep, ominous muttering ran like a rising wave up the street toward Broadway, and again down toward the river on the right.

" At length the batons of the police were seen swinging in the air, far up on the left, parting the crowd and pressing it back to make way for a carriage that moved slowly and with difficult jogs, through the compact multitude. Suddenly the silence was broken, and the cry of ' Butler ! Butler ! Butler !' rang out with tremendous and thrilling effect, and was taken up by the people. But not a hurrah ! Not one ! It was the cry of a great people, asking to know how their President died. The blood bounded in our veins, and the tears ran like streams down our faces. How it was done I forget, but Butler was pulled through, and pulled up, and entered the room, where we had just walked back to meet him. A broad crape, a yard long, hung from his left arm—terrible contrast with the countless flags that were waving the nation's victory in the breeze. We first realized then the truth of the sad news that Lincoln was dead. When Butler entered the room we shook hands. Some spoke, some couldn't. All were in tears. The only word Butler had for us all at the first break of the silence was : ' Gentlemen, he died 'in the fulness of his fame ! ' and as he spoke it his lips quivered, and the tears ran fast down his cheeks.

" Then, after a few moments, came the speaking. And you can imagine the effect, as the crape fluttered in the wind, while his arm was uplifted. Dickinson, of New York State, was fairly wild. The old man leaped over the iron railing of the balcony and stood on the very edge overhanging the crowd, gesticulating in the most vehement manner, and next thing to bidding the crowd ' burn up the rebel seed, root and branch,' while a bystander held on to his coat-tails to keep him from falling over. By this time the wave of popular indignation had swelled to its crest. Two men lay bleeding on one of the side streets, the one dead, the other next to dying ; one on the pavement, the other in the gutter. They had said a moment before that ' Lincoln ought to have been shot long ago ! ' They were not allowed to say it again ! Soon two long pieces of scantling stood out above the heads of the crowd, crossed at the top like the letter X, and a looped halter pendent from the junction, a dozen men following its slow motion through the masses, while ' Vengeance !' was the cry.

" On the right, suddenly, the shout rose, ' *The World !*' ' *The World !*' ' The office of *The World !*' ' *World ! World !*' and a movement of perhaps 8,000 or 10,000 turning their faces in the direction of that building began to be executed. It was a critical moment. What might come no one could tell, did that crowd get in front of that office. Police and military would have availed little or been too late. A telegram had just been read from Washington, ' Seward is dying.' Just then at that juncture a man stepped forward with a small flag in his hand, and beckoned to the crowd. ' Another telegram from

Washington ! '  And then, in the awful silence of the crisis,
taking advantage of the hesitation of the crowd, whose steps
had been arrested a moment, a right arm was lifted skyward,
and a voice clear and steady, loud and distinct, spoke out :
' Fellow-citizens !  Clouds and darkness are round about Him !
His pavilion is dark waters and thick clouds of the skies !
Justice and judgment are the establishment of His throne !
Mercy and truth shall go before His face !  Fellow-citizens !
God reigns and the Government at Washington still lives !'

   " The effect was tremendous.  The crowd stood riveted to
the ground in awe, gazing at the motionless orator, and thinking of God and the security of the Government in that hour.
As the boiling wave subsides and settles to the sea when some
strong wind beats it down, so the tumult of the people sank
and became still.  All took it as a divine omen.  It was a triumph of eloquence, inspired by the moment, such as falls to
but one man's lot, and that but once in a century.  The genius
of Webtser, Choate, Everett, Seward, never reached  it.
Demosthenes never equalled it.  What might have happened
had the surging and maddened mob been let loose, none can
tell.  The man for the crisis was on the spot, more potent than
Napoleon's guns at Paris.  I inquired what was his name.  The
answer came in a low whisper, ' It is General Garfield, of
Ohio !' "

## CHAPTER XVII.

### GENERAL GARFIELD AS A LAWYER.

   GARFIELD formed the intention of studying law while in college, but his poverty and his debt for his college expenses made
it necessary for him to earn money at once, and for many years,
while teaching in the Hiram Institute he saw no way of carrying out his plan.  He managed to read law books, however,

and his election to the State Senate giving him more time for study, he entered his name in a Cleveland law office, and began a systematic course while serving in the Legislature. In 1861, as stated in a foregoing chapter, he was admitted to the bar of the Supreme Court of the State. His army service and his subsequent busy career in Congress prevented him from practising for a long time, but he always entertained the idea of settling in Cleveland when his public career should close, and devoting himself to the legal profession. His constituents refused to retire him from public life, however, and kept on returning him to Congress term after term, by unanimous nominations and large majorities at the polls. Being always a working member, giving up his time during the sessions to the business of legislation, and spending most of the vacations of Congress helping his party by his efforts upon the stump, he has found little opportunity for making briefs and pleas. Some business that was pressed upon him and that he could attend to without interfering with his public duties, he has accepted. His first case was that of the Indiana conspirators, Bowles and Mulligan, who were tried and convicted by a military commission in 1864 for treason. The case was brought before the Supreme Court on a question involving the right of a military tribunal to try civilians in a State not the theatre of actual war. General Garfield undertook the defense of the men, not from any desire to shield them from punishment, but because he believed the civil law should be supreme where not necessarily suspended by the operations of hostile armies. He made an argument of great abilty and won the case. For his action in defending the conspirators, he was severely criticised by many of his Republican friends at home. In reference to these criticisms he said in a speech at Warren, Ohio, that he argued the case " in defense of what I believe to be a most vital and important principle, not only to the Republican Party, but to the nation—namely : that in no part of our civil community must the military be exalted above the civil authority. . . . I believe that all over this land one of the great landmarks of civilization and civil liberty is the self-restraining liberty of the American people, curbing themselves and governing themselves by the limitation of the civil law."

In the spring of 1868 he was engaged to defend the will of Alexander Campbell, the founder of the sect of Disciples and of their college at Bethany, West Virginia. This case he also won. Since then he has been engaged in fifteen cases before the United States Supreme Court, most of them of considerable importance, one case in the Supreme Court of Pennsylvania, one in the United States Circuit Court at Mobile, Ala., and one in the Equity Court of Lawrence County, Pa. In these cases he has been associated with several of the leading lawyers of the country. His powers of analysis, his habit of going to the bottom of a subject at no matter what cost of hard study, and his ability to carry on a closely-interwoven logical argument, make him a formidable advocate. If he had devoted his life to the law, there is no doubt that he would rank with the five or six lawyers who by the general verdict of their confrères stand at the head of the profession in this country. He has an immense capacity for work, and his remarkable intellect, always kept in harness by his will, together with his oratorical powers, peculiarly fit him for the higher walks of the legal calling.

---

## CHAPTER XVIII.

### HOME AND FAMILY LIFE.

THE first years of General Garfield's married life were passed in Hiram, boarding with families of friends, and it was not until he went to the war that he saved money enough to buy a home. In 1862 he purchased a small frame cottage facing the college

green, paying for it $800. About $1000 more were spent in enlarging it by a wing and fitting it up. It had a small front
yard ornamented with a few shade trees and evergreen shrubs,
and at the back of the lot was a barn and kitchen garden. The
rooms were small and the ceilings low, as was the fashion in
village houses of moderate pretensions, but the young house-
wife soon made the place cosey and homelike. This was the
only home of the family for many years. While in Washington
they lived in apartments. The lack of a settled home at the
capital, where the children could grow up amid wholesome influences, was seriously felt early in General Garfield's Congressional career, but it was not until he had been three times elected that he began to regard that career as likely to continue for
an indefinite period, and sought the means of escaping from
the disagreeable features of hotel and boarding-house life. He
bought a lot on the corner of Thirteenth and I Streets, facing
Franklin Square, and with money loaned him by an old army
friend put up a plain, square, substantial brick house, big
enough to hold his family and two or three guests. Some
years later the wing of the house was extended to enlarge the
dining-room and library, the requirements of the household
having outgrown the capacity of the one and those of the
General's library that of the other. The cottage in Hiram was
sold and the family life for several years centred in the Washington house ; but in order not to be without a foothold in his
own district General Garfield built a small cottage on Little
Mountain, in Lake County, for a summer sojourning place.

As the boys grew older, however, and needed more range for
their activities than a city house could afford, the desire to own
a farm which he had always felt increased upon him. When
he had paid off the mortgage on his house and had a little
money ahead, he thought he could safely gratify his desire, and
after a good deal of thought about localities, decided to settle in
the vicinity of the Lake Shore Railroad on one of the hand-

some productive ridges that run parallel to Lake Erie. A farm of 160 acres was bought in the town of Mentor, Lake County, a mile from a railway and telegraph station and half a mile from a post-office. The buildings consisted of a tumble-down barn and an ancient farm-house a story and a half high ; but the land was fertile, the summer climate, tempered by breezes from the neighboring lake, was delightful, and the people in the vicinity were of the best class of farmers to be found in Ohio. The old house was somewhat modernized with paint and paper and a new piazza, a barn was built, and the family migrated to the new home. All were delighted with the change. The children ran wild in the orchards and hay-fields, the mother took pleasure in the new duties of a farmer's household, the good old grandmother rejoiced to get back to rural scenes like those amid which her early years had been spent, and the General revived all the farming skill of his boyhood days, holding the plow or loading the hay wagon or driving the ox team. Drainage, fencing, and other improvements absorbed all the money the place brought in, but the time spent upon it was highly enjoyed by all the members of the household, and every winter they looked forward to the adjournment of Congress and their release from Washington with pleasant anticipations.

After three summers in the cramped, low-ceiled little house it was resolved that it must be enlarged. Plans were made last winter, mainly by Mrs. Garfield, who has considerable natural talent for architecture, and in the spring a new house grew around and over the old one, just in time for the throng of old frends and new that poured in after the nomination of its owner for the Presidency. The house faces the Ridge Road which runs from Cleveland eastward to Erie, through a string of pretty towns and villages. It is broad, high, and spacious. Its two stories are capped by a steep red roof, which shelters a big garret lighted by dormer windows. A wide piazza extends the whole length of the front—a wide hall runs through to a

back porch. Below is the parlor, dining-room, kitchen and two
large bed-rooms, the pleasantest being the room of " grandma,"
the venerable mother of the General, who is now nearly eighty
years old. Above are numerous sleeping-rooms and the study
of the master of the house. A few steps from the house, in the
edge of the orchard is a little building of a single room, called
the library, with its walls lined with bookcases, its windows :
on all sides through which the lake breeze pours. A pleasanter
working place for a summer day could not be desired.

The farm raises good crops of wheat, oats, corn, hay, and
potatoes, and the big barns hardly hold the products of the
harvest.   There is a good orchard, a little vineyard, and a large
vegetable garden which comes up unabashed beside the croquet
lawn and crowds its cabbage-heads and pea-vines against the
roadside fence.   The railroad runs through the meadows on the
lower end of the farm ; the village of Mentor, with a score of
neat white houses, three little churches, and a fine brick school-
house, is half a mile distant ; Painesville, the county town, with
a population of 5000, is six miles eastward by an excellent
gravel road ; Willoughby, a village where the census-taker has
found just 999 inhabitants, is four miles westward on the high
road to Cleveland ; over the wooded hills to the southward,
three miles distant is the half-deserted village of Kirtland, where
the first temple built by the Mormons is still standing, an enduring monument to folly and superstition ; Lake Erie is three
miles north, and on the southeastern horizon that dark green
elevation is the hemlock-covered summit of Little Mountain,
and the white fleck on its brow is the hotel from whose portico
can be seen thirty miles of the blue waters and fertile shores of
Lake Erie.   The County of Lake is strongly Republican, every
town in it giving a heavy Republican majority.   The people are
of New England descent—an unmixed race of Yankees modified
in their characteristics only by the influence of a climate less
severe and conditions of life less rigorous than prevail in rural

New England. A thriftier or more intelligent farming population cannot be found in the United States. With all these pleasant surroundings, it is no wonder that the Garfields are greatly attached to their farm. Whatever may be the result of the next election, they will keep it as a permanent home.

General Garfield has had seven children and five are living. The oldest, Mary, died when he was in the army and the youngest, Edward, died in Washington about four years ago. Of the surviving children, the oldest, Harry, is fourteen; after him come James, Molly, Irwin (named after General McDowell), and Abram. Harry and James are preparing for college at St. Paul's School in Concord, New Hampshire. Harry is the musician of the family and plays the piano well. James, who more resembles his father, is the mathematician. Molly, a handsome girl of thirteen, is ruddy, sweet-tempered, vivacious, and blessed with perfect health. The younger boys are still in the period of boisterous animal life. All the children have quick brains and are strongly individualized. All learned to read young except Abe, who hearing that his father had years ago said in a lecture on education, that no child of his should be forced to read until he was seven years old, took refuge behind the parental theory and declined to learn his letters until he had reached that age.

Mrs. Garfield superintends all the duties of the household and helps in its active labors during a portion of each day. Her tastes are for a quiet domestic life, brightened by reading and study and by the society of a few intimate friends. Few women have as wide a range of culture. She reads Greek and Latin, German and French, has considerable knowledge of the natural sciences, and keeps up with the best of the literature of the day. She is the companion of her husband's intellectual life as well as the devoted mother of his children, the skilful manager of his household, and the cordial hostess of the many guests attracted by his fame and his social qualities.

The manner of life in the Garfield household, whether in Washington or on the Mentor farm, is simple and quiet. The long table is bountifully supplied with plainly-cooked food, and there is always room for any guest who may drop in at meal-time. No alcoholic drinks are used. There is no effort at fol lowing fashions in furniture or table service. No carriage is kept in Washington, but on the farm there are vehicles of vari-ous sorts and two teams of stout horses. Comfort, neatness, and order prevail without the least attempt at keeping up with styles of dress and living, or any desire to sacrifice the health-ful regularity of household customs adopted before the General won fame and position, to the artificial usages of what is called good society.

## CHAPTER XIX.

### GENERAL GARFIELD'S RELIGION.

AT the centre of Mentor Township stands a little white church surmounted by a little white steeple. Within, the plain, straight-backed pews give seating accommodations for about two hundred people. There is no pulpit. Upon a broad car-peted platform stands an old-fashioned mahogany table, which, with the aid of a big red curtain, forms a reading-desk. After the sermon is over, the cushion and the Bible which it sup-ports are removed. A white cloth is spread upon the table, the communion service is brought out from a cupboard near at hand, and the sacrament, called by the Disciples the Lord's Supper, is partaken of by all the congregation who are so disposed. The choir sit in the centre of the auditorium, in the midst of the pews. A large framed motto—" Blessed be the Peacemakers "—hangs on the wall near the platform. The windows of common glass are screened by green shutters, and the place suggests a simple, primitive form of worship, without

ritual, ceremonial, or adjuncts of any sort to impress the imagination. This is the home church of General Garfield, where
he and his family attend worship regularly, while living upon
their farm. Garfield joined the Disciples when a lad of eighteen, and has been a member of that denomination ever since.

The full name of the sect is Disciples of Christ. Members of
other denominations frequently call them Campbellites. They
number about 500,000, and have the centre of their strength in
Western Pennsylvania, West Virginia, Ohio, Kentucky, and Indiana, within the radius of the labors of their founder, Alexander Campbell, of Bethany, West Virginia. In the East they
are almost unknown, but they have scattered churches throughout the Gulf States, are numerous in Illinois and Missouri, and
are pretty well organized in other States west of the Mississippi.
Campbell was a Presbyterian preacher of remarkable force of
mind and powers of oratory, who came from Ireland, in 1809,
with his father, and settled in Washington County, Pennsylvania. He established an independent church at Brush Run, in
that county, on the theory that all creeds were human, and,
therefore, without authority, and that every Christian was his
own judge of the meaning of the Scriptures. It was an epoch
of intense doctrinal differences, when Protestantism in this country seemed to have degenerated into a battle of creeds. This
sturdy reformer, preaching no creed but the Bible, and claiming
for all believers liberty of conscience and judgment with regard
to the meaning of the sacred book, struck a responsive chord
in the public mind. Hundreds joined his standard wherever
he preached, and within a few years after he commenced his independent ministry in 1827, a new sect had arisen acknowledging him as its leader. His discourses formed a body of doctrine for this sect, although its members, owning no authority
but the Bible itself, did not acknowledge them as in any sense
authoritative. To all intents and purposes, however, he was
the founder of Discipleism, as much as Calvin was of Presby-

terianism and Wesley of Methodism. In 1841 he established a college at Bethany, near Wheeling, which soon became the educational and doctrinal centre of the new denomination, and began to publish a periodical called the *Millennial Harbinger*, which was everywhere received as its organ, and is still in existence.

The Disciples endeavored to restore the spirit and methods of primitive Christianity. They admit to their membership any one who will receive the rite of baptism by immersion and answer in the affirmative the following question : " Do you believe that Jesus Christ is the Son of God and your Saviour ?" Nothing is asked about doctrinal points. Indeed, it is difficult to ascertain the precise points of difference between the Disciples and other denominations, because few of them can be got to formulate their faith. The New Testament, they say, is their guide of faith and practice, and they have no catechism or books of reference to settle questions of dispute. Practically, they agree on a few general doctrines, such as the necessity of immersion for the remission of sins, but on most controverted theological points they allow a wide latitude for individual opinion. They are not Calvinists. They believe in the power of every human soul to obtain salvation. They do not, as a rule, believe in the eternal Sonship of Christ, although agreeing with Trinitarians respecting His divine nature. They do not invest the Lord's Supper with a sacramental idea, but regard it only as a memorial festival designed to quicken their love of Christ and strengthen the ties of brotherhood between themselves. Sunday they call the Lord's Day, and they do not apply to it the law of the Jewish Sabbath to the extent that most of the older sects do. In church government they are purely Congregational, recognizing no authority either to direct or advise, superior to the individual congregation. They support a missionary society, have a book concern, with branches at Cincinnati and at Oskaloosa, Iowa, and maintain a large number of colleges and seminaries. Indeed, they claim that they have more institutions of learning in proportion to their membership than any other denomination.

The Disciples are a friendly, sociable people. They are fond of calling each other by their first names, prefaced often by the affectionate term brother or sister, and are very cordial in their personal intercourse with fellow-members. They care less for the Old Testament than do the Calvinists and Methodists, and do not speculate much about the Book of Revelations. The Gospels, the Acts, and the Epistles are studied closely. They are very hospitable and entertain travelling brethren at their houses in the manner of the apostolic times. They have communion service in their churches every Sunday after the morning discourse. Of late years they have supported a settled ministry, but their early successes were achieved by travelling preachers speaking in the woods, or in tents which were transported in big wagons around the country. Any member can speak in their pulpits, administer the communion, and baptize converts. The ministry is not a peculiar class, although there is a form of ordination for men who wish to devote themselves to it.

General Garfield's father and mother sat under the powerful preaching of Alexander Campbell, when he visited their locality during one of his tours, and were converted to the new faith without creed or catechism, discipline, or formulated statement of belief of any sort. It was natural that their son should connect himself with the same denomination. Most of his early education before he went to college was got at a new struggling Disciples' school at Hiram. His gift of public speaking soon drew him into the way of talking at religious meetings, and he was constantly encouraged in this habit by the members of the denomination, who saw that his powerful intellect and unusual oratorical powers would be of great help to them. Although he spoke regularly in the churches of Hiram, Solon, and Newburg for nearly three years, he never had the thought of de-

voting himself to the ministry. Law was then his chosen profession. He was never ordained, but was what might be called a lay preacher, filling pulpits on Sundays while teaching
week-days. Those who remember his preaching say that it was
characterized by the vigor, magnetism, wealth of illustration,
and intellectual force of his later political addresses. The war
put a stop to both his teaching and his pulpit work. He has
since kept up his association with the church of his boyhood,
but has not taken an active part in its religious services, save
now and then to offer a prayer in the church at Mentor, in response to a call from the minister.

With General Garfield's breadth of mind and keen interest in
scientific research and philosophical discussion, it would be impossible for him to run in any narrow rut of sectarianism.
His religious views are characterized by great tolerance and lib-
erality. His Christianity is of a very broad pattern, and is
without a trace of bigotry. In form it is the religion of his
parents ; in spirit it is enlightened, elevated, and imbued with
the progressive thought of the age ; a Christianity not of cere-
monies and statements, but of humanity and the heart.

# GENERAL GARFIELD

AS A

## STATESMAN AND ORATOR.

# PARAGRAPHS

FROM

# GENERAL GARFIELD'S SPEECHES.

———•••———

## THE DEATH OF SLAVERY.

[From a Speech in the House of Representatives, Jan. 13, 1865, on the
Constitutional Amendment to abolish slavery.]

WE shall never know why slavery dies so hard in this Republic
and in this hall until we know why sin has such longevity and Satan
is immortal. With marvellous tenacity of existence, it has outlived
the expectations of its friends and the hopes of its enemies. It has
been declared here and elsewhere to be in all the several stages of
mortality—wounded, moribund, dead. The question was raised
by my colleague [Mr. Cox] yesterday, whether it was indeed dead
or only in a troubled sleep. I know of no better illustration of its
condition than is found in Sallust's admirable history of the great
conspirator, Catiline, who when his final battle was fought and lost,
his army broken and scattered, was found far in advance of his own
troops, lying among the dead enemies of Rome, yet breathing a
little, but exhibiting in his countenance all that ferocity of spirit
which had characterized his life. So, sir, this body of slavery lies
before us among the dead enemies of the Republic, mortally
wounded, impotent in its fiendish wickedness, but with its old
ferocity of look, bearing the unmistakable marks of its infernal
origin.

Who does not remember that thirty years ago—a short period in
the life of a nation—but little could be said with impunity in these
halls on the subject of slavery? How well do gentlemen here remember the history of that distinguished predecessor of mine,

Joshua R. Giddings, lately gone to his rest, who, with his forlorn hope of faithful men, took his life in his hand, and in the name of justice protested against the great crime, and who stood bravely in his place until his white locks, like the plume of Henry of Navarre, marked where the battle for freedom raged fiercest !

We can hardly realize that this is the same people, and these the same halls, where now scarcely a man can be found who will venture to do more than falter out an apology for slavery, protesting in the same breath that he has no love for the dying tyrant. None I believe, but that man of supernal boldness from the City of New York [Mr. Fernando Wood], has ventured this session to raise his voice in favor of slavery for its own sake. He still sees in its features the reflection of beauty and divinity, and only he. "How art thou fallen from heaven, O Lucifer, son of the morning ! How art thou cut down to the ground, which didst weaken the nations !"

Many mighty men have been slain by thee, many proud ones have humbled themselves at thy feet ! All along the coast of our political sea these victims of slavery lie like stranded wrecks, broken on the headlands of freedom. How lately did its advocates, with impious boldness, maintain it as God's own, to be venerated and cherished as divine ! It was another and higher form of civilization. It was the holy Evangel of America dispensing its mercies to a benighted race, and destined to bear countless blessings to the wilderness of the West. In its mad arrogance it lifted its hand to strike down the fabric of the Union, and since that fatal day it has been a "fugitive and a vagabond on the earth." Like the spirit Jesus cast out, it has since then been "seeking rest and finding none."

It has sought in all the corners of the Republic to find some hiding place in which to shelter itself from the death it so richly deserves.

It sought an asylum in the untrodden Territories of the West, but with a whip of scorpions indignant freemen drove it thence. I do not believe that a loyal man can now be found who would consent that it should again enter them. It has no hope of harbor there. It found no protection or favor in the hearts or consciences of the freemen of the Republic, and has fled for its last hope of safety behind the shield of the Constitution. We propose to follow it there, and drive it thence as Satan was exiled from heaven.

---

## SUPREMACY OF THE CIVIL LAW.

[From an Argument made in the Supreme Court, March 6, 1866, in the Indiana Conspiracy Case.]

YOUR decision will mark an era in American history. The just and final settlement of this great question will take a high place among the great achievements which have immortalized this decade. It will establish forever this truth, of inestimable value to us and to mankind, that a Republic can wield the vast enginery of war without breaking down the safeguards of liberty ; can suppress insurrection and put down rebellion, however formidable, without destroying the bulwarks of law ; can by the might of its armed millions preserve and defend both nationality and liberty. Victories on the field were of priceless value, for they plucked the life of the Republic out of the hands of its enemies ; but

> " Peace hath her victories
> No less renowned than war ;"

and if the protection of law shall, by your decision, be extended over every acre of our peaceful territory, you will have rendered the great decision of the century.

When Pericles had made Greece immortal in arts and arms, in liberty and law, he invoked the genius of Phidias to devise a monument which should symbolize the beauty and glory of Athens. That artist selected for his theme the tutelar divinity of Athens, the Jove-born goddess, protectress of arts and arms, of industry and law, who typified the Greek conception of composed, majestic, unrelenting force.

He erected on the heights of the Acropolis a colossal statue of Minerva, armed with spear and helmet, which towered in awful majesty above the surrounding temples of the gods. Sailors on far-off ships beheld the crest and spear of the goddess and bowed with reverent awe. To every Greek she was the symbol of power and glory. But the Acropolis, with its temples and statues is now a heap of ruins. The visible gods have vanished in the clearer light of modern civilization. We cannot restore the decayed emblems of ancient Greece ; but it is in your power, O judges, to erect in this citadel of our liberties a monument more lasting than brass ; invisible indeed to the eye of flesh, but visible to the eye of the spirit as the awful form and figure of Justice, crowning and adorning the Republic ; rising above the storms of political strife, above the din of battle, above the earthquake shock of rebellion ; seen from afar and hailed as protector by the oppressed of all nations ; dispensing equal blessings, and covering with the protecting shield of law the weakest, the humblest, the meanest, and, until declared by solemn law unworthy of protection, the guiltiest of its citizens.

### RESTORATION OF THE REBEL STATES.

[From a Speech in the House of Representatives, Feb. 1, 1866.]

AND first, we must recognize in all our action the stupendous facts of the war. In the very crisis of our fate, God brought us face to face with the alarming truth that we must lose our own freedom or grant it to the slave. In the extremity of our distress we called upon the black man to help us save the Republic, and amid the very thunder of battle we made a covenant with him, sealed both with his blood and ours, and witnessed by Jehovah, that when the nation was redeemed he should be free and share with us the glories and blessings of freedom. In the solemn words of the great proclamation of emancipation, we not only declared the slaves forever free, but we pledged the faith of the nation " to maintain their freedom"—mark the words, " *to maintain their freedom*." The omniscient witness will appear in judgment against us if we do not fulfil that covenant. Have we done it ? Have we given freedom to the black man ? What is freedom ? Is it a mere negation—the bare privilege of not being chained, bought and sold, branded and scourged ? If this be all, then freedom is a bitter mockery, a cruel delusion, and it may well be questioned whether slavery were not better.

But liberty is no negation. It is a substantive, tangible reality. It is the realization of those imperishable truths of the Declaration " that all men are created equal," that the sanction of all just government is " the consent of the governed." Can these truths be realized until each man has a right be to heard on all matters relating to himself ?

Mr. Speaker, we did more than merely to break off the chains of the slaves. The abolition of slavery added four million citizens to the Republic. By the decision of the Supreme Court, by the decision of the Attorney-General, by the decision of all the departments of our Government, those men made free are, by the act of freedom, made citizens. As another has said, they must be " four million disfranchised, disarmed, untaught, landless, thriftless, non-producing, non-consuming, degraded men, or four million land-holding, industrious, arms-bearing, and voting population. Choose between the two !"

Mr. Speaker, let us learn a lesson from the dealing of God with the Jewish nation. When his chosen people, led by the pillar of cloud and fire, had crossed the Red Sea and traversed the gloomy wilderness with its thundering Sinai, its bloody battles, disastrous defeats, and glorious victories ; when near the end of their perilous pilgrimage they listened to the last words of blessing and warning from their great leader before he was buried with immortal honors by the angel of the Lord ; when at last the victorious host, sadly joyful, stood on the banks of the Jordan, their enemies drowned in the sea or slain in the wilderness, they paused and made solemn preparation to pass over and possess the land of promise. By the command of God, given through Moses and enforced by his great

successor, the ark of the covenant, containing the tables of the law
and the sacred memorials of their pilgrimage, was borne by chosen
men two thousand cubits in advance of the people. On the further
shore stood Ebal and Gerizim, the mounts of cursing and blessing,
from which, in the hearing of all the people, were pronounced the
curses of God against injustice and disobedience, and his blessing
upon justice and obedience. On the shore, between the mountains
and in the midst of the people, a monument was erected, and on it
were written the words of the law, "to be a memorial unto the children of Israel forever and ever." Let us learn wisdom from this
illustrious example. We have passed the Red Sea of slaughter ;
our garments are yet wet with its crimson spray. We have crossed
the fearful wilderness of war, and have left our four hundred thousand heroes to sleep beside the dead enemies of the Republic. We
have heard the voice of God amid the thunders of battle commanding us to wash our hands of iniquity, to "proclaim liberty throughout all the land unto all the inhabitants thereof." When we spurned
his counsels we were defeated, and the gulfs of ruin yawned before
us. When we obeyed his voice, he gave us victory. And now
at last we have reached the confines of the wilderness. Before us
is the land of promise, the land of hope, the land of peace, filled
with possibilities of greatness and glory too vast for the grasp of the
imagination. Are we worthy to enter it ? On what condition may
it be ours to enjoy and transmit to our children's children ? Let us
pause and make deliberate and solemn preparation. Let us, as
representatives of the people, whose servants we are, bear in
advance the sacred ark of republican liberty, with its tables of the
law inscribed with the "irreversible guaranties"[1] of liberty. Let
us here build a monument on which shall be written not only the
curses of the law against treason, disloyalty, and oppression, but
also an everlasting covenant of peace and blessing with loyalty,
liberty, and obedience ; and all the people will say, Amen.

---

## ABRAHAM LINCOLN.

[Remarks at the Memorial Services in the House of Representatives,
April 14, 1865.]

It was no one man who killed Abraham Lincoln ; it was the embodied spirit of treason and slavery, inspired with fearful and
despairing hate, that struck him down, in the moment of the nation's
supremest joy.

Sir, there are times in the history of men and nations when they
stand so near the veil that separates mortals and immortals, time

from eternity, and men from their God, that they can almost hear the beatings and feel the pulsations of the heart of the Infinite.

Through such a time has this nation passed. When two hundred and fifty thousand brave spirits passed from the field of honor, through that thin veil, to the presence of God, and when at last its parting folds admitted the martyr President to the company of these dead heroes of the Republic, the nation stood so near the veil that the whispers of God were heard by the children of men. Awe-stricken by his voice, the American people knelt in tearful reverence and made a solemn covenant with him and with each other, that this nation should be saved from its enemies, that all its glories should be restored, and on the ruins of slavery and treason the temples of justice and freedom should be built and should survive forever.

It remains for us, consecrated by that great event and under a covenant with God, to keep that faith, to go forward in the great work until it shall be completed. Following the lead of that great man, and obeying the higher behests of God, let us remember that

" He has sounded forth a trumpet that shall never call retreat :
He is sifting out the hearts of men before his judgment seat.
Be swift my soul to answer Him, be jubilant my feet ;
    For God is marching on."

## PUBLIC DEBT AND SPECIE PAYMENTS.

[From a Speech in the House of Representatives, March 16, 1866.]

I PROPOSE, sir, to let the House take the responsibility of adopting or rejecting this measure. On the one side it is proposed to return to solid and honest values ; on the other, to float on the boundless and shoreless sea of paper money, with all its dishonesty and broken pledges. We leave it to the House to decide which alternative it will choose. Choose the one, and you float away into an unknown sea of paper money that shall know no decrease until you take just such a measure as is now proposed to bring us back again to solid values. Delay the measure, and it will cost the country dear. Adopt it now, and with a little depression in business and a little strigency in the money market the worst will be over, and we shall have reached the solid earth. Sooner or later such a measure must be adopted. Go on as you are now going on, and a financial crisis worse than that of 1837 will bring us to the bottom. I for one am unwilling that my name shall be linked to the fate of a paper currency. I believe that any party which commits itself to paper money will go down amid the general disaster, covered with the curses of a ruined people.

Mr. Speaker, I remember that on the monument of Queen Elizabeth, where her glories were recited and her honors summed up, among the last and the highest, recorded as the climax of her honors, was this—that she had restored the money of her kingdom to its just value. And when this House shall have done its work, when it shall have brought back values to their proper standard, it will deserve a monument.

---

## A NATIONAL BUREAU OF EDUCATION.

[From a Speech in the House of Representatives, June 8, 1866.]

WHEN the history of the Thirty-ninth Congress is written it will be recorded that two great ideas inspired it, and made their impress upon all its efforts, viz., to build up free States on the ruins of slavery, and to extend to every inhabitant of the United States the rights and privileges of citizenship.

Before the divine Architect builded order out of chaos, he said, "Let there be light." Shall we commit the fatal mistake of building up free States without first expelling the darkness in which slavery had shrouded their people? Shall we enlarge the boundaries of citizenship and make no provision to increase the intelligence of the citizen? I share most fully in the aspirations of this Congress, and give my most cordial support to its policy ; but I believe its work will prove a disastrous failure unless it makes the schoolmaster its ally, and aids him in preparing the children of the United States to perfect the work now begun.

The stork is a sacred bird in Holland, and is protected by her laws, because it destroys those insects which would undermine the dikes and let the sea again overwhelm the rich fields of the Netherlands. Shall this Government do nothing to foster and strengthen those educational agencies which alone can shield the coming generation from ignorance and vice, and make it the impregnable bulwark of liberty and law?

---

## REFUSAL TO RETURN FUGITIVE SLAVES.

[From a Speech in the House of Representatives, Feb. 8, 1867.]

I CANNOT forget that less than five years ago I received an order from my superior officer in the army commanding me to search my camp for a fugitive slave, and if found to deliver him up to a Kentucky captain, who claimed him as his property, and I had the honor to be perhaps the first officer in the army who peremptorily refused to obey such an order. We were then trying to save the Union without hurting slavery. I remember, sir, that when we undertook to agitate in the army the question of putting arms into the hands of the slaves, it was said, " Such a step will be fatal ; it will alienate half our army and lose us Kentucky." By and by, when our necessities were imperious, we ventured to let the negroes dig in the trenches, but it would not do to put muskets into their hands. We ventured to let the negro drive a mule team, but it would not do to have a white man or a mulatto just in front of him, or behind him ; all must be negroes in that train : you must not disgrace a white soldier by putting him in such company. " By and by," some one said, " rebel guerillas may capture the mules ; so for the sake of the mules let us put a few muskets in the wagons, and let the negroes shoot the guerillas if they come." So for the sake of the mules we enlarged the limits of liberty a little. By and by we allowed the negroes to build fortifications and armed them.

---

## TAXATION OF UNITED STATES BONDS.

[From a Speech in the House of Representatives, July 5, 1868.]

THERE was a declaration made by an old English gentleman in the days of Charles the Second which does honor to human nature. He said he was willing, at any time, to give his life for the good of his country, but he would not do a mean thing to save his country from ruin. So, sir, ought a citizen to feel in regard to our financial affairs. The people of the United States can afford to make any sacrifice for their country, and the history of the last war has proved their willingness ; but the humblest citizen cannot afford to do a mean or dishonorable thing to save even this glorious Republic.

For my own part I will consent to no act of dishonor. And I look upon this proposition—though I cannot think the gentleman meant it to be so—as having in itself the very essence of dishonor. I shall, therefore, to the utmost of my ability, resist it.

Mr. Speaker, I desire to say, in conclusion, that in my opinion all these efforts to pursue a doubtful and unusual, if not dishonorable policy in reference to our public debt, spring from a lack of faith in the intelligence and conscience of the American people. Hardly an hour passes when we do not hear it whispered that some such policy as this must be adopted, or the people will by and by repudiate the debt. For my own part I do not share that distrust. The people of this country have shown by the highest proofs human nature can give that, wherever the path of honor and duty may lead, however steep and rugged it may be, they are ready to walk in it. They feel the burden of the public debt, but they remember that it is the price of blood—the precious blood of half a million brave men who died to save to us all that makes life desirable or property secure. I believe they will, after a full hearing, discard all methods of paying their debts by sleight of hand, or by any scheme which crooked wisdom may devise. If public morality did not protest against any such plan, enlightened public selfishness would refuse its sanction. Let us be true to our trust a few years longer, and the next generation will be here with its seventy-five millions of population and its sixty billions of wealth. To them the debt that then remains will be a light burden. They will pay the last bond according to the letter and spirit of the contract, with the same sense of grateful duty with which they will pay the pensions of the few surviving soldiers of the great war for the Union.

## THE CONSTITUTIONAL AMENDMENTS.

[From a Speech in the House of Representatives, April 4, 1871.]

Now, Mr. Speaker, to review briefly the ground travelled over : The changes wrought in the Constitution by the last three amendments in regard to the individual rights of citizens are these : that no person within the United States shall be made a slave ; that no citizen shall be denied the right of suffrage because of his color or because he was once a slave ; that no State, by its legislation or the enforcement thereof, shall abridge the privileges or immunities of citizens of the United States ; that no State shall, without due process of law, disturb the life, liberty, or property of any person within its jurisdiction ; and finally, that no State shall deny to any person within its jurisdiction the equal protection of the laws.

Thanks to the wisdom and patriotism of the American people, these great and beneficent provisions are now imperishable elements of the Constitution, and will, I trust, remain forever among the irreversible guaranties of liberty.

## THE TARIFF.

[From a Speech in the House of Representatives, April 1, 1870.]

I STAND now where I have always stood since I have been a member of this House. I take the liberty of quoting, from the

*Congressional Globe* of 1866, the following remarks which I then made on the subject of the tariff :

" We have seen that one extreme school of economists would place the price of all manufactured articles in the hands of foreign producers by rendering it impossible for our manufacturers to compete with them : while the other extreme school, by making it impossible for the foreigner to sell his competing wares in our market, would give the people no immediate check upon the prices which our manufacturers might fix for their products. I disagree with both these extremes. I hold that a properly adjusted competition between home and foreign products is the best gauge by which to regulate international trade. Duties should be so high that our manufacturers can fairly compete with the foreign product, but not so high as to enable them to drive out the foreign article, enjoy a monopoly of the trade, and regulate the price as they please. This is my doctrine of protection. If Congress pursues this line of policy steadily, we shall, year by year, approach more nearly to the basis of free trade, because we shall be more nearly able to compete with other nations on equal terms. I am for a protection which leads to ultimate free trade. I am for that free trade which can only be achieved through a reasonable protection."

Mr. Chairman, examining thus the possibilities of the situation, I believe that the true course for the friends of protection to pursue is to reduce the rates on imports wherever we can justly and safely do so, and, accepting neither of the extreme doctrines urged on this floor, endeavor to establish a stable policy that will commend itself to all patriotic and thoughtful people.

---

## DEMOCRATIC RESPONSIBILITY FOR THE REBELLION.

[From a Speech in the House of Representatives, March 14, 1870.]

MY friend from Indiana [Mr. Niblack] is not himself an extreme partisan. But he has said some things just now which deserve an answer. He says that if the glory of the war belongs to the Republican party, then the results of the war, the expenditures of the war, and the burdens laid upon the people in consequence of the war, fall also to our share. A part of this statement I indorse. But, Mr. Chairman, I desire to ask that gentleman and his party a question. Suppose that in the year 1861 every Democrat north of the Potomac and the Ohio had followed the lead of Grant, and Douglas, and Dickinson, and Tod, and all the other great lights of the Democratic party, had thrown away the Democratic name and said that they would be Democrats no longer, as we said we would be Republicans no longer, but all would be Union men, and stand together around the flag until the rebellion had been put under our feet. I desire to ask the gentlemen, if these things had happened, how long the war would have lasted, how much the war would have cost? I do not hesitate to say that it could not have lasted a month, and the expenditures of the war would never have exceeded $10,000,000. I say, as a matter of current history, that it was the great hope of the rebels of the South that the assistance of the Democratic party of the North would divide our forces and overcome all our efforts ; that at the ballot-box the Democrats at home would help the cause which they were maintaining in the field. It was that, and that alone, which protracted the war and created our immense debt.

I come, therefore, to the door of your party, gentlemen on the other side, and I lay down at your threshold every dollar of the debt, every item of the stupendous total which expresses the great cost of the war : and I say if you had followed Douglas there would have been no debt, no blood, no burden.

---

## THE WOMAN QUESTION.

[From an Address before the Business College, Washington, D. C., June 29, 1869.]

LAUGH at it as we may, put it aside as a jest if we will, keep it out of Congress or political campaigns, still, the woman question is rising in our horizon larger than the size of a man's hand ; and some solution, ere long, that question must find. I have not yet committed my mind to any formula that embraces the whole question. I halt on the threshold of so great a problem ; but there is one point on which I have reached a conclusion, and that is, that this nation must open up new avenues of work and usefulness to the women of the country, so that everywhere they may have something to do. This is, just now, infinitely more valuable to them than the platform or the ballot-box. Whatever conclusion shall be reached on that subject by and by, at present the most valuable gift which can be bestowed on women is something to do, which they can do well and worthily, and thereby maintain themselves. Therefore I say that every thoughtful statesman will look with satisfaction upon such business colleges as are opening a career for our young women. On that score we have special reason to be thankful for the establishment of these institutions.

## BANK-NOTES AND GREENBACKS.

[From a Speech in the House of Representatives, June 7, 1870.]

In the first place, it is the experience of all nations, and it is the almost unanimous opinion of all eminent statesmen and financial writers, that no nation can safely undertake to supply its people with a paper currency issued directly by the government. And, to apply that principle to our own country, let me ask if gentlemen think it safe to subject any political party who may be in power in this government to the great temptation of overissues of paper money in lieu of taxation? In times of high political excitement, and on the eve of a general election, when there might be a deficiency in the revenues of the country, and Congress should find it necessary to levy additional taxes, the temptation would be overwhelming to supply the deficit by an increased issue of paper money. Thus the whole business of the country, the value of all contracts, the prices of all commodities, the wages of labor, would depend upon a vote in Congress. For one, I dare not trust the great industrial interests of this country to such uncertain and hazardous chances.

But even if Congress and the administration should be always superior to such political temptations, still I affirm, in the second place, that no human legislature is wise enough to determine how much currency the wants of this country require. Test it in this House to-day. Let every member mark down the amount which he believes the business of the country requires, and who does not know that the amounts will vary by hundreds of millions?

But a third objection, stronger even than the last, is this : that such a currency possesses no power of adapting itself to the business of the country. Suppose the total issues should be five hundred millions, or seven hundred millons, or any amount you please ; it might be abundant for spring and summer, and yet when the great body of agricultural products were moving off to market in the fall that amount might be totally insufficient. Fix any volume you please, and if it be just sufficient at one period it may be redundant at another, or insufficient at another. No currency can meet the wants of this country unless it is founded directly upon the demands of business, and not upon the caprice, the ignorance, the political selfishness of the party in power.

What regulates now the loans and discounts and credits of our national banks? The business of the country. The amount increases or decreases, or remains stationary, as business is fluctuating or steady. This is a natural form of exchange, based upon the business of the country and regulated by its changes. And when that happy day arrives when the whole volume of our currency is redeemable in gold at the will of the holder, and recognized by all nations as equal to money, then the whole business of banking, the whole volume of currency, the whole amount of credits, whether in the form of checks, drafts, or bills, will be regulated by the same general law, the business of the country. The business of the country is like the level of the ocean, from which all measurements are made of heights and depths. Though tides and currents may for a time disturb, and tempests vex and toss its surface, still, through calm and storm the grand level rules all its waves and lays its measuring-lines on every shore. So the business of the country, which, in the aggregated demands of the people for exchange of values, marks the ebb and flow, the rise and fall of the currents of trade, and forms the base line from which to measure all our financial legislation, is the only safe rule by which the volume of our currency can be determined.

---

## A NON-EXPORTABLE CURRENCY.

[From a Speech in the House of Representatives, June 15, 1870.]

COULD anything but a predetermined purpose to defend, maintain, and increase our irredeemable paper money lead so able and distinguished a statesman as the gentleman from Pennsylvania [Mr. Kelley] to say, as he did the other day, concerning the greenback currency :

" Beyond the sea, in foreign lands, it fortunately is not money ; but, sir, when have we had such a long and unbroken career of prosperity in business as since we adopted this non-exportable currency ?"

It is reported of an Englishman who was wrecked on a strange shore that, wandering along the coast, he came to a gallows with a victim hanging upon it, and that he fell down on his knees and thanked God that he at last beheld a sign of civilization. But this is the first time I ever heard a financial philosopher express his gratitude that we have a currency of such bad repute that other nations will not receive it ; he is thankful that it is not exportable. We have a great many commodities in such a condition, that they are not exportable. Mouldy flour, rusty wheat, rancid butter, damaged cotton, addled eggs, and spoiled goods generally are not exportable. But it never occurred to me to be thankful for this putrescence. It is related in a quaint German book of humor, that the inhabitants of Schildeberg, finding that other towns, with more public spirit than their own, had erected gibbets within their precincts, resolved that the town of Schildeberg should also have a gallows ; and one patriotic member of the town council offered a resolution that the benefits of this gallows should be reserved exclusively for the inhabitants of Schildeberg.

The gentleman from Pennsylvania would reserve for our exclusive benefit all the blessings of a fluctuating, uncertain, and dishonored paper currency. In his view this irredeemable, non-exportable currency is so full of virtue that for the want of it California is falling into decay. That misguided State has seen fit to cling to the money that all nations receive, and ruin impends over her golden shores. I doubt if the business men of California will ask my friend to prescribe for their financial maladies. Quite in keeping with the gentleman's other opinions on this subject is the following. He says " the volume of currency does not, as has often been asserted, regulate the price of commodities." According to this we have not only a non-exportable currency, but one regulated by some trick of magic, so as to defy the universal laws of value, of supply and demand, and that neither the increase or decrease of its volume can affect the price of commodities. Argument on such a doctrine is useless.

----

## A FIXED STANDARD OF VALUE.

[From a Speech in the House of Representatives, April 8, 1874.]

With what care has our government protected its standards ! The gentleman from Massachusetts [Mr. Butler] sneeringly asked, Why does not some one argue in favor of redeeming the yard-stick, the quart-pot, or the Fairbanks scales ? In that paragraph he uses words without significance. We do not redeem these standards, but we do in regard to them what is analogous to the redemption of our standard of value. Our yard-stick is a metallic bar copied from the standard yard of England, which is nearly three hundred years old. It is deposited in the office of the Coast Survey, and is sacredly guarded from diminution or injury. The best efforts of science have been brought to bear to make the yard-stick as little liable as possible to mutilation or change.

Two methods have been adopted by science to test the accuracy of the standard and preserve it from loss. One is to find a pendulum which, swinging *in vacuo*, will make one vibration a second, at a given altitude from the level of the sea ; the other was a method adopted by France, when in the last century she sent her surveyors to measure six hundred miles of a meridian line, from Dunkirk to Barcelona. Thus she made her metre a given aliquot part of the earth's circumference, so that should her standard be lost the measure of the globe itself would furnish the means of restoring it. Both these standards are deposited in the Coast Survey, and together with the standard measures of capacity are furnished to the several States as the standards to which all our State and municipal laws refer. Every contract for the sale and delivery of anything that can be weighed or measured is based upon these standards, and the citizen who changes the weight or the measurement commits a misdemeanor for which he is punished by the law. The false weight and balance are still an abomination.

Sir, we do not redeem our yard-stick ; but we preserve it, and by the solemn sanctions of the law demand that it shall be applied to all transactions where extension is an element. Let us with equal care restore and preserve our standard of value, which must be applied to every exchange of property between man and man. An uncertain and fluctuating standard is an evil whose magnitude is too vast for measurement.

---

## THE BATTLE OF HISTORY.

[From a Speech in the House of Representatives, August 4, 1876.]

PEACE from the shock of battle ; the higher peace of our streets, of our homes, of our equal rights, we must make secure by making the conquering ideas of the war everywhere dominant and permanent. With all my heart I join with the gentleman in rejoicing that the war-drums throb no longer and the battle-flags are furled ; and I look forward with joy and hope to the day when our brave people, one in heart, one in their aspirations for freedom and peace, shall see that the darkness through which we have passed was a part of that stern but beneficent discipline by which the Great Disposer of events has been leading us on to a higher and nobler national life.

But such a result can be reached only by comprehending the whole meaning of the revolution through which we have passed and are still passing. I say still passing ; for I remember that after the battle of arms comes the battle of history. The cause that triumphs in the field does not always triumph in history. And those who carried the war for union and equal and universal freedom to a victorious issue can never safely relax their vigilance until the ideas for which they fought have become embodied in the enduring forms of individual and national life.

Has this been done ? Not yet. I ask the gentleman, in all plainness of speech, and yet in all kindness, Is he correct in his statement that the conquered party accept the results of the war ? Even if they do, I remind the gentleman that *accept* is not a very strong word. I go further : I ask him if the Democratic party have *adopted* the results of the war ? Is it not asking too much of human nature to expect such unparalleled changes to be not only accepted, but in so short a time adopted by men of strong and independent opinions ? The antagonisms which gave rise to the war and grew out of it were not born in a day, nor can they vanish in a night.

---

## THE EVIL GENIUS OF THE SOUTH.

[From a Speech in the House of Representatives, August 4, 1876.]

I HOPE my public life has given proof that I do not cherish a spirit of malice or bitterness toward the South. Perhaps they will say I have no right to advise them ; but at the risk of being considered impertinent I will express my conviction that the bane of the Southern people, for the last twenty-five years, has been that they have trusted the advice of the Democratic party. The very remedy which the gentleman from Mississippi offers for the ills of his people has been and still is their bane. The Democratic party has been the evil genius of the South in all these years. They yielded their own consciences to you on the slavery question, and led you to believe that the North would always yield. They made you believe that if we ever dared to cross the Potomac or Ohio to put down your rebellion, we could only do so across the dead bodies of many hundred thousands of Northern Democrats. They made you believe that the war would begin in the streets of our Northern cities ; that we were a community of shopkeepers, of sordid money-getters, and would not stand against your fiery chivalry. You thought us cold, slow, lethargic ; and in some respects we are. There are some differences between us that spring from origin and influences of climate—differences not unlike the description of the poet, that

> " Bright and fierce and fickle is the South,
> And dark and true and tender is the North"—

differences that kept us from a good understanding.

You thought that our coldness, our slowness, indicated a lack of spirit and of patriotism, and you were encouraged in that belief by most of the Northern Democracy ; but not by all. They warned you at Charleston in 1860.

And when the great hour struck there were many noble Democrats in the North who lifted the flag of the Union far above the flag of party ; but there was a residuum of Democracy, called in the slang of the time " copperheads," who were your evil genius from the beginning of the war till its close, and ever since. Some of them sat in these seats, and never rejoiced when we won a victory, and never grieved when we lost one. They were the men who sent your Vallandigham's to give counsel and encouragement to your rebellion, and to buoy you up with the false hope that at last you would conquer by the aid of their treachery. I honor you, gentlemen of the South, ten thousand times more than I honor such Democrats of the North.

---

## NO STEPS BACKWARD.

[From a Speech in the House of Representatives, Aug. 4, 1876.]

I WILL close by calling your attention again to the great problem before us. Over this vast horizon of interest North and South, above all party prejudices and personal wrong-doing, above our battle hosts and our victorious cause, above all that we hoped for and won, or you hoped for and lost, is the grand onward movement of the Republic to perpetuate its glory, to save liberty alive, to preserve exact and equal justice to all, to protect and foster all these priceless principles, until they shall have crystallized into the form of enduring law, and become inwrought into the life and habits of our people.

And until these great results are accomplished it is not safe to take one step backward. It is still more unsafe to trust interests of such measureless value in the hands of an organization whose members have never comprehended their epoch, have never been in sympathy with its great movements, who have resisted every step of its progress, and whose principal function has been "To lie in cold obstruction" across the pathway of the nation. It is most unsafe of all to trust that organization, when for the first time since the war it puts forward for the first and second place of honor and command men who in our days of greatest danger esteemed party above country, and felt not one throb of patriotic ardor for the triumph of imperilled Union, but from the beginning to the end hated the war and hated those who carried our eagles to victory. No, no, gentlemen ; our enlightened and patriotic people will not follow such leaders in the rearward march. Their myriad faces are turned the other way, and along their serried lines still rings the cheering cry, "Forward ! till our great work is fully and worthily accomplished."

---

## REBELLION IN THE REAR.

[From a Speech in the House of Representatives, Jan. 12, 1876.]

AND now, Mr. Speaker, I close as I began. Toward those men who gallantly fought on the field I cherish the kindest feeling. I feel a sincere reverence for the soldierly qualities they displayed on many a well-fought battle-field.   I hope the day will come when their swords and ours will be crossed over many a doorway of our children, who will remember the glory of their ancestors with pride. The high qualities displayed in that conflict now belong to the whole nation.   Let them be consecrated to the Union and its future peace and glory.   I shall hail that consecration as a pledge and symbol of our perpetuity.

But there is a class of men referred to in the speech of the gentleman yesterday, for whom I have never yet gained the Christian grace necessary to say the same thing.   The gentleman said that amid the thunder of battle, through its dim smoke and above its roar, they heard a voice from this side, saying, " Brothers, come."   I do not know whether he meant the same thing, but I heard that voice behind us.   I heard that voice, and I recollect that I sent one of those who uttered it through our lines—a voice owned by Vallandigham.   General Scott said, in the early days of the war, " When this war is over, it will require all the physical and moral power of the Government to *restrain the rage and fury of the non-combatants."*

It was that non-combatant voice behind us that cried " Halloo ?" to the other side ; that always gave cheer and encouragement to the enemy in our hour of darkness.   I have never forgotten and have not yet forgiven those Democrats of the North whose hearts were not warmed by the grand inspirations of the Union, but who stood back finding fault, always crying disaster, rejoicing at our defeat, never glorying in our victory.   If these are the voices the gentleman heard, I am sorry he is now united with those who uttered them.   But to those most noble men, Democrats and Republicans, who together fought for the Union, I commend all the lessons of charity that the wisest and most beneficent men have taught. I join you all in every aspiration that you may express to stay in this Union, to heal its wounds, to increase its glory, and to forget the evils and the bitternesses of the past ; but do not for the sake of the three hundred thousand heroic men who, maimed and bruised, drag out their weary lives, many of them carrying in their hearts horrible memories of what they suffered in the prison-pen—do not ask us to vote to put back into power that man who was the cause of their suffering—that man still unaneled, unshrived, unforgiven, undefended.

---

## POPULAR SUFFRAGE MADE SAFE BY EDUCATION.

[From an Address on the Future of the Republic, delivered before the Literary Societies of Hudson College.]

. WE are apt to be deluded into false security by political catchwords, devised to flatter rather than instruct.   We have happily escaped the dogma of the divine right of kings. Let us not fall into the equally pernicious error that multitude is divine because it is a multitude. The words of our great publicist, the late Dr. Lieber, whose faith in republican liberty was undoubted, should never be forgotten. In discussing the doctrine of " *Vox populi, vox Dei,*" he said :

" Woe to the country in which political hypocrisy first calls the people almighty, then teaches that the voice of the people is divine, then pretends to take a mere clamor for the true voice of the people, and lastly, gets up the desired clamor."

This sentence ought to be read in every political caucus. It would make an interesting and significant preamble to most of our political platforms. It is only when the people speak truth and justice that their voice can be called " the voice of God." Our faith in the democratic principle rests upon the belief that intelligent men will see that their highest political good is in liberty, regulated by just and equal laws ; and that in the distribution of political power it is safe to follow the maxim, " Each for all, and all for each." We confront the dangers of the suffrage by the blessings of universal education. We believe that the strength of the state is the aggregate strength of its individual citizens ; and that the suffrage is the link, that binds in a bond of mutual interest and responsibility, the fortunes of the citizen to the fortunes of the state. Hence, as popular suffrage is the broadest base ; so, when coupled with intelligence and virtue it becomes the strongest, the most enduring base on which to build the superstructure of government.

---

## THE DEMOCRACY CONVICTED OF A REVOLUTIONARY PURPOSE.

[From a Speech in the House of Representatives, April 26, 1879.]

GENTLEMEN, I took upon myself a very grave responsibility in the opening of this debate when I quoted the declarations of leading members on the other side and said that the programme was revolution and, if not abandoned, would result in the destruction of this Government. I declared that you had entered upon a scheme which if persisted in would starve the Government to death. I say that I took a great risk when I made this charge against you, as a party. I put myself in your power, gentlemen. If I had misconceived your purposes and misrepresented your motives, it was in your power to prove me a false accuser. It was in your power to ruin me in the estimation of fair-minded, patriotic men, by the utterance of one sentence. The humblest or the greatest of you could have overwhelmed me with shame and confusion in one short sentence. You could have said, " We wish to pass our measures of legislation in reference to elections, juries, and the use of the army : and we will, if we can do so constitutionally ; but if we cannot get these measures in accordance with the Constitution we will pass the appropriation bills like loyal representatives ; and then go home and appeal to the people."

If any man, speaking for the majority, had made that declaration, uttered that sentence, he would have ruined me in the estimation of fair-minded men, and set me down as a false accuser and slanderer. Forty-five of you have spoken. Forty-five of you have deluged the ear of this country with defeat ; but that sentence has not been spoken by any one of you. On the contrary, by your silence, as well as by your affirmation, you have made my accusation overwhelmingly true.

---

## A PARTY OF POSITIVE IDEAS.

[From a Debate with Geo. H. Pendleton, at Springfield, Ohio, Sept. 27, 1877.]

AND now, in looking over this long discussion, let me say that the Republican party, though it has made mistakes, has been a party of great courage, a party of great faith. It has had positive ideas— ideas it was willing to stand up by, and, if need be, die by. It believed in the Union ; it believed in the public faith ; it believed in a public trust ; it believed in enlarging the borders of liberty ; it believed in paying the public obligations, and it believes now in sustaining all it has so worthily achieved. It dares appeal to the country, as it is deserving of the confidence of the country. It dares appeal to the country as against a vacillating and uncertain and unwise and in many cases the unpatriotic spirit of the Democratic party.

---

## THE DEMOCRATIC CREED.

[From a Speech at London, Ohio, Sept. 19, 1877.]

THERE was a time when the Democratic party was a party of ideas. No party ever did any good unless it was a party of ideas. While it had ideas the Democratic party prospered. But twenty years ago an explosion occurred in its camp. From then until the present time it has not been a party of ideas. For twenty years it has been a party simply of opposition, of obstruction. Its creed may be summed up in one little word of two letters—-No! The

Democratic party for twenty years has said no. It has built nothing, but against all progress it has pulled back and snarled its opposition No. The Republican party is a party that builds something ; it is a party of aggressive ideas ; it believes in the Union and its perpetuity ; it believes in freedom against slavery ; it believes in the equality of all against class ; it believes in the public faith, in the public credit, in the payment of the public debt. It is the exponent of all great national things that make our country respected and prosperous. And to all this there has come one grumbling voice—No—from the Democracy. I hold myself open to debate this assertion with any Democratic speaker in Ohio. The Democracy have not in twenty years advanced one great national idea of public polity that they have held to for three consecutive years. Like an army building a bridge and burning each span behind it, they have builded and burned until at last they stand out isolated in the swamp, unable to get to either shore.

---

## THE SAVINGS OF THE PEOPLE.

[From a Speech in the House of Representatives, Nov. 16, 1877.]

GENTLEMEN assail the bondholders of the country as the rich men who oppress the poor. Do they know how vast an amount of the public securities are held by poor people ? I took occasion, a few years since, to ask the officers of a bank in one of the counties of my district—a rural district—to show me the number of holders and amounts held of United States bonds on which they collected the interest. The total amount was $416,000. And how many people held them ? One hundred and ninety six. Of these, just eight men held from $15,000 to $20,000 each ; the other one hundred and eighty-eight ranged from $50 up to $2500. I found in that list, fifteen orphan children and sixty widows, who had a little left them from their fathers' or husbands' estates, and had made the nation their guardian. And I found one hundred and twenty-one laborers, mechanics, ministers, men of slender means, who had saved their earnings and put them in the hands of the United States that they might be safe. And they were the bloated " bondholders," against whom so much eloquence is fulminated in this House. There is another way in which poor men dispose of their money. A man says, I can keep my wife and babies from starving while I live and have my health ; but if I die they may be compelled to go over the hill to the poorhouse ; and, agonized by that thought, he saves of his hard earnings enough to take out and keep alive a small life-insurance policy, so that, if he dies, there may be something left, provided the insurance company to which he intrusts his money is honest enough to keep its pledges. And how many men do you think have done that in the United States? I do not know the number for the whole country; but I do know this, that from a late report of the insurance commissioners of the State of New York it appears that the companies doing business in that State had 774,625 policies in force, and the face value of these policies was $1,922,000,000. I find, by looking over the returns, that in my State there are 55,000 policies outstanding; in Pennsylvania, 74,000; in Maine, 17,000; in Maryland, 25,000, and in the State of New York, 160,000. There are, of course, some rich men insured in these companies, but the majority are poor people, for the policies do not average more than $2200 each. What is done with the assets of these companies, which amount to $445,000,000? They are loaned out. Here again the creditor class is the poor, and the insurance companies are the agents of the poor to lend their money for them. It would be dishonorable for Congress to legislate either for the debtor class or for the creditor class alone. We ought to legislate for the whole country. But when gentlemen attempt to manufacture sentiment against the Resumption act, by saying it will help the rich and hurt the poor, they are overwhelmingly answered by the facts.

Suppose you undo the work that Congress has attempted—to resume specie payment—what will result? You will depreciate the value of the greenback. Suppose it falls ten cents on the dollar. You will have destroyed ten per cent of the value of every deposit in the savings-banks, ten per cent of every life-insurance policy and fire-insurance policy, of every pension to the soldier, and of every day's wages of every laborer in the nation.

---

## THE DEMOCRATIC PROGRAMME OF COERCING THE PRESIDENT.

[From a Speech in the House of Representatives, March 29, 1879.]

OUR theory of law is free consent. That is the granite foundation of our whole superstructure. Nothing in this Republic can be law without consent—the free consent of the House, the free consent of the Senate, the free consent of the Executive, or, if he refuse it, the free consent of two thirds of these bodies. Will any man deny that? Will any man challenge a line of the statement that free consent is the foundation of all our institutions? And yet the programme announced two weeks ago was that, if the Senate refused to consent to the demand of the House, the Government should stop. And the proposition was then, and the programme is now, that, although there is not a Senate to be coerced, there is still a third independent branch in the legislative power of the Government whose consent is to be coerced at the peril of the destruction of this Government ; that is, if the President, in the discharge of his duty, shall exercise his plain constitutional right to refuse his consent to this proposed legislation, the Congress will so use its voluntary powers as to destroy the Government. This is the proposition which we confront ; and we denounce it as revolution.

It makes no difference, Mr. Chairman, what the issue is. If it were the simplest and most inoffensive proposition in the world, yet if you demand, as a measure of coercion, that it shall be adopted against the free consent prescribed in the Constitution, every fair-minded man in America is bound to resist you as much as though his own life depended upon his resistance.

Let it be understood that I am not arguing the merits of any one of the three amendments. I am discussing the proposed method of legislation ; and I declare that it is against the Constitution of our country. It is revolutionary to the core, and is destructive of the fundamental principle of American liberty, the free consent of all the powers that unite to make laws.

In opening this debate I challenge all comers to show a single instance in our history where this consent has been thus coerced. This is the great, the paramount issue which dwarfs all others into insignificance.

---

### EFFECTS OF RESUMPTION.

[From an Address in Chicago, Jan. 2, 1879.]

SUCCESSFUL resumption will greatly aid in bringing into the murky sky of our politics what the signal service people call " clearing weather." It puts an end to a score of controversies which have long vexed the public mind, and wrought mischief to business. It ends the angry contention over the difference between the money of the bondholder and the money of the plough-holder. It relieves enterprising Congressmen of the necessity of introducing twenty-five or thirty bills a session to furnish the people with cheap money, to prevent gold-gambling, and to make custom duties payable in greenbacks. It will dismiss to the limbo of things forgotten such Utopian schemes as a currency based upon the magic circle of interconvertibility of two different forms of irredeemable paper, and the schemes of a currency " based on the public faith," and secured by " all the resources of the nation" in general, but upon no particular part of them. We shall still hear echoes of the old conflict, such as " the barbarism and cowardice of gold and silver," and the virtues of " fiat money ;" but the theories which gave them birth will linger among us like belated ghosts, and soon find rest in the political grave of dead issues. All these will take their places in history alongside of the resolution of Vansittart, in 1811, that " British paper had not fallen, but gold had risen in value," and the declaration of Castlereagh, in the House of Commons, that " the money standard is a sense of value in reference to currency as compared with commodities," and the opinion of another member, who declared that "the standard is neither gold nor silver, but *something set up in the imagination to be regulated by public opinion.*"

When we have fully awakened from these vague dreams, public opinion will resume its old channels, and the wisdom and experience of the fathers of our Constitution will again be acknowledged and followed.

We shall agree, as our fathers did, that the yard-stick shall have length, the pound must have weight, and the dollar must have value in itself, and that neither length, nor weight, nor value can be created by the fiat of law. Congress, relieved of the arduous task of regulating and managing all the business of our people, will address itself to the humbler but more important work of preserving the public peace, and managing wisely the revenues and expenditures of the Government. Industry will no longer wait for the legislature to discover easy roads to sudden wealth, but will begin again to rely upon labor and frugality as the only certain road to riches. Prosperity, which has long been waiting, is now ready to come. If we do not rudely repulse her she will soon revisit our people, and will stay until another periodical craze shall drive her away.

---

## THE ABSURDITY OF FIAT MONEY.

[From a Speech at Flint, Michigan, Oct. 22, 1878.]

Now, fellow-citizens, to sum up all I have tried to say thus far, when you can have more cloth by shortening your yard-stick ; when you can have more wheat by reducing the size of your bushel ; when you can have more land by changing the figures of your deed, and having it read " 200" where it read " 100 ;" when your dairyman can make more butter and cheese by watering his milk—then, and *not till then*, can you make wealth in this country by printing pieces of paper and calling them dollars. Why, I met a gentleman on your streets to-day, a man hardly past middle age, that told me he was here when there were but two log-cabins in this place. And I say that this beautiful city, with its beautiful gardens and its circling river, with its homes and happiness—I say that all that has been done here since the time that man first came, has been done by the hard struggling and earnest toil of courageous men, who have for a generation back battled with the wilderness and brought it up to the glory of to-day. Well, friends, what fools these people were, to speak plainly, to have endured so much when they might have set up a printing-press and just printed themselves rich, if this idea of fiat money be true. Why, fellow-citizens, do you really believe that if we should in Washington print pieces of paper saying, "This is 1,000,000," and send one to each man, woman, and child in the United States, that we should all in fact be millionaires the next morning? Now does anybody believe that? It is the wildest hallucination that ever struck upon a people. It is wholly wild, and wholly without foundation.

---

## A REPLY TO THE DEMOCRATIC THREAT TO DESTROY THE ARMY.

[Remarks in the House of Representatives, April 4, 1879.]

I SAY, if the gentleman from Virginia puts that proposition before the American people, we will debate it in the forum of every patriotic heart, and will abide the result. If the party which, after eighteen years' banishment from power, has come back, as the gentleman from Kentucky [Mr. Blackburn] said yesterday, to its "birthright of power," or "heritage," as it is recorded in the record of this morning, is to signalize its return by striking down the gallant and faithful army of the United States, the people of this country will not be slow to understand that there are reminiscences of that army which these gentlemen would willingly forget, by burying both the army and the memories of its great service to the Union in one grave.

We do not seek to revive the unhappy memories of the war ; but we are unwilling to see the army perish at the hands of Congress, even if its continued existence should occasionally awaken the memory of its former glories.

Now, let it be understood, once for all, that we do not deny, we have never denied your right to make such rules for this House as you please. Under those rules, as you make or construe them, you may put all your legislation upon these bills as "riders." But we say that, whatever your rules may be, you must make or repeal a law in accordance with the Constitution, by the triple consent to which I referred the other day, or you must do it by violence.

Now, as my friend from Connecticut [Mr. Hawley] well said, if you can elect a President and a Congress in 1880, you have only to wait two years, and you have the three consents. You can then, without revolution, tear down this statute and all the rest. You can follow out the programme which some of your members have suggested, and tear out one by one the records of the last eighteen years. Some of them are glorious with the unquenchable light of liberty ; some of them stand as the noblest trophies of freedom. With full power in your hands, you can destroy them. But we ask you to restrain your rage against them until you have the lawful power to smite them down.

———

## PROTECTION OF THE NATIONAL BALLOT-BOX.

[From a Speech in the House of Representatives, March 29, 1879.]

LET it be remembered that the avowed object of this new revolution is to destroy all the defences which the nation has placed around its ballot-box to guard the fountain of its own life. You say that the United States shall not employ even its civil power to keep peace at the polls. You say that the marshals shall have no power either to arrest rioters or criminals who seek to destroy the freedom and purity of the ballot-box.

I remind you that you have not always shown this great zeal in keeping the civil officers of the General Government out of the States. Only six years before the war your law authorized marshals of the United States to enter all our hamlets and households to hunt for fugitives slaves. Not only that, it empowered the marshals to summon the *posse comitatus*, to command all bystanders to join in the chase and aid in remanding to eternal bondage the fleeing slave. And your Democratic Attorney-General, in his opinion published in 1854, declared that the marshal of the United States might summon to his aid the whole able-bodied force of his precinct, all bystanders, including not only the citizens generally, " but any and all organized armed forces, whether militia of the State, or officers, soldiers, sailors, and marines of the United States," to join in the chase and hunt down the fugitive. Now, gentlemen, if, for the purpose of making eternal slavery the lot of an American, you could send your marshals, summon your *posse*, and use the armed force of the United States, with what face or grace can you tell us that this Government cannot lawfully employ the same marshals with their armed *posse* of citizens, to maintain the purity of our own elections and keep the peace at our own polls. You have made the issue and we have accepted it. In the name of the Constitution and on behalf of good government and public justice, we make the appeal to our common sovereign.

## THE NEW REBELLION.

[From a Speech in the House of Representatives, March 29, 1879.]

LET it be understood that I am not discussing the merits of this law. I have merely turned aside from the line of my argument to show the inconsistency of the other side in proposing to stop the Government if they cannot force the repeal of a law which they themselves made. I am discussing a method of revolution against the Constitution now proposed by this House, and to that issue I hold gentlemen in this debate, and challenge them to reply.

And now, Mr. Chairman, I ask the forbearance of gentlemen on the other side while I offer a suggestion, which I make with reluctance. They will bear me witness that I have, in many ways, shown my desire that the wounds of the war should be healed ; that the grass which has grown green over the graves of the dead of both armies might symbolize the returning spring of friendship and peace between citizens who were lately in arms against each other.

But I am compelled by the conduct of the other side to refer to a chapter of our recent history. The last act of Democratic domination in this Capitol, eighteen years ago, was striking and dramatic, perhaps heroic. Then the Democratic party said to the Republicans, " If you elect the man of your choice as President of the United States we will shoot your Government to death ;" but the people of this country, refusing to be coerced by threats or violence, voted as they pleased, and lawfully elected Abraham Lincoln as President of the United States.

Then your leaders, though holding a majority in the other branch of Congress, were heroic enough to withdraw from their seats and fling down the gage of mortal battle. We called it rebellion : but we recognized it as courageous and manly to avow your purpose, take all the risks, and fight it out in the open field. Notwithstanding your utmost efforts to destroy it, the Government was saved. Year by year, since the war ended, those who resisted you have come to believe that you have finally renounced your purpose to destroy, and are willing to maintain the Government. In that belief you have been permitted to return to power in the two Houses.

To-day, after eighteen years of defeat, the book of your domination is again opened, and your first act awakens every unhappy memory, and threatens to destroy the confidence which your professions of patriotism inspired. You turned down a leaf of the history that recorded your last act of power in 1861, and you have now signalized your return to power by beginning a second chapter at the same page, not this time by a heroic act that declares war on the battle-field, but you say, if all the legislative powers of the Government do not consent to let you tear certain laws out of the statute-book, you will not shoot our Government to death as you tried to do in the first chapter, but you declare that if we do not consent against our will, if you cannot coerce an independent branch of this Government, against its will to allow you to tear from the statute-book some laws put there by the will of the people, you will starve the Government to death. [Great applause on the Republican side.]

Between death on the field and death by starvation I do not know that the American people will see any great difference. The end. if successfully reached, would be death in either case. Gentlemen, you have it in your power to kill this Government; you have it in your power, by withholding these two bills, to smite the nerve-centres of our Constitution with the paralysis of death; and you have declared your purpose to do this, if you cannot break down that fundamental principle of free consent which, up to this hour has always ruled in the legislation of this Government.

---

## AN APPEAL TO YOUNG MEN.

[From a Speech at Cleveland, on the Saturday evening before the Ohio election of 1879.]

NOW, fellow-citizens, a word before I leave you, on the very eve of the holy day of God—a fit moment to consecrate ourselves finally to the great work of next Tuesday morning. I see in this great audience to-night a great many young men—young men who are about to cast their first vote. I want to give you a word of suggestion and advice. I heard a very brilliant thing said by a boy the other day, up in one of our northwestern counties. He said to me, " General, I have a great mind to vote the Democratic ticket." That was not the brilliant thing. I said to him, " Why ?" " Why," said he, " my father is a Republican, and my brothers are Republicans, and I am a Republican all over ; but I want to be an independent man, and I don't want anybody to say, ' That fellow votes the Republican ticket just because his dad does,' and I have half a mind to vote the Democratic ticket just to prove my independence." I did not like the thing the boy suggested, but I did admire the spirit of the boy that wanted to have some independence of his own.

Now, I tell you, young man, don't vote the Republican ticket just because your father votes it. Don't vote the Democratic ticket, even if he does vote it. But let me give you this one word of advice, as you are about to pitch your tent in one of the great political camps. Your life is full and buoyant with hope now, and I beg you, when you pitch your tent, pitch it among the living and not among the dead. If you are at all inclined to pitch it among the Democratic people and with that party, let me go with you for a moment while we survey the ground where I hope you will not shortly lie. It is a sad place, young man, for you to put your young life into. It is to me far more like a graveyard than like a camp for the living. Look at it ! It is billowed all over with the graves of dead issues, of buried opinions, of exploded theories, of disgraced doctrines. You cannot live in comfort in such a place. Why, look here ! Here is a little double mound. I look down on it and I read, " Sacred to the memory of Squatter Sovereignty and the Dred Scott Decision." A million and a half of Democrats voted for that, but it has been dead fifteen years—died by the hand of Abraham Lincoln, and here it lies. Young man, that is not the place for you.

But look a little further. Here is another monument, a black tomb, and beside it, as our distinguished friend said, there towers to the sky a monument of four million pairs of human fetters taken from the arms of slaves, and I read on its little headstone this : " Sacred to the memory of Human Slavery." For forty years of its infamous life the Democratic party taught that it was divine—God's institution. They defended it, they stood around it, they followed it to its grave as a mourner. But here it lies, dead by the hand of Abraham Lincoln ; dead by the power of the Republican party ; dead by the justice of Almighty God. Don't camp there, young man.

But here is another—a little brimstone tomb—and I read across its yellow face, in lurid, bloody lines, these words : " Sacred to the memory of State Sovereignty and Secession." Twelve millions of Democrats mustered around it in arms to keep it alive ; but here it lies, shot to death by the million guns of the Republic. Here it lies, its shrine burned to ashes under the blazing rafters of the burning Confederacy. It is dead ! I would not have you stay in there a minute, even in this balmy night air, to look at such a place.

But just before I leave it I discover a new-made grave, a little mound—short. The grass has hardly sprouted over it, and all around I see torn pieces of paper with the word " fiat " on them, and I look down in curiosity, wondering what the little grave is, and I read on it : " Sacred to the memory of the Rag Baby ;" nursed in the brain of all the fanaticism of the world ; rocked by Thomas Ewing, George H. Pendleton, Samuel Cary, and a few others throughout the land. But it died on the 1st of January, 1879, and the one hundred and forty millions of gold that God made, and not fiat power, lie upon its little carcass to keep it down forever.

Oh, young man, come out of that ! That is no place in which to put your young life. Come out, and come over into this camp of liberty, of order, of law, of justice, of freedom, of all that is glorious under these night stars.

Is there any death here in our camp? Yes ! yes ! Three hundred and fifty thousand soldiers, the noblest band that ever trod the earth, died to make this camp a camp of glory and of liberty forever. But there are no dead issues here. There are no dead ideas here. Hang out our banner from under the blue sky this night until it shall sweep the green turf under your feet. It hangs over our camp. Read away up under the stars the inscription we have written on it, lo ! these twenty-five years.

Twenty-five years ago the Republican party was married to liberty, and this is our silver wedding, fellow-citizens. A worthily married pair love each other better on the day of their silver wedding than on the day of their first espousals ; and we are truer to liberty to-day and dearer to God than we were when we spoke our first word of liberty. Read away up under the sky across our starry banner that first word we uttered twenty-five years ago ! What was it ? "Slavery shall never extend over another foot of the territory of the great West." Is that dead or alive ? Alive, thank God, forevermore ! And truer to-night than it was the hour it was written. Then it was a hope, a promise, a purpose. To-night it is equal with the stars—immortal history and immortal truth.

Come down the glorious steps of our banner. Every great record we have made we have vindicated with our blood and with our truth. It sweeps the ground, and it touches the stars. Come here, young man, and put in your young life where all is living and where nothing is dead but the heroes that defended it. I think these young men will do that.

---

## THE DEMOCRATIC GRAVEYARD.

[From a Speech in the House of Representatives, Aug. 4, 1876.]

I WALK across that Democratic camping-ground as in a graveyard. Under my feet resound the hollow echoes of the dead. There lies Slavery ; a black marble column at the head of its grave, on which I read, Died in the flames of the civil war ; loved in its life, lamented in its death ; followed to its bier by its only mourner, the Democratic party, but dead ! And here is a double grave : Sacred to the memory of Squatter Sovereignty. Died in the campaign of 1860. On the reverse side : Sacred to the memory of the Dred Scott-Breckinridge doctrine. Both dead at the hands of Abraham Lincoln. And here a monument of brimstone : Sacred to the memory of the Rebellion ; the war against it is a failure ; Tilden et Vallandigham fecerunt, A.D. 1864. Dead on the field of battle ; shot to

death by the million guns of the Republic.   The doctrine of Secession, of State Sovereignty.   Dead ; expired in the flames of civil
war, amid the blazing rafters of the Confederacy, except that the
modern Æneas, fleeing out of the flames of that ruin, bears on his
back another Anchises of State Sovereignty, and brings it here in
the person of the honorable gentleman from the Appomattox district
of Virginia.   All else is dead.

Now, gentlemen, are you sad, are you sorry for these deaths ?
Are you not glad that secession is dead ? that slavery is dead ? that
squatter sovereignty is dead ? that the doctrine of the failure of the
war is dead ?   Then you are glad that you were outvoted in 1860,
1864, in 1868, and in 1872.   If you have tears to shed over these
losses, shed them in the graveyard, but not in this House of living
men.   I know that many a Southern man rejoices that these issues
are dead.   The gentleman from Mississippi has clothed his joy with
eloquence.   Now, gentlemen, if you yourselves are glad that you
have suffered defeat during the last sixteen years, will you not be
equally glad when you suffer defeat next November ?

---

### RELATION OF CURRENCY TO PRICES.

[From a Speech in the House of Representatives, May 15, 1868.]

LET us examine more minutely the effect of such a currency upon
prices.   Suppose that the business transactions of the country at
the present time require $350,000,000 in gold.   It is manifest that
if there are just $350,000,000 of legal-tender notes, and no other
money in the country, each dollar will perform the full functions of
a gold dollar, so far as the work of exchange is concerned.   Now,
business remaining the same, let $350,000,000 more of the same
kind of notes be pressed into circulation.   The whole volume, as
thus increased, can do no more than all the business. Each dollar will
accomplish just half the work that a dollar did before the increase,
but as the nominal dollar is fixed by law, the effect is shown in
prices being doubled.   It requires two of these dollars to make the
same purchase that one dollar made before the increase.   It would
require some time for the business of the country to adjust itself to
the new conditions, and great derangement of values would ensue ;
but the result would at last be reached in all transactions which are
controlled by the law of demand and supply.

No such change of value can occur without cost.   Somebody
must pay for it.   Who pays in this case ?   We have seen that
doubling the currency finally results in reducing the purchasing power

of each dollar one half ; hence every man who held a legal-tender note at the time of the increase, and continued to hold it till the full effect of the increase was produced, suffered a loss of fifty per cent of its value ; in other words, he paid a tax to the amount of half of all the currency in his possession. This new issue, therefore, by depreciating the value of all the currency, cost the holders of the old issue $175,000,000 ; and if the new notes were received at their nominal value at the date of issue, their holders paid a tax of $175,000,000 more. No more unequal or unjust mode of taxation could possibly be devised. It would be tolerated only by being so involved in the transactions of business as to be concealed from observation ; but it would be no less real because hidden.

----

### SURPLUS AND DEFICIT IN THE TREASURY.
[From a Speech in the House of Representatives, March 5, 1874.]

REVENUES and expenditures may be considered from two points of view—in relation to the people and their industries, and in rela-tion to the government and the effective working of its machinery. So far as the people are concerned, they willingly bear the burdens of taxation, when they see that their contributions are honestly and wisely expended to maintain the government of their choice, and to accomplish those objects which they consider necessary for the general welfare. So far as the government is concerned the sound-ness of its financial affairs depends upon the annual surplus of its revenues over expenditures. A steady and constant revenue drawn from sources that represent the prosperity of the nation—a revenue that grows with the growth of national wealth and is so adjusted to the expenditures that a constant and considerable surplus is annually left in the treasury above all the necessary current demands ; a surplus that keeps the treasury strong, that holds it above the fear of sudden panic ; that makes it impregnable against all private com-binations ; that makes it a terror to all stock jobbing and gold-gambling—this is financial health. This is the situation that wise statesmanship should endeavor to support and maintain.

Of course in this discussion I leave out the collateral though im-portant subject of banking and currency. The surplus, then. is the key to our financial situation. Every act of legislation should be studied in view of its effects upon the surplus. Two sets of forces are constantly acting upon the surplus. It is increased by the growth of the revenue and by the decrease of expenditure. It is decreased by the repeal or reduction of taxation, and by the increase of expenditures. When both forces conspire against it, when taxes are diminished and expenditures are increased, the surplus disappears.

With the disappearance of the surplus comes disaster—disaster to the treasury, disaster to the public credit, disaster to all the public interests. In times of peace, when no sudden emergency has made a great and imperious demand upon the treasury, a deficit cannot occur except as the result of unwise legislation or reckless and unwarranted administration. That legislation may consist in too great an increase of appropriations, or in too great a reduction of taxation, or in both combined.

---

## HEROES IN POLITICS.

### [From an Oration delivered at Ravenna, Ohio, July 4, 1860.]

As a people we are brimfull of enthusiasm and excitement. To Europeans our Presidential campaigns are a source of profound astonishment. Mackay in his late tour among us expressed his wonder that such an intensely exciting mass-meeting should be held in the City of New York without the restraining influence of military force. But they do not understand the omnipotence of majorities among us. Let a contest rage never so fiercely, with all the intensity which excited partisans can feel, and though each will fight for his man or party to the bitter end yet, when once the voice of the majority has been clearly and fairly expressed, the waves of strife are still, and ninety-nine in the hundred of that fiery throng would fight to their death to sustain the will of that majority. This strong element of national enthusiasm has given a peculiar character to our hero-worship. We are never without a man or a motto to shout over. Still our Hosannas are not so much for the man as for the doctrine he represents. Our political heroes we very appropriately call " standard-bearers." We applaud the motto inscribed on the banner rather than him who bears it. He may soon pass out of sight, but the motto is preserved. And here we are reminded of that proverbial ingratitude charged upon republics for their treatment of their great men. It must be conceded that for the last quarter of a century few of our first men have been elevated to the highest positions. This has at least demonstrated the virtue and strength of the Government, that with only mediocre men at the helm its functions could be so easily and well discharged. It may be fairly questioned whether the welfare of the whole people does not demand that the power and control of great men should be jealously watched and in a measure abridged. As a giant tree absorbs all the elements of growth within its reach, and leaves only a sickly vegetation in its shadow, so do towering great men absorb all the strength and glory of their surroundings.

## TREASON IN CONGRESS.

[From Remarks in the House Jan. 1874 in answer to a speech by Alexander Long
in favor of recognizing the Southern Confederacy.]

FIRST of all, the gentleman tells us that the right of secession is a constitutional right. I do not propose to enter into the argument. I have expressed myself hitherto upon State sovereignty and State rights, of which this proposition is the legitimate child. But the gentleman takes higher ground, and in that I agree with him, namely, that five million or eight million people possess the right of revolution. Grant it : we agree there. If fifty-nine men can make revolution successful, they have the right of revolution. If one State wishes to break its connection with the Federal Government, and does it by force, maintaining itself, it is an independent nation. If the eleven Southern States are determined and resolved to leave the Union, to secede, to revolutionize, and can maintain that revolution by force, they have the revolutionary right to do so. Grant it. I stand on that platform with the gentleman.

And now the question comes, Is it our constitutional duty to let them do it ? That is the question, and in order to reach it I beg to call your attention, not to an argument, but to the condition of affairs which would result from such action, the mere statement of which becomes the strongest possible argument. What does this gentleman propose ? Where will he draw the line of division ? If the rebels carry into successful secession what they desire to carry ; if their revolution envelops as many States as they intend it shall envelop ; if they draw the line where Isham G. Harris, the rebel Governor of Tennessee, in the rebel camp near our lines, told Mr. Vallandigham they would draw it—along the line of the Ohio and the Potomac ; if they make good their declaration to him that they will never consent to any other line, then I ask, what is this thing that the gentleman proposes to do ? I tell you, and I confess it here, that while I hope I have something of human courage, I have not enough to contemplate such a result. I am not brave enough to go to the precipice of successful secession and look down into its damned abyss. If my vision were keen enough to pierce to its bottom, I would not dare to look. If there be a man here who dare contemplate such a spectacle, I look upon him as the bravest of the sons of women or as a downright madman. Secession to gain peace ! Secession is the tocsin of eternal war. There can be no end to such a war as will be inaugurated of this thing be done, and leave a dearth of greatness for a whole generation. A monopoly of popular honors is as much a tyranny as a monopoly of wealth. The good of the many should be dearer to the American heart than the good of the few.

# GEN. GARFIELD'S LETTER OF ACCEPTANCE.

MENTOR, O., July 12.

DEAR SIR : On the evening of the 8th of June last I had the honor to receive from you, in the presence of the committee of which you were chairman, the official announcement that the Republican National Convention at Chicago had that day nom-inated me as their candidate for President of the United States. I accept the nomination with gratitude for the confidence it im-plies, and with a deep sense of the responsibility it imposes. I cordially endorse the principles set forth in the platform adopted by the Convention. On nearly all the subjects of which it treats, my opinions are on record among the published pro-ceedings of Congress. I venture, however, to make special mention of some of the principal topics which are likely to be-come subjects of discussion.

Without reviewing the controversies which have been settled during the last twenty years, and with no purpose or wish to revive the passions of the late war, it should be said that while the Republicans fully recognize and will strenuously defend all the rights retained by the people and all the rights reserved to the States, they reject the pernicious doctrine of State suprem-acy which so long crippled the functions of the National Gov-ernment, and at one time brought the Union very near to de-struction. They insist that the United States is a nation, with ample power of self-preservation ; that its Constitution and the laws made in pursuance thereof are the supreme law of the land ; that the right of the Nation to determine the method by which its own Legislature shall be created cannot be surrendered without abdicating one of the fundamental powers of government ; that the national laws relating to the election of Representatives in Congress shall neither be violated nor evaded ; that every elector shall be permitted freely and without intimidation to cast his lawful ballot at such election and have it honestly counted, and that the potency of his vote shall not be destroyed by the fraudulent vote of any other person.

The best thoughts and energies of our people should be directed to those great questions of national well-being in which all have a common interest.   Such efforts will soonest restore perfect peace to those who were lately in arms against each other ; for justice and good-will will outlast passion.   But it is certain that the wounds of the war cannot be completely healed, and the spirit of brotherhood cannot fully pervade the whole country, until every citizen, rich or poor, white or black, is secure in the free and equal enjoyment of every civil and political right guaranteed by the Constitution and the laws.   Wherever the enjoyment of these rights is not assured, discontent will prevail, immigration will cease, and the social and industrial forces will continue to be disturbed by the migration of laborers and the consequent diminution of prosperity.   The National Government should exercise all its constitutional authority to put an end to these evils, for all the people and all the States are members of one body, and no member can suffer without injury to all.   The most serious evils which now afflict the South arise from the fact that there is not such freedom and toleration of political opinion and action that the minority party can exercise an effectve and wholesome restraint upon the party in power.   Without such restraint party rule becomes tyrannical and corrupt.   The prosperity which is made possible in the South by its great advantages of soil and climate will never be realized until every voter can freely and safely support any party he pleases.

Next in importance to freedom and justice is popular education, without which neither freedom nor justice can be permanently maintained. Its interests are entrusted to the States and to the voluntary action of the people. Whatever help the Nation can justly afford should be generously given to aid the States in supporting common schools ; but it would be unjust to our people and dangerous to our institutions to apply any portion of the revenues of the Nation, or of the States, to the support of sectarian schools. The separation of the Church and the State in everything relating to taxation should be absolute.

On the subject of national finances my views have been so frequently and fully expressed that little is needed in the way of additional statement. The public debt is now so well secured and the rate of annual interest has been so reduced by refunding, that rigid economy in expenditures and the faithful application of our surplus revenues to the payment of the principal of the debt will gradually but certainly free the people from its burdens, and close with honor the financial chapter of the war. At the same time the Government can provide for all its ordinary expenditures and discharge its sacred obligations to the soldiers of the Union, and to the widows and orphans of those who fell in its defence. The resumption of specie payments, which the Republican Party so courageously and successfully accomplished, has removed from the field of controversy many questions that long and seriously disturbed the credit of the Government and the business of the country. Our paper currency is now as national as the flag, and resumption has not only made it everywhere equal to coin, but has brought into use our store of gold and silver. The circulating medium is more abundant than ever before, and we need only to maintain the equality of all our dollars to insure to labor and capital a measure of value from the use of which no one can suffer loss. The great prosperity which the country is now enjoying should not be endangered by any violent changes or doubtful financial experiments.

In reference to our customs laws a policy should be pursued which will bring revenues to the Treasury, and will enable the labor- and capital employed in our great industries to compete fairly in our own markets with the labor and capital of foreign producers. We legislate for the people of the United States, and not for the whole world, and it is our glory that the American laborer is more intelligent and better paid than his foreign competitor. Our country cannot be independent unless its people, with their abundant natural resources, possess the requisite skill at any time to clothe, arm, and equip themselves for war, and in time of peace to produce all the necessary implements of labor. It was the manifest intention of the founders of the Government to provide for the common defence, not by standing armies alone, but by raising among the people a greater army of artisans whose intelligence and skill should powerfuly contribute to the safety and glory of the nation.

Fortunately for the interests of commerce, there is no longer any formidable opposition to appropriations for the improvement of our harbors and great navigable rivers, provided that the expenditures for that purpose are strictly limited to works of national importance. The Mississippi River, with its great tributaries, is of such vital importance to so many millions of people that the safety of its navigation requires exceptional consideration. In order to secure to the Nation the control of all its waters, President Jefferson negotiated the purchase of a vast territory, extending from the Gulf of Mexico to the Pacific Ocean. The wisdom of Congress should be invoked to devise some plan by which that great river shall cease to be a terror to those who dwell upon its banks, and by which its shipping may safely carry the industrial products of 25,000,000 of people. The interests of agriculture, which is the basis of all our material prosperity, and in which seven-twelfths of our population are engaged, as well as the interests of manufactures and commerce,

demand that the facilities for cheap transportation shall be increased by the use of all our great water-courses.

The material interests of this country, the traditions of its
settlement, and the sentiment of our people have led the Government to offer the widest hospitality to immigrants who seek our
shores for new and happier homes, willling to share the burdens
as well as the benefits of our society, and intending that their
posterity shall become an undistinguishable part of our population.    The recent movement of the Chinese to our Pacific Coast
partakes but little of the qualities of such an immigration either
in its purpose or its result. It is too much like an importation to
be welcomed without restriction ; too much like an invasion to
be looked upon without solicitude.    We cannot consent to allow any form of servile labor to be introduced among us under
the guise of immigration.    Recognizing the gravity of this subject, the present Administration, supported by Congress, has
sent to China a commission of distinguished citizens for the purpose of securing such a modification of the existing treaty as
will prevent the evils likely to arise from the present situation.
It is confidently believed that these diplomatic negotiations will
be successful without the loss of commercial intercourse between the two Powers, which promises a great increase of re-
ciprocal trade and the enlargement of our markets.    Should
these efforts fail, it will be the duty of Congress to mitigate the
evils already felt, and prevent their increase by such restrictions
as, without violence or injustice, will place upon a sure foundation the peace of our communities and the freedom and dig-
nity of labor.

The appointment of citizens to the various executive and judicial offices of the Government is, perhaps, the most difficult of
all duties which the Constitution has imposed on the Executive.
The Convention wisely demands that Congress shall co-operate
with the executive departments in placing the Civil Service on a
better basis.    Experience has proved that with our frequent

changes of administration no system of reform can be made effective and permanent without the aid of legislation. Appointments to the military and naval service are so regulated by law and custom as to leave but little ground for complaint. It may not be wise to make similar regulations by law for the Civil Service. But without invading the authority or necessary discretion of the Executive, Congress should devise a method that will determine the tenure of office, and greatly reduce the uncertainty which makes that service so uncertain and unsatisfactory. Without depriving any officer of his rights as a citizen, the Government should require him to discharge all his official duties with intelligence, efficiency, and faithfulness. To select wisely from our vast population those who are best fitted for the many offices to be filled, requires an acquaintance far beyond the range of any one man. The Executive should, therefore seek and receive information and assistance of those whose knowledge of the communities in which the duties are to be performed best qualifies them to aid in making the wisest choice.

The doctrines announced by the Chicago Convention are not the temporary devices of a party to attract votes and carry an election ; they are deliberate convictions resulting from a careful study of the spirit of our institutions, the events of our history, and the best impulses of our people. In my judgment these principles should control the legislation and administration of the Government. In any event, they will guide my conduct until experience points out a better way.

If elected, it will be my purpose to enforce strict obedience to the Constitution and the laws, and to promote, as best I may, the interest and honor of the whole country, relying for support upon the wisdom of Congress, the intelligence and patriotism of the people, and the favor of God. With great respect, I am very truly yours, J. A. GARFIELD.

*To the Hon.* GEORGE F. HOAR, *Chairman of Committee.*

LIFE OF

# CHESTER A. ARTHUR

## OF NEW YORK.

BY

E. L. MURLIN.

CHESTER A. ARTHUR.

LIFE OF

# CHESTER A. ARTHUR.

## CHAPTER I.

### BOYHOOD AND COLLEGE LIFE.

The traveller through Washington County, New York, and the bordering counties of Southwestern Vermont finds a land that has many of the characteristics of a mountain region. There are long and narrow valleys adorned with rich meadows, shut in by hills approaching the height of mountains—their bases covered with farms and their crests hidden by dense forests. To the northward the dwellers on these hills see, low-lying on the horizon line, the Adirondacks ; at the south the curving line of the blue Catskills ; while cleaving their land is a great mountain range, a huge ridge of rock and forest lifted high in the air—the Green Mountains. The inhabitants of this region, as in all mountainous countries, have always been a liberty-loving people and very energetic in their action when they thought it endangered. From them went forth Ethan Allen to conquer Ticonderoga, "in the name of God and the Continental Congress." From them again, in 1851, there came forth a young man who loved liberty and believed in human freedom, and who, from these native traits, was to take a great part in the liberation and enfranchisement of four million slaves then in bondage.

Chester Alan Arthur was born in Franklin County, Vermont, on the 5th day of October, 1830. He was the eldest of two

sons ; he had four sisters older and one younger than himself.
His father, the Rev. Dr. William Arthur, was a Baptist clergy-
man, who came to the United States from Ballymena, County
Antrim, Ireland, when only 18 years old, and died at an
advanced age in Newtonville, near Albany, on October 27th,
1875.   Dr. Arthur was a finely-educated man ; a graduate of
Belfast University, Ireland.     For several years he published
*The Antiquarian*, a journal devoted, as its title indicates, to antiquarian research.  A work of his own, " Family Names," is still
highly esteemed by the collectors of this kind of literature.
While devoting himself to literature, he yet fulfilled faithfully
all the duties of his special calling.     He was pastor of the
Calvary Baptist Church, Albany ; and also of Baptist churches
at Bennington, Hinesburg, Fairfield and Williston, in Vermont ;
and at  York,  Perry,  Greenwich,  Schenectady, Lansingburg,
Hoosic, West Troy, and Newtonville, in New York State.   The
second son, William Arthur, highly distinguished himself in the
Union army during the war of the Rebellion.   He is now a pay-
master of the regular army with the rank of major.

  Chester A. Arthur found his father's fine knowledge of the
Latin and Greek classics of great advantage to him when he
came to prepare for college.   His preparation first began in
Union Village, now Greenwich, a beautiful village of Washington County, New York ; and was concluded at the grammar
school at Schenectady.   Thanks to his fine training young
Arthur took a high position in Union College, which he entered
in 1845, when only 15 years old.     Every year of his college
course he was declared to be one of those who had taken
" maximum honors " ; and at the conclusion of his college
course, out of a class of one hundred members he was one
of six who were elected members of the Phi Beta Kappa
Society, the condition of entrance to which is the highest schol-
arship.  This was the more creditable to him as he was compelled
to absent himself from Union two winters during his course, to

earn money to go on with his education. His father was receiving a salary of only $500, and with a large family to support with it, found that he could not aid his eldest son through college. When 16 years old, therefore, and a Sophomore, young Arthur left college, and obtaining a school at Schaghticoke, Rensselaer County, taught there throughout the winter. He had " to board around " and received only $15 a month compensation. He also had to keep up his studies in college. In the last year of his college course he again taught during the winter at Schaghticoke. He was graduated, at 18 years of age, from Union College in the class of 1848. In college he had been very popular with his fellow-students and had become a member of the Psi Upsilon fraternity—in whose welfare he ever after took a keen interest.

## CHAPTER II.

### AT WORK FOR THE SLAVE.

AT college he had determined to become a lawyer. Accordingly, upon graduation he went to a law school at Ballston Springs, and there remained diligently studying for several months. He then returned to Lansingburg, where his father then resided and there studied law. In 1851 he obtained a situation as principal of an academy at North Pownal, Bennington County, Vermont. He prepared boys for college, all the while studying law. Two years after he left North Pownal, or in 1853, a student from Williams College named James A. Garfield came to the place, and in the same academy building taught penmanship throughout one winter. It was a singular circumstance that after nearly a quarter of a century both these men should meet at a great political convention and unexpectedly to themselves be picked out as the candidates of the Republican Party for President and Vice-President.

Mr. Arthur came to New York in 1853 and entered the law office of E. D. Culver as a law student. By the strictest economy he had saved $500, and with this determined to start out in business life. He had known Mr. Culver when the latter was a Congressman from Washington County and when Mr. Arthur's father was pastor of the Baptist Church in the village. Mr. Culver was celebrated in Congress for his firm anti-slavery principles, and his law office in New York was one of the depots of " The Underground Railway " patronized by runaway slaves. It was from Mr. Culver that Mr. Arthur imbibed his anti-slavery ideas. Admitted to the Bar in 1853 he became, at once a member of the firm of Culver, Parker & Arthur, where he remained until the dissolution of that firm in 1857. He then formed a law partnership with Henry D. Gardiner, an intimate friend, the firm being Arthur & Gardiner. They had intended to practice law in the West, but after a three months' tour through the West they concluded that their prospects were better in New York City. They accordingly returned to New York, and very soon acquired a very lucrative practice.

Already there were tokens of the coming struggle over slavery. Mr. Arthur's fame as a lawyer had begun earlier with his management of a very celebrated slave case. In 1852, a slaveholder of Virginia named Jonathan Lemmon determined to take eight slaves to Texas. He brought them by steamer from Norfolk to New York, intending to reship them from New York for Texas. While in New York these slaves were discovered by a free colored man named Louis Napoleon. He had been told that slaves could not legally be held in the State of New York. He accordingly presented a petition to Elijah Paine, a Justice of the Superior Court of New York, asking that a writ of habeas corpus be issued to the persons having the slaves in charge, commanding them to bring the slaves into court at once. Mr. Culver and John Jay appeared as counsel for the slaves, and H. D. Lapaugh and Henry L. Clinton for

Lemmon. Judge Paine, after hearing long arguments, ordered the slaves released, affirming that the fugitive-slave law did not apply to them and that no human creature could be held in bondage in the State, except under that national law. This decision created great excitement in the slave States, as it practically made every slave free who should put foot on the soil of a free State. Governor Cobb of Georgia thought the decision would be " a just cause for war." Governor Johnson, of Virginia said : " In importance it is of the first magnitude, and in spirit it is without a parallel. If sustained, it will not only destroy that comity which should have subsisted between the several States composing this Confederacy, but must seriously affect the value of slave property wherever found." Inspired by this message, the Legislature of Virginia directed the Attorney-General of the State to employ counsel to appeal from the decision of Judge Paine to the higher courts of New York. Mr. Arthur went to Albany and after persistent effort induced the Legislature of New York to take up the challenge ; and he procured the passage of a joint resolution requesting the Governor to appoint counsel to defend the interests of the State. Ogden Hoffman, then Attorney-General, E. D. Culver, and Joseph Blunt were appointed the counsel of the State. Mr. Arthur was the State's attorney in the matter, and upon the death of Ogden Hoffman at the suggestion he associated with him William M. Evarts as counsel. The Supreme Court sustained Judge Paine's decision. Thereupon to strengthen their cause the slaveholders engaged Charles O'Conor to argue the case before the Court of Appeals. But there again the counsel for the State were successful in defending Judge Paine's decision ; and thenceforth no slaveholder dared venture with his slaves into the State of New York.

Mr. Arthur became such a champion of their interests in the eyes of the colored people by his connection with this case that it was natural they should seek his aid when next in trouble. The street car companies of New York, cringing to the sentiments of the slaveholders, made almost no provision for the transportation of colored people. Upon several of the lines occasionally there could be seen passing by an old and shabby-looking car labelled, "Colored persons allowed in this car." Several of the lines did not make even this provision. This was the case with the rich Fourth Avenue line. One Sunday in 1855 a neatly-dressed colored woman named Lizzie Jennings, who had just come from fulfilling her duties as superintendent of a colored Sunday-school, hailed a Fourth Avenue car. The car stopped, she took a seat, and the conductor took her fare —thus silently acknowledging her right to ride on the car. The car went on a block and then a drunken white man said to the conductor : "Are you going to let that —— nigger ride in this car ?"

"Oh, I guess it won't make any difference," said the conductor.

"Yes, but it will," answered the pro-slavery man ; "I have paid my fare, and I want a decent ride, and I tell you you've got to give me a decent ride."

Thereupon the conductor went to Lizzie Jennings and asked her to leave the car, offering to return her fare. She refused to comply with the request. The car was stopped and the conductor attempted to put her off by force. She strenuously resisted, all the while crying : "I have paid my fare and I am entitled to ride." Her clothing was almost torn from her body, but still she resisted, and resisted successfully. Finally, the conductor had to call in several policemen, and by their efforts she was finally removed from the car. Influential colored people soon heard of her treatment, and going to the office of Culver, Parker & Arthur told them all about it. They at once told them that her wrongs should be righted. A suit was brought against the railway company in her behalf in Judge Rockwell's court in Brooklyn. Public sentiment was still on the side of the slaveholder, however, and even the judge was prejudiced.

When Mr. Arthur handed him the papers in the case he said : " Pshaw ! do you ask me to try a case against a corporation for the wrongful act of its agent ?'' Mr. Arthur immediately pointed out a section of the Revised Statutes under which the action had been brought, making the corporation liable for the acts of its servants. It could not be disputed, and upon trial of the case, judgment in favor of Lizzie Jennings to the amount of $500 was rendered. Without further contest the railroad company paid the $500. It then issued orders to its conductors that colored people should be allowed to ride on the cars. All the city railroad companies followed the example. The " Colored People's Legal Rights Association " annually for years celebrated the anniversary of the day on which Mr. Arthur conducted and won this celebrated case.

---

## CHAPTER III.

### FIRST STEPS IN POLITICS.

It was in the year 1856 that Mr. Arthur began to be prominent in politics in New York City. He had taken an active interest in politics at a very early age. He sympathized with the Whig Party and was an ardent admirer of Henry Clay. It is related of him that during the contest between Polk and Clay, he was the leader of the boys of Whig parentage in Greenwich village, who determined to raise an ash pole in honor of Henry Clay. They were attacked by the boys of Democratic parentage while doing so, and for a time driven off the village green. But they were rallied by young Arthur, and he leading a desperate charge, the Democrats were driven with broken heads from the field. Then, with a shout of triumph, the Whig boys raised the ash pole. His first vote was cast in 1852—for Winfield Scott for President. In New York City Mr. Arthur identified himself with the "practical men" in politics by joining political associations of his party and sitting at the polls and acting as inspector of election on election day. A far higher class of men then served as inspectors at most of the polls in New York City ,on election days than do now in any part of the city. They were regularly elected each year, and prominent ctizens then were willing to serve. For many years Mr. Arthur served as an inspector of elections at a polling-place in a carpenter's shop at Broadway and Twenty-third Street, New York, the Hippodrome being on the lower corner of the same block. The carpenter's shop and the Hippodrome were removed to give place to the present Fifth Avenue Hotel. In the formation of the Republican Party Mr. Arthur took a very prominent part. His name can be found appended to many calls like the following, which was printed in the New York *Herald* at the opening of the campaign of 1856 :

"Eighteenth Ward Young Men's Fremont Vigilance Committee. Grand rally. The first public meeting under the auspices of the Eighteenth Ward Young Men's Fremont Vigilance Committee will be held at the Demilt Dispensary, corner of Twenty-third Street and Second Avenue, on Wednesday evening, the 8th inst., at 7.30, which will be addressed by A. Oakey Hall, Esq., of this city, and Joseph J. Couch, Esq., of Brooklyn. The Fremont and Dayton Glee Club will be in attendance. All are invited to attend. *Executive Committee:* John H. Burleson, William D. Chase, George T. Strong, Henry D. Sedgwick, Joseph Wales, Samuel Brown, Chester A. Arthur, Richard T. Deming, John A. Foster, Henry G. Hallock, Curtis Beane, Benjamin F. Manierre, Peter T. Woodbury, Charles E. Strong."

He was a delegate to the convention at Saratoga that founded the Republican Party. During these political labors he became acquainted with Edwin D. Morgan and gained his ardent friendship. Mr. Morgan, when re-elected Governor in 1860, testified to his high esteem for Mr. Arthur by making him En-

gineer-in-Chief on his staff. Mr. Arthur had for several years
previously taken a great interest in the militia organization of
the State and had been appointed Judge Advocate General of
the Second Brigade. In this position he was associated with
many men who took part in the War of the Rebellion afterward and held high positons. Brigadier-General Yates, who
commanded the Second Brigade, was a very thorough disciplinarian, and for several years required all the brigade and staff
officers to meet every week for instruction. They in this manner
became very proficient in military tactics and regulations, and
the instruction proved to be of inestimable advantage to General Arthur in the great and exceedingly responsible duties to
which he was soon to be called.

## CHAPTER IV.

### NEW YORK'S SECRETARY OF WAR.

THE breaking out of the War of the Rebellion in April,
1861, found him still Engineer-in-Chief. It was a merely orna-
mental office, and he probably never imagined he would do a
day's duty in the position. The day after Fort Sumter was
fired upon, while on his way to his law office, he received a
dispatch from Governor Morgan summoning him to Albany.
Upon reaching there Governor Morgan directed him to open a
branch Quartermaster's Department in New York City, and to
fulfil all the duties there of Quartermaster General. General
Arthur was young, strong, and as Governor Morgan saw, of a
vigorous nature. The Governor put in his hands the duty of
quartering, subsisting, uniforming, equipping, and arming New
York's soldiers for the war. It was not only a herculean task,
but was one of special difficulty, for there was no broad road
of experience to guide the young man. There had been no war

for many years, and moreover, this one was palpably to be prosecuted on a scale, in regard to the number of men engaged in it,
of which no American could have a conception who had not
been an eye-witness of some recent European war.  Men who
had been trained in the small regular army, or in the still
smaller State militia regiments, were staggered by the enormous tasks set before them in the equipment and forwarding of
several hundred thousand men to the seat of war.  There was
nothing for which General Arthur afterward received higher
praise than the way he rose to the height of the occasion in all
difficulties that beset him in the toilsome years which followed.
He was the brains, the organizing force, that took the raw
levies of New York, put uniforms on their backs, muskets in
their hands, and sent them on to the war.  Governor Morgan
practically made him the War Minister of the State, shifting
him from place to place on his staff, and from time to time trans-
ferring to him the dutes of other military officers of the State,
in order that the work might be properly done.  He was virtually the centre round which all the military operations of the
State revolved.  He did not go near his law office during the
first two years of the war.  It was the creation of a great department for the provision of an army, out of nothing ; but he
succeeded and had the proud satisfaction of seeing that New
York had sent one-fifth of all the soldiers that marched to sub-
due the Rebellion—a splendid contingent of 690,000 men.

It is well to relate what he did in detail.  When he began in
New York, in April, 1861, to perform the work of Quartermaster
General, there were thousands of enlisted men in the city to be
fed and equipped, the militia regiments were departing for the
war from this State, and New England regiments were passing
through the city.  All these regiments had to be fed and quarters provided for them—where none existed.  Wealthy citizens
of New York aided General Arthur generously ; giving him the
right to occupy their buildings.  Mr. Astor, Mr. Devlin, and

Mr. Goelet were conspicuous in this service. The number of troops passing through the city finally became so great that it was found necessary to provide more quarters for them. Then it was that barracks were erected in the City Hall Park. To get them ready for the troops, workmen under General Arthur's direction worked night and day. The populace thought that the war would be over in thirty days, and the barracks be removed. But the barracks remained there four years, or till the end of the war, the latter part of the time being used as a hospital. Meanwhile the work of creating a Quartermaster's Department went on. General Arthur advertised for proposals for subsistence for the troops, and succeeded in making a contract at rates one-third lower than those of the United States Government. This saved the State many thousands of dollars. Everything was done in a business-like way ; the quartermaster's stores were issued on regular army requisitions and receipts were demanded for everything. The result of his care was that although the accounts of the State of New York with the United States Government were very much greater than those of any other State, his accounts were the first audited and allowed at Washington. Not a dollar was deducted from them, whereas the accounts of some other States were cut down from $1,000,000 to $10,000,000. It was natural that contractors should seek to ingratiate themselves with a man who was buying such enormous quantities of supplies. But every present that reached him with this motive was at once returned to the sender. A great clothing firm proffered him a costly saddle and trappings—they were contemptuously returned. He was a comparatively poor man when he became Quartermaster General—he was far poorer when he gave up the office. Some of the greatest contracts ever made in America were under his direction and control. The interests of the Government, however, were treated as though they were his interests. A friend describing his course at this period says : " So jealous was he of his integrity that I have known instances where he could have made thousands of dollars legitimately, and yet he refused to do it on the ground that he was a public officer and meant to be like Cæsar's wife, ' above suspicion.' "

## CHAPTER V.

### WAR DIFFICULTIES MASTERED.

THE troops poured into New York by the thousand, and it was found necessary every day to provide additional quarters. General Arthur built more barracks at various places on Long Island, on Staten Island, and Riker's Island. The first quota of the State, outside of the militia regiments, was for thirty-eight regiments. These regiments were organized in different parts of the State in the spring of 1861. The work of quartering, subsisting, uniforming, equipping, and arming these regiments went on without regard to Sunday or the hours of sleep. For several months General Arthur did not sleep over three hours a night. Whoever had any business connected with the army came to the State headquarters in Elm Street (afterward in Walker Street), and consequently General Arthur's office was constantly besieged by crowds. All sorts of adventurers went on to Washington, obtained commissions to raise troops, and returning to New York, began their work. All these classes required supervision from General Arthur, as they would endeavor to act independently of his office. His ability to deal with these men, many of whom were of a very rough character, was highly praised at the time. Several instances of his energetic action are remembered to this day. One of the adventurers was " Billy " Wilson, who had been the representative in the New York Board of Aldermen of the roughest element of the city population, and who had been authorized at Washington to raise a regiment from this class. The regiment at one time refused to eat the Government rations and supported itself by raiding on the restaurants in the vicinity of its barracks. General Arthur, hearing of these outrages, sent for Wilson, and told him that he must put an end to them. Wilson thereupon said, in an impudent manner :

" Neither you nor the Governor has anything to do with me. I am a colonel in the United States service, and you've got no right to order me."

" You are not a colonel," indignantly replied General Arthur, " and you will not be until you have raised your regiment to its quota of men and received your commission."

" Well, I've got my shoulder-straps, anyway," said Wilson, " and as long as I wear them, I don't want no orders from any of you fellows."

He had scarcely made this insolent reply, when General Arthur, who is a very strong man, sprang toward him, saying :

" We'll make short work of your shoulder-straps," and tearing the straps from Wilson's shoulders, put him under arrest.

General Arthur had a similar experience with Colonel Ellsworth's Fire Zouaves, who were quartered in Devlin's building on Canal Street. One day the members of the regiment refused to unpack their muskets. General Arthur having been applied to by Colonel Ellsworth, went among the throng with several policemen, had the ringleaders in the revolt pointed out to him, and said : " Arrest that man, and that one, and that one." His orders were obeyed, the regiment was cowed, and there were no more revolts of that nature. The regiment had an amusing experience on starting for the war. It was organized on the very original plan of having attached to it a battery of light artillery and a troop of cavalry. Furthermore, it had 120 men to the company, being more than the regulation complement. The War Department sent orders to Governor Morgan that the regiment should not be mustered into the ser-

vice or leave the city until it had equalized or reduced its companies. But that very day the regiment, 1300 strong, had received a stand of colors from Mrs. Astor, in Canal Street, and
was on its way to the Baltic steamer to take passage for the
South. General Wool had reviewed the regiment, and induced
by the persuasion of the officers of the regiment, had rescinded
the order for its detention. The regiment had then marched
proudly to the troop-ship, which soon afterward steamed
down the harbor. An hour after the steamer had sailed an
officer strolled into the Elm Street headquarters and said acci-
dentally :

" Well, the Fire Zouaves have got off at last."

" Got off !" said General Arthur, in amazement ; " that's
not possible. Orders have been received from Washington,
forbidding them to leave, and there is not a pound of provisions of any sort on the troop-ship, as I countermanded the
order which had been given."

It was clear that the regiment must be fed at short notice.
General Arthur jumped into a carriage, drove to an army contractor, and ordered the rations. " Impossible to supply them
at such short notice," said the contractor. " It is not impossible, and you must do it. I will pay you fifty cents, instead
of the usual rate of thirty-five cents a ration, and will have
them transported myself to the Baltic." Stimulated by this
reward, the contractor got together five days' rations for 1300
men in two hours. General Arthur, meanwhile, had hired
every tug he could obtain. He put the rations on these tugs,
caught up with the Baltic at the Narrows—where the regimental
officers had discovered the deficiency, and stopped the ship—
and provisioned the ship. The ship sailed the same night.
The regiment was again insubordinate, when it was encamped
at Washington after the battle of Bull Run, and was ordered
back to New York, and quartered in tents on the Battery.
There the men refused to obey the officers, and wandered

about the city like marauders, stealing food in the restaurants, as had Wilson's Zouaves. General Arthur (then Inspector General) was directed to disband them ; but he thought something could yet be done with them. With the aid of the police he arrested every soldier of the regiment found wandering about the city and had him taken on board a transport ship which he had procured to be placed in the harbor, and imprisoned. When he had thus " hived " four hundred of them, the ship sailed for Hampton Roads. There the regiment was consolidated with another and put under the strict discipline of General Wool, and subsequently did good service in the war.

The " Ulster County Guards," in which the present General George H. Sharpe was a captain, was a regiment of far higher character. It was composed of men from the finest families of Ulster County. On their way to Washington they occupied the Park Barracks on the night they were completed. They had hardly got possession before orders came from the War Department to Governor Morgan that the regiment should return home, as no more three-months regiments were to be accepted. The regiment was almost beside itself with rage and disappointment. Thereupon General Arthur took a night train for Albany, described to Governor Morgan the martial character of the regiment, and the damaging effect of its being compelled to return home, and insisted upon its being sent on to Washington. He obtained the necessary permission and returned to New York by a special train. He reached the barracks at one A.M. and told the good news. The joy of the regiment was indescribable. A volunteer regiment was thus saved the service, for nearly all re-enlisted for three years at the end of their three months' service. The regiment, throughout the war, named its camps " Camp Arthur " in gratitude for this service of General Arthur. It was his readiness to deal with such matters that led Governor Morgan to intrust General Arthur with the management of the war affairs of the State. As the immediate repre-

sentative of Governor Morgan he became known to army officers
from every section and this was the foundation of his large
personal acquaintance in the State.

In the fall of 1861, after 38 regiments had been furnished, it
was seen that the Government would be glad to accept troops
without limit ; and as the State had furnished the full quota of
those regularly called for through the Governor, numbers of men
of desperate fortunes, adventurers, went on to Washington and
obtained authority to raise regiments. They came to New
York and began to raise troops, claiming to be independent of
State authority.   There were parts of over a hundred regiments
being raised at one time.   General Arthur made an investigation as to the character of these adventurers, and found that
many of them were men of bad antecedents.   One of them who
afterward adorned Ludlow Street Jail, advertised for " young
gentlemen of pious character " for his regiment, and sold commissions in the regiment.   Another hired the old New York
Club House, then vacant—ordered a service of plate, furnished
the house handsomely, and ran into debt to tradesmen all over
the city, ostensibly in behalf of the regiment. These men defied
the authority of the State officers.   General Arthur advised
Governor Morgan to claim from the United States Government
supervision over all the troops raised in New York ; and for
this purpose to obtain the office of major-general in the United
States service.     Governor Morgan, accompanied by General
Arthur, went on to Washington.   There General Arthur depict-
ed to the War Department officials the character of the men
they had commissioned.   The officials were amazed and readily
consented to the suggestion that Governor Morgan should be
made a major-general, that a Department of New York should
be established, and that all the independent organizations
should be put under Governor Morgan's authority. Thenceforth
there were no more disputes as to authority in New York ; and
the example set by this State was followed by all the other

loyal States in raising troops for the war. At this time General Arthur was acting Adjutant-General of New York ; and was also actually doing the work of the Engineer-in-Chief, Inspector General, and Quartermaster-General. As Inspector General, he afterward consolidated the odds and ends of regiments spoken of before.

## CHAPTER VI.

### TERRORS OF WAR TIMES.

It was while Inspector General that he had an exciting and amusing experience. One Sunday in March, 1862, there came hurrying into his office, almost breathless, and flushed a deep red, General Gustavus Loomis, the oldest regular infantry officer in the service.

" What in the world has happened, General ?" said General Arthur, offering the aged officer a chair.

" The rebel ram Merrimac ! the rebel ram Merrimac," faintly said General Loomis.

" Well, what about her ?"

" I have a despatch from General McClellan saying that she has sunk two United States ships—that she is coming to New York to shell the city—may be expected at any moment—I'm so out of breath running to tell you the news I can hardly speak."

" *Running* to tell me the news ! Why on earth didn't you hire a carriage ?"

" Hire a carriage," answered Loomis with apparent horror ; " hire a carriage ! why that would cost me $2.50. I can't afford to spend so much out of my own pocket, and if I made such an extraordinary expenditure on account of the Government it would take all the rest of my official life to explain why I did so."

General Arthur thought that General Loomis did not realize
" that time was worth a million an hour at such a time," and
sent out for several carriages while reading the following
dispatch from General M'Clellan :

"WAR DEPARTMENT, Washington, March 9, 1862.
"*Commanding Officer, New York Harbor :*
" The rebel iron-clad steamer Merrimac has destroyed two of
our frigates near Fortress Monroe, and finally retired last night to
Craney Island.    She may succeed in passing the batteries and go
to sea.    It is necessary that you at once place your post in the
best possible condition for defence and do your best to stop
her should she endeavor to run by.    Anything that can be
effected in the way of temporary batteries should be done at
once.                                                          -
                         "G. B. MCCLELLAN, Major-General."

He then took a carriage and speeding to General Sandford,
got him to detail artillerists from the militia regiments in the
city who had been trained to the use of heavy guns to the forts
in the harbor, General Loomis having reported that the forts
were filled with recruits who didn't know how to handle the
guns.    It was reported also that there was no powder in the
forts ; but fortunately a schooner arrived from Connecticut
loaded with powder that day, and General Arthur sent it down
the harbor to the forts.    He also went to the house of Mayor
Opdyke, to inform him of the situaton.    As General Arthur
drove up Fifth Avenue to the Mayor's residence on that pleasant Sunday afternoon and saw the gayly-dressed throngs going
to church, he thought with horror of what might be their fate if
the city should be bombarded by the Merrimac.    Mayor Opdyke,
on receiving General Arthur's alarming news, summoned to his
house many eminent citizens.    They proposed to sink ships
loaded with stone in the Narrows, and thus bar the approach of
the Merrimac to the city.    General Arthur protested that he
would have nothing to do with such a scheme.    The council

broke up without adopting any plan for the protection of the city. Fortunately for New York, news came during the night that the Monitor had reached Hampton Roads that day and had sunk the Merrimac.

This was not the first occasion when General Arthur had to do with the defence of the seaport of New York during the war. When Mason and Slidell were taken from the Trent by Captain Wilkes, and war seemed imminent with England, one day in December, 1861, General Arthur was summoned to Albany in his capacity of Engineer-in-Chief. He knew that he had been summoned to receive orders regarding the defence of New York. He also knew that the forts of masonry in New York harbor were practically obsolete before modern naval cannon ; that most of the cannon in them were "shell guns," *i.e.*, unsafe to fire. On reaching Albany he stated to Governor Morgan that, not being an engineer, he came to resign his position in order that some eminent engineer might be appointed. Governor Morgan replied that there were plenty of engineers, but that for the present duty he preferred to keep a man of the energy, skill, and executive ability of his present Engineer-in-Chief. Governor Morgan insisting upon his keeping the office, General Arthur set about his task. On December 24th, 1861, he summoned together a Board of the most eminent engineers in the State ; requesting them to meet him in New York two days later to consult about the defences of the harbor. For two months this board, of which General Arthur was a member, labored constantly, and at the end of that time produced a plan for the defence of the harbor which won universal praise. The plan is still in existence and may be of great value to New York in some emergency. Before its completion, war with England seeming at hand, the erection of a temporary barrier across the harbor was proposed. Colonel Delafield, of the United States Engineers, had suggested that it would be practicable to construct a barrier consisting of floats loaded with stone, and con-

nected and held in place by chain cables.   An immense amount
of timber was needed for such a barrier and there was no State
appropriation with which to buy it.   General Arthur took upon
himself the responsibility of buying it.   He went to Albany and
in a day had the refusal of all the timber there and along the
river.   The purchase was made so quietly and secretly that the
price of lumber did not advance.   He also made a contract for
the timber being rafted down the Hudson.   Unluckily, the day
after the purchase was made the Hudson froze up, and it was
therefore plain that it would be impossible to deliver it before
spring.    Undaunted, General Arthur returned immediately to
New York and bought up most of the timber there.   Before the
barrier could be erected, however, Mason and Slidell were surrendered to England and all danger of war passed away.    But
the State had upon its hands the immense quantity of timber
General Arthur had bought, and grumblers severely criticised
the purchase in the State Senate.   General Arthur having been
sent for by the Governor to advise about the disposition of the
timber, went to Albany and had a bill then before the Legislature in regard to war expenditures amended so as to provide
for the sale of unused war material.   The bill passed, was at
once signed by Governor Morgan, and the timber was sold soon
afterward at a profit to the State.

Immediately after his convening of the Board of Engineers to
consider the defence of the harbor of New York, General Arthur
made a thorough, while rapid, inspection of all the forts and
defences in the State, both on the seacoast and inland border.
He wrote an admirable report to the Legislature of this inspection, which was submitted to that body January 18th, 1862, or a
little more than three weeks after his attention was called to
the subject by Governor Morgan.   In this report the armament
of every fort is described, and its condition for defence stated
with the minutest details. The *New York Herald*, of January 25th,
1862, says editorially :  " The report of the Engineer-in-Chief,

General Arthur, which appeared in yesterday's *Herald*, is one of the most important and valuable documents that has been this year presented to our Legislature. It deserves perusal, not only an account of the careful analysis it contains of the condition of the forts, but because the recommendations with which it closes coincide precisely with the wishes of the administration with respect to securing a full and complete defence of the entire Northern coast.

In February, 1862, General Arthur was appointed Inspector General, there being duty to do in the army. In May, 1862, he went to Fredericksburg, and inspected the New York troops there under the command of General McDowell. From there he went to the Army of the Potomac, then on the Chickahominy, and carefully inspected the New York troops there, with a view of having the depleted regiments then in service filled by enlistments to their proper strength, instead of having new regiments raised. As an advance on Richmond was then daily expected, General Arthur volunteered for duty on the staff of his friend, Major-General Hunt, commander of the reserve artillery. It is well to state here that shortly after the commencement of the war General Arthur was elected Colonel of the Ninth New York Militia, which enlisted in the United States service for two years, and desired to accept the post, but Governor Morgan would not release him from the more important work. The year afterward, when four regiments had been formed through the efforts of the Metropolitan Police Commissioners of the City of New York, in which they were largely aided by General Arthur, the colonels of the regiments offered him the command of the brigade, known as the "Metropolitan Brigade." He thereupon made formal application to the Governor for permission to accept the command, saying that it had long been his desire to have active service in the field. Governor Morgan replied that he could not be spared from the service of the State, and that while he appreciated

General Arthur's desire for war service, he knew he would do far more valuable service for the country by continuing at his post of duty in New York State.

---

## CHAPTER VII.

### ARMING SIXTY THOUSAND MEN.

In June, 1862, the affairs of the country looked desperate. There had been defeats, regiments were getting thinned out, and it was evident a great levy would have to be made. Governor Morgan telegraphed General Arthur, then with the Army of the Potomac, to return to New York. He did so, and was immediately requested 'to act as secretary at a secret meeting of the Governors of loyal States, held at the Astor House on July 28th, 1862. At this meeting President Lincoln was requested by the Governors to call for more men. President Lincoln, on July 1st, issued a proclamation thanking the Governors for their patriotism and calling for 300,000 volunteers and 300,000 militia for nine months' service. Private knowledge that such a call was to be issued would have enabled contractors to have made millions. General Arthur was approached by one of these men, and an interest offered him in immense contracts if he would reveal what had been done. The secret was kept by all, however, till the proclamation was issued. The quota of New York under the call for 300,000 volunteers was 59,705. It was desired that these sixty regiments should be recruited and got to the seat of war at the earliest possible moment. In view of the fact that the greater part of the labor would fall upon the Quartermaster's Department, the request was made by Governor Morgan to General Arthur that he should take his old post as Quartermaster General. General Arthur complied on July 7th, 1862, and set energetically to work. He devised

a new system for enlisting and caring for the troops, which was
found to work very successfully. He established a camp in
each one of the thirty-two Senatorial districts of the State. The
Governor had provided for the appointment of committees
of prominent citizens from both political parties, in each district, to stimulate recruiting. This the committees did by holding public meetings. The State fairly resounded with the din
of war-meetings. At this time a new system for the recruiting
and organization of the regiments enlisted at the several camps
was suggested to the War Department by General Arthur,
which was approved and put in operation. All previous regiments
recruited had been for months during the enlistment, a disor-
ganized body of men dressed in civilian garb—until mustered
into the United States service. General Arthur now changed all
this. He recommended that the executive officers of each regiment being raised—the adjutant, quartermaster, and surgeon—
be at the outset mustered into the service of the United States,
and so have complete authority and control in their respective
departments to enforce military regulations, order, and discipline in the camp. The men, as soon as enlisted were put in
uniform and subjected to the restraint and drill of military life.
The camps immediately had a military appearance and became
attractive places of resort to the population surrounding them
for miles. So attractive were they to young men that in many
cases half a second regiment was enlisted before the first left
the camp. The quartermasters of all regiments, as soon as appointed, were required by General Arthur to come to New York
and were there, at the office of the Quartermaster General, taught
their duties. They were informed of their great responsibilities
and shown how to keep their accounts. Large amounts were
thus saved the State, for in other States the accounts of the un-
instructed quartermasters were so badly prepared that there
was great loss. General Arthur also had many of the barrack
buildings at the various camps constructed by the enlisted

men, thus saving a great deal of money. The barracks erected in the whole State for this levy of troops thus cost altogether only $27,000. General Arthur made special contracts with the railroads for transporting the soldiers to the front, and in this way saved $43,144 to the State from the rates allowed by the Government. In his annual report, dated January 27th, 1863, he says :

" In summing up the operations of the department during the last levy of troops, I need only state as the result the fact that through the single office and clothing department of this Department in the City of New York, from August 1st to December 1st, the space of four months, there were completely clothed, uniformed, and equipped, supplied with camp and garrison equipage, and transported from this State to the seat of war, 68 regiments of infantry, 2 battalions of cavalry, and 4 battalions and 10 batteries of artillery.'

The incoming of a Democratic State Administration deprived him of his office in December, 1863. His Democratic successor made the following comment upon General Arthur's administration in his annual report to Governor Seymour :

" STATE OF NEW YORK, Q. M. G. DEPARTMENT,
NEW YORK, December 31, 1863.

" *To his Excellency* HORATIO SEYMOUR, *Governor, Commander-in-Chief, State of New York :*

" GOVERNOR : I have the honor to submit the following report of the operations of this department since the 1st day of January last.

\*　　\*　　\*　　\*　　\*　　\*　　\*

" I found, upon entering on the discharge of my duties, a well-organized system of labor and accountability, for which the State is chiefly indebted to my predecessor, General Chester A. Arthur, who, by his practical good sense and unremitting exertion, at a period when everything was in confusion, reduced the operations of the department to a matured plan, by which large

amounts of money were saved to the Government, and great
economy of time secured in carrying out the details of the same.

\*       \*       \*       \*       \*       \*       \*

" [Signed.]      S. V. TALCOTT,
                        " *Quartermaster-General.*"

## CHAPTER VIII

### COLLECTOR OF NEW YORK.

UPON his retirement from office General Arthur resumed the
active duties of his profession. His partnership with Mr. Gar-
diner ceased only with that gentleman's death in 1866. Alone
for over five years he carried on his business. It then became
so large that he formed, in 1871, the now well-known firm of
Arthur, Phelps, Knevals & Ransom. He became counsel to
the Department of Taxes and Assessment, at a salary of $10,000
yearly ; but abruptly resigned the position when the Tammany
Hall officials at the head of the New York departments attempted to coerce the Republicans connected with those departments.

Gradually he was drawn into political life again. He was
very much interested in promoting the first election of President Grant, being chairman of the Central Grant Club of New
York. He also served as chairman of the Executive Committee
of the Republican State Committee of New York. He re-en-
tered official life on November 20th, 1871, being appointed Collector of the Port of New York by President Grant. The post
of Collector came to him unsought and unexpectedly, and was
accepted with much hesitation.

The appointment met with the general approval of the business community, many of the merchants having become personally acquainted with General Arthur during the war. He instituted many reforms in the management of the Custom House,

all calculated to render contact with the institution less vexatious than it ordinarily is to the mercantile classes. He also executed the work of a Collector in the matter of appointments and removals in the Custom House in such a manner as to cause less than the usual amount of commotion among politicians. The number of removals during his administration was far less than during the rule of any other Collector, since 1857. New appointees were put in the lowest grades of Custom House service and compelled to work their way up to higher positions. So satisfactory was his work that upon the close of his term of office, in December, 1875, he was renominated by President Grant. The nomination was unanimously confirmed by the Senate without referring it to a committee—a compliment never given before except to ex-Senators. He was the first Collector of the Port ever reappointed for a second term, and was, with only one or two exceptions, the only one who in fifty years ever held the office for more than the whole term of four years. The administration of President Hayes was deeply interested in civil service reform, and sent a commission headed by John Jay to learn the operation of the principle in the New York Custom House. Commenting upon their report in a letter to John Sherman, Secretary of the Treasury, Collector Arthur said :

" The essential elements of a correct civil service I understand to be : First, permanence in office, which, of course, prevents removals, except for cause. Second, promotion from the lower to the higher grades, based upon good conduct and efficiency. Third, prompt and thorough investigation of all complaints and prompt punishment of all misconduct. In this respect I challenge comparison with any department of the Government, either under the present or under any past national administration. I am prepared to demonstrate the truth of this statement on any fair investigation." In a table which was appended to this letter, Collector Arthur showed that during the six years he had managed the office the yearly percentage of removals for all causes had been only 2¾ per cent, against an annual average of 28 per cent under his three immediate predecessors, and an annual average of about 24 per cent. since 1857, when Collector Schell took office. Out of 923 persons who held office when he became Collector on December 1st, 1871, there were 531 still in office on May 1st, 1877, having been retained during his entire term. Concerning promotions, the statistics of the office show that during his entire term the uniform practice was to advance men from the lower to the higher grades, and almost without exception on the recommendation of heads of departments. All the appointments, except two, to the 100 persons receiving over $2,000 salary a year, were made on this method. The expense of collecting the revenue was also kept low. Under Collector Schell, from 1857 to 1861, the expense was an average of about 59 per cent. ; under Mr. Barney, from 1861 to 1865, about 87⅓ per cent. ; under Mr. Draper, in 1864 and 1865, 1.30 per cent. ; under Mr. Smythe, from 1866 to 1869, about 74 per cent. ; under Mr. Grinnell, in 1869 and 1870, about 85 per cent. ; under Mr. Murphy, in 1870 and 1871, about 60 per cent. ; under Mr. Arthur, from 1871 to 1877, about 62 per cent. Mr. Arthur was succeeded as Collector in 1878 by General E. A. Merritt, and has since been engaged in the practice of law. In the fall of 1879 he was elected chairman of the Republican State Committee, and conducted the victorious campaign which ended in the election of all but one of the candidates of the Republican Party for six State offices.

In June, 1880, he was nominated for Vice-President by the National Republican Convention, held at Chicago. General Stewart L. Woodford proposed his name in the convention ; and the nomination was seconded by ex-Governor Dennison, of Ohio ; General Kilpatrick, of New Jersey ; Emery A. Storrs, of Illinois ; Denis McCarthy, of New York, and many others. Vice-President Wheeler in a speech afterward said : " It is my good fortune to know well General Arthur, the nominee for Vice-President.    In unsullied character and in devotion to the principles of the Republican Party no man in the organization surpasses him.    No man has contributed more of time and means to advance the just interests of the Republican Party than he."

General Arthur was married in 1859 to Ellen Lewis Herndon, of Fredericksburg, Virginia.    She was a daughter of Captain William Lewis Herndon, U. S. N., whose heroic death, in command of the ill-fated Central America in 1857, is remembered as one of the deeds of which the American Navy is proud.    Captain Herndon discovered that his ship was sinking, loaded his boats with women and children, and calmly went down with his ship.    Over three hundred lives were lost.    Mrs. Arthur became the mother of two children : Chester Alan Arthur, now aged 15, and Ellen Herndon Arthur, now aged 8.    It was few women's fortune to inspire such ardent friendships.    She had a winning manner, a charming voice, and a finely-cultivated mind. She was the centre of a refined circle of friends in New York when, to the great grief of her husband, she died in the early part of January, 1880.    Her funeral in New York was attended by some of the most distinguished men in the nation.

# GENERAL ARTHUR'S LETTER OF ACCEPTANCE.

New York, July 15, 1880.

DEAR SIR : I accept the position assigned me by the great party whose action you announce. This acceptance implies approval of the principles declared by the convention, but recent usage permits me to add some expression of my own views. The right and duty to secure honesty and order in popular elections is a matter so vital that it must stand in front. The authority of the National Government to preserve from fraud and force elections at which its own officers are chosen is a chief point on which the two parties are plainly and intensely opposed. Acts of Congress for ten years have, in New York and elsewhere, done much to curb the violence and wrong to which the ballot and the count have been again and again subjected— sometimes despoiling great cities, sometimes stifling the voice of a whole State, often seating, not only in Congress, but on the Bench and in Legislatures, numbers of men never chosen by the people. The Democratic Party, since gaining possession of the two houses of Congress, has made these just laws the ob- ject of bitter, ceaseless assault, and, despite all resistance, has hedged them with restrictions cunningly contrived to baffle and paralyze them. This aggressive majority boldly attempted to extort from the Executive his approval of various enactments destructive of these election laws by revolutionary threats that a constitutional exercise of the veto power would be punished by withholding the appropriations necessary to carry on the Government. And these threats were actually carried out by refusing the needed appropriations, and by forcing an extra ses- sion of Congress, lasting for months and resulting in conces- sions to this usurping demand which are likely, in many States, to subject the majority to the lawless will of a minority. Ominous signs of public disapproval alone subdued this arrogant power into a sullen surrender for the time being of a part of its demands.    The Republican Party has strongly approved the stern refusal of its representatives to suffer the overthrow of statutes believed to be salutary and just.    It has always insisted, and now insists, that the Government of the United States of America is empowered and in duty bound to effectually protect the elections denoted by the Constitution as national.

More than this, the Republican Party holds, as a cardinal point in its creed, that the Government should, by every means known to the Constitution, protect all American citizens everywhere in the full enjoyment of their civil and political rights. As a great part of its work of reconstruction, the Republican Party gave the ballot to the emancipated slave as his right and defence.    A large increase in the number of members of Congress and of the Electoral College, from the former slaveholding States, was the immediate result.    The history of recent years abounds in evidence that in many ways and in many places—especially where their number has been great enough to endanger Democratic control—the very men by whose elevation to citizenship this increase of representation was effected have been debarred and robbed of their voice and their vote.    It is true that no State statute or Constitution in so many words denies or abridges the exercise of their political rights ; but the modes employed to bar their way are no less effectual.    It is a suggestive and startling thought that the increased power derived from the enfranchisement of a race now denied its share in governing the country—wielded by those who lately sought the overthrow of the Government—is now the sole reliance to defeat the party which represented the sovereignty and nationality of the American people in the greatest crisis of our history. Republicans cherish none of the resentments which may have animated them during the actual conflict of arms.    They long for a full and real reconciliation between the sections which were needlessly and lamentably at strife ; they sincerely offer the hand of good-will, but they ask in return a pledge of good faith. They deeply feel that the party whose career is so illustrious in great and patriotic achievement will not fulfil its destiny until peace and prosperity are established in all the land, nor until liberty of thought, conscience and action, and equality of opportunity shall be not merely cold formalities of statute, but living birthrights, which the humble may confidently claim and the powerful dare not deny.

The resolution referring to the public service seems to me deserving of approval. Surely, no man should be the encumbent of an office the duties of which he is, for any cause, unfit to perform, who is lacking in the ability, fidelity, or integrity which a proper administration of such office demands. This sentiment would doubtless meet with general acquiescence, but opinion has been widely divided upon the wisdom and practicability of the various reformatory schemes which have been suggested, and of certain proposed regulations governing appointments to public office. The efficiency of such regulations has been distrusted, mainly because they have seemed to exalt mere educational and abstract tests above general business capacity, and even special fitness for the particular work in hand. It seems to me that the rules which should be applied to the management of the public service may properly conform, in the main, to such as regulate the conduct of successful private business. Original appointments should be based upon ascertained fitness. The tenure of office should be stable. Positions of responsibility should, so far as practicable, be filled by the promotion of worthy and efficient officers. The investigation of all complaints, and the punishment of all official misconduct, should be prompt and thorough. These views, which I have long held, repeatedly declared, and uniformly applied when called upon to act, I find embodied in the resolution, which, of course, I approve. I will add that by the acceptance of public office, whether high or low, one does not, in my judgment, escape any of his responsibilities as a citizen, or lose or impair any of his rights as a citizen, and that he should enjoy absolute liberty to think and speak and act in political matters according to his own will and conscience, provided only that he honorably, faithfully, and fully discharges all his official duties.

The resumption of specie payments—one of the fruits of Republican policy—has brought the return of abundant prosperity, and the settlement of many distracting questions. The restoration of sound money, the large reduction of our public debt and of the burden of interest, the high advancement of the public credit, all attest the ability and courage of the Republican Party to deal with such financial problems as may hereafter demand solution. Our paper currency is now as good as gold, and silver is performing its legitimate function for the purpose of change. The principle which should govern the relations of these elements of the currency are simple and clear. There must be no deteriorated coin, no depreciated paper. And every dollar, whether of metal or paper, should stand the test of the world's fixed standard.

The value of popular education can hardly be overstated. Although its interests must of necessity be chiefly confided to voluntary effort and the individual action of the several States, they should be encouraged, so far as the Constitution permits, by the generous co-operation of the National Government. The interests of the whole country demand that the advantages of our common school system should be brought within the reach of every citizen, and that no revenues of the nation or of the States should be devoted to the support of sectarian schools.

Such changes should be made in the present tariff and system of taxation as will relieve any overburdened industry or class, and enable our manufacturers and artisans to compete successfully with those of other lands.

The Government should aid works of internal improvement

national in their character, and should promote the development of our water-courses and harbors wherever the general interests of commerce require.

Four years ago, as now, the nation stood at the threshold of a Presidential election, and the Republican Party, in soliciting a continuance of its ascendency, founded its hope of success, not upon its promises, but upon its history. Its subsequent course has been such as to strengthen the claims which it then made to the confidence and support of the country. On the other hand, considerations more urgent than have ever before existed forbid the accession of its opponents to power. Their success, if success attends them, must chiefly come from the united support of that section which sought the forcible disruption of the Union, and which, according to all the teachings of our past history, will demand ascendency in the councils of the party to whose triumph it will have made by far the largest contribution.

There is the gravest reason for apprehension that exorbitant claims upon the public Treasury, by no means limited to the hundreds of millions already covered by bills introduced in Congress within the past four years, would be successfully urged if the Democratic Party should succeed in supplementing its present control of the National Legislature by electing the Executive also.

There is danger in intrusting the control of the whole law-making power of the Government to a party which has in almost every Southern State repudiated obligations quite as sacred as those to which the faith of the nation now stands pledged.

I do not doubt that success awaits the Republican Party, and that its triumph will assure a just, economical, and patriotic administration. I am, respectfully, your obedient servant,

C. A. ARTHUR.

"*To the Hon.* GEORGE F. HOAR, *President of the Republican National Convention.*

# APPENDIX.

---

## ABANDONED

# DEMOCRATIC PRINCIPLES,

SELECTED FROM THE

National Platforms of the Democratic Party

SINCE 1856.

## FROM THE DEMOCRATIC PLATFORM OF 1856 ; RE-ADOPTED IN 1860.

### INTERNAL IMPROVEMENTS UNCONSTITUTIONAL.

THE Constitution does not confer upon the General Government the power to commence and carry on a general system of internal improvements.

### SLAVERY NOT TO BE INTERFERED WITH.

That all efforts of the Abolitionists or others, made to induce Congress to interfere with questions of slavery, or to take incipient steps in relation thereto, are calculated to lead to the most alarming and dangerous consequences, and that all such efforts have an inevitable tendency to diminish the happiness of the people and endanger the stability and permanence of the Union, and ought not to be countenanced by any friend of our political institutions.

### THE FUGITIVE-SLAVE LAW NOT TO BE REPEALED OR CHANGED.

The foregoing proposition covers and was intended to embrace the whole subject of slavery agitation in Congress, and therefore the Democratic Party of the Union, standing on this national platform, will abide by and adhere to a faithful execution of the acts known as the Compromise Measures, settled by the Congress of 1850, " the act for reclaiming fugitives from service or labor " included, which act being designed to carry out an express provision of the Constitution, cannot, with fidelity thereto, be repealed or so changed as to destroy or impair its efficiency.

### NOTHING TO BE SAID AGAINST SLAVERY.

The Democratic Party will resist all attempts at renewing, in Congress or out of it, the agitation of the slavery question, under whatever shape or color the attempt may be made.

### EXTREME STATE RIGHTS DOCTRINE ENDORSED.

The Democratic Party will faithfully abide by and uphold the principles laid down in the Kentucky and Virginia resolutions of 1798 and 1799, and in the report of Mr. Madison to the Virginia Legislature in 1799—that it adopts these principles as constituting one of the main foundations of its political creed and is resolved to carry them out in their obvious meaning and import.      [NOTE.—The Kentucky and Virginia resolutions affirmed the right of each State to judge for itself of the constitutionality of the acts of the General Government, and to refuse to submit if it deems those acts unconstitutional.     These resolutions formed the basis of the doctrine of secession.]

### SLAVERY IN THE TERRITORIES AND THE DISTRICT OF COLUMBIA.

The American Democracy recognize and adopt the principles contained in the organic laws establishing the Territories of Kansas and Nebraska, as embodying the only sound and safe solution of the slavery question upon which the great national idea of the people of this whole country can repose in its determined conservation of the Union ; and non-interference of Congress with slavery in the District of Columbia.

## FROM BOTH DEMOCRATIC PLATFORMS OF 1860.

### LAWS AGAINST KIDNAPPING DENOUNCED.

THE enactments of State Legislatures to defeat the faithful execution of the fugitive-slave law are hostile in character, subversive of the Constitution, and revolutionary in their effect. [NOTE.—This refers to laws passed by several Northern States to protect persons from being captured on their soil by slave-hunters, and carried to the South without a trial by jury to determine whether they were slaves or not.]

### PROTECTION TO CITIZENS.

It is the duty of the United States to afford ample and complete protection to all its citizens, whether at home or abroad, and whether native or foreign. [NOTE.—The Democracy never applied this principle to colored people or to white people who opposed human slavery. Of late years it has abandoned it altogether, and has vehemently resisted the enactment and enforcement of laws to protect the civil rights of citizens.]

## FROM THE DEMOCRATIC PLATFORM OF 1864.

### THE WAR A FAILURE.

THIS convention does explicitly declare, as the sense of the American people, that after four years of failure to restore the Union by the experiment of war, during which, under the pretext of a military necessity of a war power higher than the Constitution, the Constitution itself has been disregarded in every part, and public and private liberty alike trodden down, and the material prosperity of the country essentially impaired, justice, humanity, liberty and the public welfare demand that immediate efforts be made for a cessation of hostilities, with a view to an ultimate convention of all the States or other peaceable means, to the end that at the earliest practicable moment peace may be restored on the basis of the Federal Union of the States.

# FROM THE DEMOCRATIC PLATFORM OF 1868.

### TAXATION OF GOVERNMENT BONDS, IN VIOLATION OF THE CONTRACT.

EQUAL taxation of every species of property including Government bonds and other public securities.

#### PAYMENT OF THE BONDS IN GREENBACKS.

Where the obligations of the Government do not expressly state upon their face, or the law under which they were issued does not provide, that they shall be paid in coin, they ought in right and justice to be paid in the lawful money of the United States.

#### A DISMAL PROPHECY.

Under its [the Republican Party's] repeated assaults the pillars of the Government are rocking on their base, and should it succeed in November next and inaugurate its President, we will meet as a subjected and conquered people amid the ruins of liberty and the scattered fragments of the Constitution.

#### THE RECONSTRUCTION ACTS DENOUNCED AS REVOLUTIONARY AND VOID.

We regard the reconstruction acts (so-called) of Congress, as such, as usurpations and as unconstitutional, revolutionary, and void.

#### THE REPUBLICAN PARTY FALSELY ACCUSED.

In demanding these measures and reforms, we arraign the Radical Party for its disregard of right and the unparalleled oppression and tyranny which have marked its career.

## FROM THE PLATFORM OF 1876.

### THE RESUMPTION LAW DENOUNCED.

WE denounce the resumption clause of the Act of 1875, and demand its repeal.

### THE PROTECTIVE TARIFF CONDEMNED.

We denounce the present tariff levied upon nearly 4,000 articles, as a masterpiece of injustice, inequality and fraud. [NOTE.—This is probably the only one of the doctrines here quoted which the Democratic Party avows to-day. Its present platform demands a tariff for revenue only.]

# Library of Universal Knowledge.

In 21 volumes, numbering over 16,000 pages. Volumes 1 to 15 comprise the verbatim reprint of the last (1879) Edinburgh and London Edition of Chambers's Encyclopædia, a Dictionary of Universal Knowledge for the People. Volumes 16 to 21 comprise further treatment of many subjects of the original work, with about 15,000 additional topics ; thus supplying the deficiencies of the original, especially in its adaptation to the wants of American readers. New, very clear-faced nonpareil type. Price per volume :

Acme edition, cloth, 50 cents; postage 10 cents.
Aldus edition, half Russia, gilt top, $1; postage 13 cents.

Any volume desired will be sold separately, and books will be delivered either all at one time or in instalments as may be ordered.

A specimen volume may be ordered by any one for examination, with the privilege of return if not found satisfactory, within ten days after date of its receipt. Price and postage must accompany the order.

### SPECIAL OFFER TO EARLY SUBSCRIBERS.

The ranks of the first 20,000 subscribers being closed, in lieu of terms heretofore given, which are hereby withdrawn, we now offer to each of

### THE THIRD 10,000 SUBSCRIBERS

A premium of any books selected from our list to the amount of $2.50 for subscriptions to the Acme edition, and to the amount of $5 for subscriptions to the Aldus edition. Under this offer orders must be accompanied by full payment of $10.50 or $21 for the edition desired; the books selected as premium will be sent at once, with the volumes of the Library of Universal Knowledge already issued, and the subsequent volumes, when published will be sent as may be directed.

## Chambers's Cyclopædia of English Literature.

A History, Critical and Biographical, of British and American Authors, with specimens of their writings. Originally edited by Robert Chambers, LL.D. New edition, revised, by Robert Carruthers, LL. D. Eight volumes, bound in four. Price, per set :

Acme edition, cloth, $2; postage 35 cents.
Aldus edition, half Russia, gilt top, $4; postage 50 cents.

## Taine's History of English Literature.

An Unabridged Reprint of the last English edition of Van Laun's translation, in four volumes, with all the author's and translator's notes and corrections. In one volume, 12mo, brevier type. Price: cloth, 75 cents; half Russia, gilt top, $1; postage 11 cents.

## The Library Magazine.

Of Select Foreign Literature. Monthly, 192 pages, brevier type, 10 cents a number, $1 a year, postage prepaid.

#### BOUND VOLUMES WITH INDEX.

Volume I., January to June, 1879, 774 pages; volume II., July to December, 1879, 804 pages. Price per volume: cloth, 50 cents; half Russia, gilt top, 75 cents; postage, per volume 9 cents.

Volume III., January to June, 1880, 1159 pages. Price, cloth, 60 cents; half Russia, gilt top, 85 cents; postage 10 cents.

# Popular History of England.

By Charles Knight. Complete in Eight volumes, bound in four. Large 12mo, bourgeois type. With 32 illustrations and very full index. Price, per set: cloth $3; half Russia, gilt top, $5; postage 52 cents.

# Milman's Gibbon's Rome.

History of the Decline and Fall of the Roman Empire. By Edward Gibbon. A new edition with the notes of H. H. Milman, and a very full index. In five volumes, bourgeois type. Price, per set:
Acme edition, cloth $2.50; postage 37 cents.
Aldus edition, half Russia, gilt top $5; postage 52 cents.

# Macaulay's History of England.

History of England from the Accession of James II. By Thomas Babington Macaulay. In three volumes, brevier type, with full index. Price, per set:
Acme edition, cloth $1,50, postage, 21 cents.
Aldus edition, half Russia, gilt top $3; postage 32 cents.

# Macaulay's Essays.

Critical, Historical, and Miscellaneous Essays and Poems. By Thomas Babington Macaulay. The most complete collection ever published In three volumes, 12mo, long primer type. Price, per set: cloth, $1.80; half Russia, gilt top, $2.70; postage 30 cents.

# Macaulay's Life and Letters.

Life and Letters of Lord Macaulay. By his nephew George Otto Trevelyan, Member of Parliament. Complete in one volume, 12mo, brevier type, leaded. Price: cloth, 50 cents; half Russia, gilt top, 75 cents; postage 10 cents.

# Rollin's Ancient History.

Ancient History of the Egyptians, Carthagenians, Assyrians, Babylonians, Medes and Persians, Grecians and Macedonians, including a history of the arts and sciences of the ancients, by Charles Rollin. In one quarto volume, 1318 double column pages, small pica type. Price: cloth, $2.25; half Russia, sprinkled edges, $2.75; postage 42 cents.

# Comic History of the United States.

By L. Hopkins. Copiously illustrated by the author from sketches taken at a safe distance. Long primer type, leaded. Price: extra cloth, illuminated, 50 cents; postage 6 cents.

# Acme Library of Standard Biography.

Twelve books in one volume for less than the price heretofore charged for each separately.

| | |
|---|---|
| I. Frederick the Great: Macaulay. | VII. Hannibal: Arnold. |
| II. Robert Burns: Carlyle. | VIII. Cæsar; Liddell. |
| III. Mahomet: Gibbon. | IX. Cromwell: Lamartine. |
| IV. Martin Luther: Bunsen. | X. William Pitt: Macaulay. |
| V. Mary, Queen of Scots: Lamartine. | XI. Columbus: Lamartine. |
| VI. Joan of Arc: Michelet. | XII. Vittoria Collona: Trollope. |

Brevier type. Price: Acme edition, cloth, black and gold, 50 cents; postage 9 cents. Aldus edition, half Russia, gilt top, $1; postage 13 cents.

# Plutarch's Lives of Illustrious Men.

Translated by John Dryden and others. In three volumes, 12mo, long primer type. Price, per set; cloth, $1,50; half Russia, gilt top, $2.25; postage 21 cents.

## Concordance to the Bible.

Young's Analytical Concordance to the Bible, with every word alphabetically arranged, showing the Hebrew or Greek original, its meaning and pronunciation; with 311,000 references, 118,000 beyond Cruden; marking 30,000 various readings in the Greek New Testament; with the latest information on biblical geography and antiquities of the Palestine Exploration Society. Designed for the simplest reader of the English Bible. In one quarto volume, about 1,100 three-column pages, nonpareil type. Price: cloth, $2.50; half Russia, sprinkled edges, $3; postage 42 cents. *In preparation.*

## Life and Words of Christ.

By Cunningham Geikie, D.D. Complete, with a full index. Brevier type. Price: Acme edition, cloth, 50 cents; postage 9 cents.
Aldus edition, half Russia, gilt top, $1; postage 13 cents.

## Kitto's Cyclopedia of Biblical Literature.

In two large octavo volumes, brevier type; illustrated by many hundred engravings on wood. Price, per set: cloth, $2; half Russia, gilt top, $3; postage 36 cents.

## Smith's Bible Dictionary.

Comprising its Antiquities, Biography, Geography, and Natural History. In one octavo volume; brevier type, double column; with numerous illustrations and maps. Price: cloth, 90 cents; half Russia, gilt top, $1.25; postage 16 cents.

## The Koran of Mahammed.

Translated into English from the Arabic by George Sale. Brevier type. Price: Acme edition, 35 cents; postage 5 cents.
Aldus edition, half Russia, gilt top, 70 cents; postage 8 cents.

## Works of Flavius Josephus.

Comprising the Antiquities of the Jews, a History of the Jewish Wars, and a Life of Josephus, written by himself, translated by William Whiston; together with numerous explanatory notes, etc. In one quarto volume, 1,142 double-column pages, pica type. Price: cloth, $2; half Russia, sprinkled edges, $2.50; postage 38 cents.

## Health by Exercise.

By George H. Taylor, M.D. What Exercises to take, and how to take them. Long primer type, leaded; with numerous illustrations. Price: cloth, 40 cents; postage 7 cents.

## Health for Women.

By George H. Taylor, M. D. Showing the causes of feebleness, and the local diseases arising therefrom; with full directions for self-treatment by special exercises. Long primer type, leaded. Price: cloth, 35 cents; postage 5 cts.

## Shakespeare's Complete Poetical Works.

From the text of Clark and Wright. With a copious glossary, an index to familiar passages, and to the characters in each play. Very large beautiful-faced nonpareil type. Price: cloth, 75 cents; half Russia, gilt top, $1.10; postage 13 cents.

## Milton's Complete Poetical Works.

With a sketch of his life. Long primer type. Price:
Acme edition, cloth, 50 cents; postage 7 cents.
Aldus edition, half Russia, gilt top, 90 cents; postage 10 cents.

## Works of Dante.

The Vision; or Hell, Purgatory, and Paradise. Translated from the Italian by H. F. Cary, A.M. With a chronological view of the age of Dante, and very full notes. Long primer type. Price:
Acme edition, cloth, 40 cents; postage 6 cents.
Aldus edition, half Russia, gilt top, 80 cents; postage 8 cents.

## Works of Virgil.

Translated by John Dryden. Brevier type. Price:
Acme edition, cloth, 40 cents; postage 6 cents.
Aldus edition, half Russia, gilt top, 80 cents; postage 8 cents.

## Cecil's Books of Natural History.

Profusely illustrated. Part I., Beasts; Part II., Birds; Part III., Insects. By Selim H. Peabody, Ph.D. Small pica type, leaded. Price: cloth, black and gold, $1; postage 11 cents.

## Stories and Ballads for Young Folks.

By Ellen Tracy Alden. New and cheaper edition. Small pica and bourgeois type, leaded; with very beautiful illustrations by Hopkins. Price: cloth, black and gold, 50 cents; postage 7 cents.

## Bunyan's Pilgrim's Progress.

Complete, with very fine illustrations by Barnard and others. Bourgeois type, leaded. Price: cloth, black and gold, 50 cents; postage 7 cents.

## The Arabian Nights.

The Thousand and One Nights. Brevier type; 16 fine full-page illustrations. Price: cloth, black and gold, 50 cents; postage 8 cents.

## Robinson Crusoe.

By Daniel De Foe. Brevier type; 16 fine full-page illustrations. Price: cloth, black and gold, 50 cents; postage 7 cents.

## Munchausen and Gulliver.

Travels and Surprising Adventures of Baron Munchausen, and Gulliver's Travels by Dean Swift. The two in one volume. Bourgeois type; with 16 full-page characteristic and humerous illustrations by Hopkins. Price: cloth, black and gold, 50 cents; postage 8 cents.

## Acme Library of Modern Classics.

Five books in one volume, for half the price usually charged for each separately.

I. Vicar of Wakefield : Goldsmith.   III. Picciola : Saintine.

II. Rasselas : Johnson.   IV.   Paul and Virginia : St. Pierre.

V. Undine and the Two Captains : Fouque.

Brevier Type.   Price : Acme edition, cloth, black and gold, 50 cents ; postage 7 cents ; Aldus edition, half Russia, gilt top, 90 cents ; postage 9 cents.

## Don Quixote.

The adventures of Don Quixote de la Mancha.   By Miguel de Cervantes.   Translated by Motteaux.   With 16 full page characteristic humorous illustrations by Hopkins.   Brevier type.   Price ; extra cloth, 50 cents; postage 9 cents.

## The Book of Fables.

Æsop's Fables, complete, with text based upon Croxall, La Fontaine, and L'Estrange, with copious additions from modern authors.   Long primer type, leaded.   Profusely illustrated by Ernest Griset.   Price : cloth, black and gold, 50 cents; postage 7 cents.

## American Patriotism.

Containing the wisdom and eloquence of the founders, builders and preservers of American Liberty, Independence, and Unity, as found in their writings, speeches, and other public papers, from the first opposition to the tyranny of Great Britain to the overthrow of the Rebellion.   Brevier type.   Price ; Acme edition, cloth, 50 cents; postage 8 cents.

Aldus edition, half Russia, gilt top, $1; postage 12 cents.

## Leaves from the Diary of an old Lawyer.

Intemperance the Great Source of Crime.   By A. B. Richmond, Esq., member of the Pennsylvania Bar.   Long primer type, leaded.   Price: extra cloth, black and gold, $1; postage 9 cents.

## Pictorial Handy Lexicon.

Containing over 25,000 words and phrases and 250 engravings.   Will answer questions of spelling, pronunciation, and meaning in more than nine-tenths of the cases which occur to the average reader, and save in time, muscle and patience more than its cost, even to owners of the big Unabridged.   Pearl type.   Price: cloth, 25 cents; postage 4 cents.

## Sayings, Wise and Otherwise.

By the author of "Sparrowgrass Papers," etc.   With a brief autobiographic sketch, and an introductory note by Donald G. Mitchell.   Small pica type, leaded.   Price: extra cloth, 35 cents; postage 6 cents.

## Mrs. Hemans' Poetical Works.

Complete in one large octavo volume.   Nonpareil type; with a critical index.   Price: cloth, 60 cents; half Russia, gilt top, 90 cents; postage 13 cents.

www.ingramcontent.com/pod-product-compliance
Lightning Source LLC
Chambersburg PA
CBHW031423270326
41930CB00007B/552